A Funny Thing Happened on the Way to Cooperstown

Mickey McDermott
with Howard Eisenberg

TRIUMPH
B O O K S
CHICAGO

Library of Congress Cataloging-in-Publication Data
McDermott, Mickey, 1928–
    A funny thing happened on the way to Cooperstown / Mickey McDermott with Howard Eisenberg.
        p. cm.
    Includes index.
    ISBN 1-57243-532-1
    1. McDermott, Mickey, 1928– 2. Baseball players—United States—Biography. I. Eisenberg, Howard, 1926– II. Title.

GV865.M3895A3 2003
796.357'092—dc21
[B]   2002045573

This book is available in quantity at special discounts for your group or organization. For further information, contact:
    Triumph Books
    601 South LaSalle Street
    Suite 500
    Chicago, Illinois 60605
    (312) 939-3330
    Fax (312) 663-3557

Printed in the United States of America
ISBN 1-57243-532-1

Interior design by Amy Flammang-Carter

To my old man, a great ballplayer, who wanted me to be a major league pitcher but ended up with a major delinquent.

To my mom (my old man's boss), with thanks for loving me in spite of everything, and for all the wisdom I wish I'd listened harder to—and would have except for the wax in my ears.

To my wife, Stevie, with thanks for taking such good care of an old has-been who happens to love her.

To my dear friend and brother Billy, whose quiet good humor and courage have inspired so many people, especially me. When they amputated his diabetic leg and foot last year, he laughed it off. "Well," he said, "they cut me down to 5'2", but it's OK. My legs never worked too good anyway."

To my four wonderful daughters: Michelle, Bobbie, Sissy, and Gail. When they call I don't say hello, I say, "How much?" But I love them anyway.

To my one and only (so far) grandson, Daniel, whose inspiring words when I hit the roof of the car I'll never forget: "Good trick, Grandpa! Do it again!" (Confused? See page 251.)

In memory of my dear friend Willie D. Fitzgerald and the crazy things we did together—escapades so wild I left them out of the book. I mean, who would believe anybody could be that nuts?

—Mickey McDermott

To Arlene, my Wonder Woman, with eternal love and grateful appreciation. After our dinner at the Waldorf (during which Mickey McDermott didn't eat much but told story after wonderfully funny story about his life in and after baseball), you said in the cab, "Wouldn't Mickey's life make a great book?" My answer was, "You bet. And I'd love to write it." Thanks to you, I have.

To Heidi, Sandee, and Evan, who dedicated their books to us. Keep writing. There's nothing we'd rather read.

And to their mates, Erik, Tim, and Freda, and at the foot of the family tree, Emma, Rachel, Wyatt, Ethan, Liz, and Sara Xing—because nine adds up to a baseball team, and because you're such great children and grandchildren I can't possibly leave you out.

—Howard Eisenberg

Table of Contents

Author's Confession and Absolution

Look, if you're a serious baseball fan (and I hope you are), you're gonna find mistakes in this book. Nobody's perfect. Especially me. So maybe it was a pelican, not an osprey, that dropped the herring on Ellis Kinder's head and knocked him out of the box at Fenway Park. (And you remember because you're a binoculars-carrying bird-watcher, and you were there.) Or maybe Ted Williams' monster Minneapolis home run didn't break a plate-glass window in a bank across the street. Actually it was a drugstore. (And you know because it was your drugstore.) Stuff like that.

But hey, I'm 74 years old, and a lot of this happened a long time ago. So don't expect a refund if I misspelled Billy Hoeft. And don't write me long letters saying I got the color of Red Rolfe's hair wrong. Do me a favor. Just sit back and enjoy the stories. All I wanna hear from you is that you loved the book.

—Mickey McDermott

Foreword

Why Nolan Ryan's Rookie Baseball Card Sells for $600 and You Can Buy Me for 15 Bucks

It's the third inning and I'm already up to my nostrils in quicksand. I'm down 3–0. Rizzuto has just singled and he's on first. Joe DiMaggio is at the plate for the second time, and a few pitches from now I could be outta here.

First time up, Joe fouls off a half-dozen pitches to the right, so I know that in his first game after two months out with heel-bone spurs his bat isn't back up to speed yet. Even so, he manages to punch one off the hands over Junior Stephens' head for a single.

I fall behind 2–0. Tebbetts, Doerr, and Dropo trot to the mound to calm me down. "You can handle him," they assure me. "Just be careful." I'm like a bull in heat. "Just gimme the f'g ball!" I explode. "He's as good as out." They shake their heads and walk back to their positions.

I give him the heater. DiMaggio swings late and pops it up in foul territory to Billy Goodman. I'm jubilant, but I celebrate too soon. The ball hits the heel of Goodman's glove, bounces out, and I have to do it all over again.

A Funny Thing Happened on the Way to Cooperstown

You can't throw Joe two fastballs in a row. I know that. And I know what my teammate Mel Parnell, who got Joe out better than anyone I know, would do: change speeds. At Louisville, Parnell was only a very good pitcher until he got lucky one afternoon. A line drive through the box broke a finger, and we didn't have a team doctor, so it stayed swollen. Poor guy. All of a sudden, he was throwing a natural slider and he became an ace. (At least that's what Parnell told me and the rest of the league. For Mel's true confession, see page 206.)

I have a change-up, but challenging a hitter is more fun. A couple of seasons later, Gus Niarhos would become my regular catcher. He refused to let me shake off his signs, forced me to change speeds, and I won 18 games. But that was still in the future; now if DiMaggio is gonna beat me, he'll have to hit my best pitch.

I rear back and do exactly what Joltin' Joe knows I'm gonna do. Prove in front of tens of thousands of standing screaming citizens that my arm can beat his bat. Prove that with men on bases and the game on the line, I am God in red socks tossing greased lightning bolts. Prove that I can dominate one of the two smartest hitters in baseball (gotta put my pal Ted first) with a fastball that will make him look like a busher.

I take a deep breath and fire the ball toward the plate as hard as it has ever been thrown. DiMaggio's cocked bat meets it head on. I don't even have to look. A bullet over the wall and it's 5–0.

Damn. I settle down and we get some runs back, but we lose it 5–4. Three months later I was replaying the season in my head as I cleaned out my locker. I suddenly realized that if I'd used my brains instead of my balls pitching to Joe that day, we could have won that game 4–3. And finished the season in the World Series a game ahead of the Yanks instead of a game behind them. Once more, Pighead McDermott, boy wonder and natural athlete, had proved that raw talent is a great thing to be born with, but that without discipline and common sense, it's not worth the genes it's imprinted on. My left arm was a God-given gift. He left it to me to take it from there.

I didn't understand that then, and it would be too late when I finally did. But if I ever get reincarnated as a Little League pitcher, I'll listen to guys with more experience than I have at getting batters out. And I'll have a work ethic like Horatio Alger.

I'll work at my craft between games like the Warren Spahns and Sandy Koufaxes of the game instead of thinking that all God's Gift to Baseball has to do is show up every fifth day and throw 125 fastballs.

My reincarnation as a pitcher is doubtful. I'm more likely to come back as a Mexican gardener. Or his donkey. So at age 74, maybe it's time to sit down, tune in to whatever brain cells I've got left, and figure out where I got lost on the road to the Baseball Hall of Fame. Hey, maybe what I've got to say will help a couple of kids find their way into it.

—Mickey McDermott

Acknowledgments

Also Known as Payback

You can't write a memoir (the fancy word publishers give books like these because it fits better on the cover than *autobiography*) without leaning on friends to refresh your aging memory. So my thanks, and many of them, to my Uncle Eddie (whose finger I break in Chapter 1). To my ex-wives, Babs and Linda, and my deceased wife, Betty—their courage, pain, and suffering while married to me entitles them to a Congressional Medal of Honor and burial in Arlington Cemetery.

To baseball buddies Walt Dropo, Johnny Pesky, Dom DiMaggio, Mel Parnell, Jimmy Piersall, Whitey Ford, Warren Spahn, Harmon Killebrew, pitcher/banker Tom Seaver, and Art Richman; they remembered things I'd hoped they'd forgotten. To pals Tino Barzie, Paul Gleason, Dick Dombro, and Michael Dante, who missed a lot of sleep because I kept saying, "Aw, come on, just one more!"

To literary representative (that sounds better than agent) Bob Markel. And, of course, to the folks at Triumph Books, who put this soon-to-be-a-major-motion-picture (well, you never know) book together, and are gonna make me richer and more famous: namely, publisher Mitch Rogatz and editorial director Tom Bast (who put their reputations in grave danger by taking on this project), managing editor Blythe Hurley (who is making sure I spell her name right), as well as Phil Springstead, Scott Rowan, and Fred Walski (who are gonna sell and promote the hell out of these pages).

To sports artist James Fiorentino, who made that sensationally handsome poster of me—thanks for persuading Robert Redford to pose for it, James. To ex-pitcher Rudy Riska, also of Heisman Trophy fame, who, come to think of it, definitely deserves a McDermott Trophy for Nice Guys Who Finish Last. To David S. Neft, lead editor of *The Sports Encyclopedia: Baseball* (St. Martin's–Griffin), for helping us get our statistical act together. To trading card authority Beckett.com, which supplied the latest humiliating price quote on my rookie card versus Nolan Ryan's. To super-doc Richard Commatucci, who has a pill in his pocket for every known disease, but sometimes reaches in the wrong pocket. To ex–New Jersey Deputy Director of Police Bernie Sweeney, a good friend who built a guest room for me at his home in Atlantic Highlands.

Did I leave anyone out? Oh, yes. To actor Jim Carrey, who doesn't know it yet, but he's gonna play me in the major motion picture I, perhaps over optimistically, mentioned earlier. Of course, I'll have to teach him how to drink and throw wild pitches.

Anyone else? Well, don't feel bad. I'm saving you for the memoir of my next life.

Coauthor's Introduction

Mickey Who?

The phenom, like fresh topsoil, happens every spring on South Florida and Arizona practice fields. One phenom in twenty lives up to his press notices. Mickey McDermott (lifetime stats: 69 wins, 69 losses, 14 saves, 3.91 ERA, nine DWIs) was among the unlucky nineteen.

So why did I spend a year writing a book with and about a dimly remembered, 74-year-old Hall of Fame might-have-been instead of, let's say, the Man with the Iron Arm, Nolan "7-No-Hit" Ryan? It's a fair question. Here's part of why.

When he was 17, Mickey became the only pitcher to hurl two no-hitters in the Double A Eastern League. (He pitched a third but lost it 1–0 on a wild pitch. Or, he prefers to believe, on a passed ball.)

When he was 18, Mickey dazzled American Association fans by striking out 20 batters in a single game.

When Mickey was 19, Al Hirshberg wrote in *Sport Magazine* after Mickey's rookie season in the majors with the Red Sox, "McDermott has the most conservative observers comparing him with Grove, Gomez, and

Feller." And Boston veteran Birdie Tebbetts, whose palm stung from catching him, did not disagree. "This kid," he declared, "could be the greatest left-hander of his generation."

"So what?" you may say. That was 50 years ago, and McDermott came nowhere near living up to all that purple praise.

So this. The Mickey McDermott story is a baseball *Tin Cup*. Like Kevin Costner, that film's stubborn golf bum hero, Mickey is a one-of-a-kind character at whom fate (if not Rene Russo) has both smiled and jeered. At film's end, Costner is en route to redemption. Mickey, for reasons he doesn't quite understand, could be said to be already there.

This book is far more than an anthology of dramatic and laugh-out-loud baseball stories about guys McDermott played with and against: Ted Williams, Mickey Mantle, Joe DiMaggio, Yogi Berra, Whitey Ford, Billy Martin, Hank Greenberg, Satchel Paige, Stan Musial, Ralph Kiner, Bob Feller, Warren Spahn, Harmon Killebrew, Don Larsen.

It's more than about how a host of managers tried (but inevitably failed) to make Mickey the consistent 20-game winner everybody thought he should be: Joe McCarthy, Lou Boudreau, Casey Stengel, Joe Cronin, Bucky Harris, and Charlie Dressen among them.

It's about the glory days of the late forties and fifties when, for the ballplayers anyway, baseball was more about fun than about big business. It's about a guy with a rifle for an arm who coulda and shoulda entered the Cooperstown Hall of Fame but, having too much fun with women, whiskey, and song (yep, he even starred in a nightclub act), never got past its hallway.

A guy who, when his life seemed to be over (he got by on his baseball pension and timely loans from pals like Ted Williams and Tino Barzie and avoided homelessness by flopping on buddies' couches), had the suddenly sobering experience of winning the Arizona lottery. "Somebody up there likes me," Mickey says, "but I'm damned if I can figure out why."

There's a message here not only for Little Leaguers but for their parents in pursuit of fame and fortune in show business or any other business: losers squander their gifts. Winners get to be winners by keeping their eye on the ball. In other words, talent don't mean a thing if you ain't got that work ethic. Happy-go-lucky Mickey, as popular among fellow ballplayers as free beer and as off-the-wall as a two-base hit, took his eye off the ball to have a ball. And the phenom fizzled.

So, "Mickey who?" This is who, say four Hall of Famers and a sportswriter turned New York Yankees executive.

Ted Williams, Boston Red Sox, Hall of Fame

At a baseball dinner, I introduce Mickey to George Bush. "Mr. President," I say, "I'd like you to meet Mickey McDermott." Mickey shoves out his big paw and says, "Hey, George, for chrissake, how the hell are you?"

The president looks stunned. I'm an ex-marine, taught to show maximum respect for my commander in chief. I bury my head in my hands and think, "Oh, brother, I should have known better."

Mickey sees my reaction. "For chrissakes, Theodore, what's your problem? George is a lefty like me. And he was a first baseman at Yale." With that, the president grins, puts up his hand, and gives Mickey a high five.

Whitey Ford, New York Yankees, Hall of Fame

Mickey and I pitched together on the Yankees in '56. But I heard about him long before that in my rookie year, 1950. I didn't have half his natural ability, so I particularly remember the spring training buzz about this 21-year-old in his third year with the Red Sox who could be the next Bob Feller. Mickey threw hard, pitched some good baseball, and had a world of talent. But he had too good of a time challenging hitters with heat to work on improving his change-up.

A few years ago, my phone woke me up at 5:00 A.M. and I figured it had to be one of two Mickeys: Mantle or McDermott. My wife, who is less trusting, wondered if it was a woman. "Listen for yourself," I said, handing her the phone. "You can tell it's McDermott. He's so drunk he thinks he won $7 million in the Arizona lottery."

Drunk or sober (and sober is what he's been for 10 years or more), Mickey's got more friends than any baseball veteran I know. He's a million laughs, and he'd give you his last 10-spot. Last time he called, it was to tell me he was think-ing of buying a Las Vegas roller-hockey team. With Mickey you never know.

Warren Spahn, Milwaukee Braves, Hall of Fame

The two greatest athletes I ever saw play baseball were Ted Williams and Mickey McDermott. Mickey was tall and rangy with a great fastball and a wicked curve. But he was as devastating a hitter as Williams, so when he wasn't pitching, he hit a lot of pinch-hit home runs. I always thought that silly son-of-a-pup could have been a great outfielder or first baseman and wondered why he didn't pursue position playing so he could be out there every day. If I'd had his talent, that would have been my choice.

Harmon Killebrew, Minnesota Twins, Hall of Fame

There's only one Mickey McDermott. I played back of him on the Senators for a couple of seasons, and I can't think of any ballplayer any-where I'd put in his category.

He could get away with being "Out All Night" McDermott even with tough managers like Bucky Harris and Charlie Dressen because he had a great talent, a great arm, and—one of the things a lot of people don't know—he was a great athlete and natural hitter. A lot of people thought when he came up to the Red Sox that he had as good a swing as Ted. There was only one Ted, but I truly believe Mickey could have been an All-Star outfielder.

For that matter, he might have been a singing star. Mickey was a darned good singer. Like a lot of other things, he didn't work very hard at it. If he had, he could have been anything.

Art Richman, longtime sportswriter and New York Yankees executive

In almost 60 years in and around baseball, I've met a lot of characters, but none loopier—or more fun to be around—than Mickey McDermott. Mickey was capable of pitching a no-hitter or clouting a homer anytime. Ask him why that great left arm of his didn't give him a half-dozen 20-game seasons and a place in the Hall of Fame, and I can tell you what he'd say: "It was injured. I bent it in a cocktail lounge."

CHAPTER 1

Growing Up Lefty

"He's Not Bob Feller. He's Just a Kid."

There were six kids in the McDermott family and we were always hungry. Breakfast was a couple of slices of Wonder Bread painted with canned evaporated milk and sugar—a formula Benjamin Moore may have borrowed from Mom for his first house paint. I helped fill the holes in our stomachs with pocketfuls of doughnuts borrowed from the bakery downstairs. Mrs. Gillespie wasn't blind. I think she just looked the other way.

But, hey, I'm not complaining. A sugar high is better than no high at all. And we were better off than most because my old man—back in the days when big and Irish was the job description—was a big Irish cop. And during the Great Depression of the thirties, that was the kind of steady paycheck that men selling apples and pencils on street corners envied.

It wasn't the job Maurice McDermott Sr. wanted. What he wanted was to use his powerful 220-pound 6'5" frame for blasting major league home runs like his and everybody's idol, the Babe. He was well on his way, playing first base at Hartford in the Eastern League, when a young upstart named Lou Gehrig came along and took his job away. They sent my old man down to Oneonta, and the way he got over his disappointment was by drowning it in tidal waves of beer. And then, because he couldn't feed his family on a bush-league pittance, he went home to make his police force job full time year-round.

It's a shame. Years later, Eddie Sawyer, who played with him then and later managed the Whiz Kid Phillies of 1950, gave me the full father appreciation course at a reunion in Scranton. "Let me tell you something, Mac," he said, "your dad was a great ballplayer. He could play first base. He could pitch. And he could hit the ball 90 miles. He could have been another Gehrig." Sawyer picked the wrong name out of his baseball cap. There was only one Gehrig, and he could hit the ball 100 miles. Which I guess is how come he took the first-base mitt away from my old man at Hartford.

Well, if he couldn't do it, one of his three sons had damn well better. It wasn't gonna be Jimmy, who was buried in a kid-sized casket at age seven. Penicillin, the new miracle drug that was supposed to cure his pneumonia, closed his throat in an allergic reaction and killed him instead. And when Billy was born with twisted legs, my father had to dump his dream on me— which was no problem because I'd been tuned in to exactly the same dream since I was old enough to throw a golf ball. But what happened to two of his sons . . . in a way, it destroyed him.

About that golf ball. My old man wasn't about to let any grass grow under my armpit, and at the age of three my hand was too small to hold a baseball, so he used the next best round thing. Out in the backyard we went, and my pitching class began with a golf ball. I turned out to be pretty good at breaking cellar windows. One day when he went to the john I broke six of them with pinpoint three-year-old accuracy before he could get out and stop me. But that was OK. A pane of glass cost only 22 cents, putty was practically free, my Uncle Eddie supplied the labor for nothing, and, hey, it was an investment.

My hands grew and so did I. In my ninth summer, baseball with my Polish buddies began at 7:00 A.M. One day I reported at game time in two-thirds of my father's old Hartford uniform. I'd found it hanging in the closet, took a scissors to it, and cut the sleeves and pant legs down to my size. Approximately. "Geez, it don't fit ya worth a damn!" was the unanimous decision, but I knew they were just jealous. My father wasn't jealous. He was furious, and my backside paid for it. My mother sewed it back together so the seams hardly showed. I got even years later. I pitched a two-hitter against his old team, Hartford.

We played on an empty lot, part of what the Sisters guardedly called St. Francis House but which we casually identified as (brace yourself—I'm going un-PC) the St. Francis Funny Farm.

Our families didn't see us again until, it being too dark to see the baseball, we were at risk for cerebral hemorrhages. Eddie Stelmach was one of us and a pretty darned good infielder. A few years later a New York Giants scout signed him. Unfortunately, he never got to first base.

First base was my father's old position, so, gangling as I was, with long arms that reached halfway to second, it's where I started and expected to stay. But at St. Mary's Grammar School when I was 12, coach John Shannon noticed that I tossed the ball across the diamond with curves as impressive as Rita Hayworth's, so he switched me to the mound.

OK, one year later on a Saturday morning there's this skinny 13-year-old kid sitting on the front porch of a beat-up frame house in Elizabeth, New Jersey. His old man says, "Go get your glove and ball."

"What for?"

"I got something in mind. Your Uncle Eddie's comin' down from Poughkeepsie. Show him your fastball. He's got connections."

Uncle Eddie pulls up in his green Chevy. He gives the kid a grizzly bear hug and slips on a fielder's glove.

"Eddie," the father says, "I think you better put on a catcher's mitt."

Eddie grins. "Whattya talkin' about? He's not Bob Feller. He's just a kid."

He turns to me, lifts his glove, and says, "OK, kid, loosen up." We throw catch for a bit and then he says, "Alright, let 'er rip." I do.

The ball explodes in my uncle's glove. He lets out a howl like a wolf with pancreatitis, yanks off the glove, and waves his fingers limply in the air. "Holy Jesus!" he exclaims.

"What's the matter, Eddie? Can't you take it? He's just a kid," my father laughs. "I can take it," Uncle Eddie groans, "but my thumb can't. I think the kid broke it."

I guess stories like that are what brought Bill McCarran, a Boston Red Sox scout, around. That and the fact that besides breaking thumbs I was breaking records—averaging 20 strikeouts a game in the parochial school league for St. Patrick's High.

One afternoon, pitching for St. Patty's against St. John's Academy, I struck out 27 batters. Not half bad, but what makes it better is it was a Catholic Conference regulation game: only seven innings, not nine. (Geez, where was Robert "Believe It or Not" Ripley when I needed him?)

Here's how it happened. At 4'2" my catcher was such a small crouching target that pitching to him was like throwing at a mole with a helmet on. I'd whip in a fastball, the batter would swing and miss the third strike, the ball would get by my midget teammate, and the batter would beat his throw to first base by half a mile. Well, the out didn't count but we counted the K, so by the time I got the side out I had collected 27 of them.

McCarran had been on my case ever since someone—probably my pop—tipped him off that fielders could do their homework in the outfield when I pitched. He laughed his butt off when I had to strike out six more than the maximum that day. But he laughed even harder—so did everybody else—the next time he was in the stands. Along about the sixth inning, a fastball got away from me and instead of whistling over the plate whistled behind the batter's ear.

It wasn't the first one, and a priest, the St. John's coach, had seen enough. He leaped up from the bench and ran onto the field. Taking up a defensive position between me and the batter, he raised his arms heavenward. "God has called my little boys," he shouted angrily. "I cannot allow you to kill them!"

After the game, he must have complained to the bishop that I was the biggest threat to the Church since the Saracens because, despite appeals from the priests at St. Patrick's, who loved to win ballgames as much as converts, my pitching arm was excommunicated. No more wild pitches—or Ks—in the Catholic Conference. For a couple of games anyway.

Wildness didn't bother McCarran. Scouts figure—years later, as a scout for the Oakland A's, I figured the same way—if a kid can throw hard, we'll teach him the rest. But nobody had to teach me how to throw a curve. Does the Lord work in mysterious ways? My big sweeping curve came naturally, a gift from the very same God who called those "little boys" to the priesthood. (My wandering fastball? I guess He just made sure it missed them.)

McCarran showed up again a few weeks later for a big game with Garfield High. After six innings with me pitching a 13-K one-hitter, he got up to leave. "What's your hurry?" my father asked. "Got another game to go to," he replied. Lucky for me. In the seventh, I lost my touch and Garfield knocked my brains out. They scored seven big runs.

The last game of the season, I wanted to knock my old man's brains out. The way I saw it high school was a convenient place to play baseball, not a place to learn. The first time I read a book cover to cover was in Durango 40 years later when I spent 60 days in the slammer for drunk driving, so my report cards featured almost as many Ds and Fs as my scorecards featured Ks. My principal, Sister Teresa, was not ecstatic about that, and, after repeated meetings in her office had not improved the quality of my scholarship, she announced that I could not play in the last game of the season for the league championship. Anyway, not 'til I passed my exams.

At the last minute she commuted my sentence. (Either she took pity on me or she was afraid she'd be crucified by an aroused student body.) I got to pitch, and I loved every moment of it—until the final play of the game.

It was the last inning of a scoreless game. Two men were out but there was a man—well, a boy—on third. The batter pulled a swinging bunt. I charged to the first-base line and fired the ball home. It was close, and maybe it's wishful thinking, but I'm sure I saw my catcher nail the runner sliding home. I was jubilant. Then I heard a roar from behind me. My old man's voice. He was umpiring, and, dammit, because his son was pitching, he was bending over backward so far that the back of his head must have been touching the ground.

"Safe!" he trumpeted.

"What!" I exclaimed, standing toe to toe with him. "He was out and you damn well know it!"

"I call them like I see them," he replied, stalking off.

I followed. I was furious. "Well, you're a ratbastardandablindsonov-abitch," I shouted, and then I added a few other exquisitely descriptive terms.

Now it was his turn to be furious. He spun around and grabbed my shirt. I twisted away and ran like hell. He chased me all over the outfield. Unsuccessfully. I didn't go home that night. I didn't want to be pounded into 110 pounds of prime hamburger.

McCarran, the Red Sox scout, wasn't the only guy who looked me over. The Ferrara Trucking Company fielded a semipro team in a league on Staten Island where major money was wagered on games every Sunday morning. With a bottle of beer in his hand, my pop frequently needled me with, "You couldn't pitch in the Epworth Sunday School League." That's girls softball. But he knew better. Especially with the promise of a good payday on Staten Island.

Ferrara paid my father $50 in singles to rent my arm. For a really important game, $75. After the game, my father would generously peel a single off the wad for me and take the rest to the nearest bar. Or, instead of pounding his beat, he'd head to the firehouse piano and pound out his favorite, "Old Mamie Riley, how do you do today? I'm going far away. Come kiss your daddy before you go. Oh Mamie, Mamie Riley." I learned those lyrics by the time I was two and a half. I flunked recess, but I never forgot Mamie.

On one occasion, pitching for the truckers, I was gung ho to show those surly muscled men on the other team that a kid could face them down. What I didn't know was who I was facing. At 13 I could zip my fastball in at 87–89 mph, and I was used to being the winning pitcher. But not that day. One after another they came up, and one after another they hit me like I really did pitch for the Epworth Sunday League, feasting on my best fastball like lumberjacks at a barbecue. The harder I threw it, the harder they whaled it. I spent five innings ducking line drives and watching unidentified white flying objects soar beyond my outfielders' outstretched gloves.

After the game, I asked, "Who are those guys?" and found out why I was so bad and they were so good. In those not-so-good-old days, major league clubs paid their peons popcorn. Established sluggers like Heinie Majeski and up-and-comers like Bobby Thomson played under aliases for semipro teams every chance they got to pick up five Cs for a morning's work. I was their morning's work, and I was shell-shocked for a week. That afternoon, someone cracked a walnut and I ducked.

Many years later in Boston, Del Rice and I stopped to have a drink after the game. The bartender bent over the bar and murmured, "Mickey, the gentleman at the other end wants to buy you a round." Gentleman? He looked like a hood right out of an Edward G. Robinson double feature, but that didn't seem to be a good reason to refuse a free drink.

A few minutes later he edged up to me. "You wouldn't remember me," he said, "but you once cost me a bundle. Remember that day you pitched for Ferrara Trucking in Staten Island?"

"Remember? How can I forget it? They hit me like I was a dartboard in a saloon."

"They sure as hell did. Well, I had $20,000 bet on that game. I'm glad I didn't see you afterward. You'd have been floatin' down the Elizabeth River as full of holes as a truckload of doughnuts."

I must have looked nervous. He held up his hand and grinned. "It's OK, kid. Easy come, easy go. I never held it against you." A good thing, too. This was a wise guy with a memory as long as his rap sheet.

I went to my first baseball tryout camp that year. Camps were the local clubs' way of getting an early look at neighborhood talent, and you can bet my father made sure I was there when the Brooklyn Dodgers announced one for Newburgh, New York. My cousin Vinnie came, too. When I finished throwing, an old scout named Mule Haas who'd been a great ballplayer with the Philadelphia Athletics beckoned to me.

"How old are you, son?" he asked.

"Thirteen," I said.

"Your father Maurice McDermott?" I admitted he was the same. "Geez," he said, "I know your pop. He was a helluva ballplayer. Give me your address. I might call him." He said he'd like to sign me, but at my age it was illegal. He bought me a glass of milk and a ham sandwich instead.

Branch Rickey held another tryout camp in Brooklyn and nothing could keep me away. It was like taking a number in a crowded bakery but finally my number came up. Again the Dodgers considered the possibility of signing me, but one of their scouts objected. "The kid's too skinny," he said. "He's never gonna be big enough for the majors." My father the man mountain stepped forward. "Not gonna be big enough?" he demanded. "He's my son!" The scout withdrew his objection, dismissed the age problem, and offered an under-the-table signing bonus of $100.

"A hundred bucks?" my pop scoffed, exaggerating slightly. "We can make that much on a Sunday in Staten Island. No thanks. We'll wait. But you'll be sorry when he beats your pants off in the World Series."

In early 1944, my father's patience ran out. I was only 15, but he was thirsty. He bought a bottle of ink eradicator at the stationer's and sat down with my birth certificate. Suddenly I was 16. "It's for your own good," he told me. "I want you to get in a year of pro ball before all the ballplayers come back from the army. But you gotta eat more; 130 pounds isn't enough for a six-footer. Stop playing so damn much basketball and put some meat on your bones."

I opened the high school season that year like Jack Armstrong, the All-American Boy. (You've gotta be a senior citizen to know Jack. If you're 65 or less, you may not remember it—my second favorite radio show. The first was *Buck Rogers in the 25th Century*. Boy, that Killer Kane was one slick villain.) I pitched a no-hitter, striking out 18 and winning the game with a home run. But it was my last game for St. Pat's. The good-news rumor about my old man signing me up with the Red Sox traveled too fast. Even if I hadn't started yet, I was a pro and, according to Catholic Conference rules, automatically suspended from playing against any of the Saints.

I could still play against lay high schools though, and I played semipro for the Garwood Question Marks (I'm not sure what the question was, but the answer was yes, they passed the hat and we got paid a few bucks) during June and July. Then in August the phone rang.

"Mr. McDermott," said Joe Cronin, GM of the Boston Red Sox, "the date on your son's birth certificate? It looked a little blurred, so I had somebody check the records. Your son will be 15 on August 28, not 16. Good Lord, man, he still needs working papers. You could get me put in jail."

But when two congenial gentlemen have your best interests at heart, somehow they're able to exorcise the devil out of the details. Shortly after that telephone conference, a check for $5,000 exchanged hands. Not exactly the $20,000 my old man had demanded, but good enough to satisfy his thirst no matter how hot the rest of the summer. The next day, two Ballantine Beer trucks rolled up to our house and some burly gents unloaded case after case of ale and stacked them gently ("Watch what you're doin'—don't break no bottles!") in our cellar.

"OK, it's official, " my father told me. "I bought you an overcoat and a bus ticket. Here's a new white shirt and a $5 bill. Don't change either one of them. You're going straight to AA ball—the Red Sox farm club in the Eastern League, the Scranton Miners. Good luck, kid, and come home with money in your pockets." (Some chance. Wherever we were, he always showed up on payday.)

With that, he broke open the first case of ale and lifted his glass in a toast. "Here's to the first McDermott in the Hall of Fame," he said.

"Amen," I said.

CHAPTER 2

Scranton

Beating the Bushes

So there I was in August 1945, not quite 16 but wearing a let's-pretend-I'm-almost-17 label, fresh out of my sophomore year in high school, off to the bush leagues to get salted, peppered, and seasoned in Scranton, Pennsylvania.

My soft-spoken, mild-mannered manager was Elmer Yoter, who'd had 96 at-bats in the majors and, even at 5'7", was a giant in my eyes. My second week I became a starter, if only in an exhibition against Elmira. Standing on the mound ready to throw out the first ball, I suddenly realized that things were different in the pros. There was that little white plate I had to hit, but why was there nothing behind it but the ump and my catcher? I waved him toward me. "Where in the hell is the backstop?" I asked. "You can't catch me without a backstop. You'll be chasing wild pitches all the way to Philadelphia." He grinned. "Just throw the ball. I'll catch it." Most of the time he did, but I sure missed that backstop.

I missed my winter long johns, too, when we rode the bus to upstate New York one unsummerly summer night. Our bus was a disabled war veteran. No springs, cracked windows through which sultry breezes—this night icy 30-degree winds—wafted over us. Baseball windbreakers did nothing to protect our frostbite-endangered fannies. Sitting in the back of the bus, Al Kozar and I, by a vote of 2–0, agreed that we had to do something.

Something we did. We built a bonfire in the back of the bus and warmed our hands for as long as our supply of discarded Cracker Jack boxes held out. Afraid of fire? Not us. We had more to fear from the holes in the floorboards through which fumes silently swirled around us. ("Al, are you sleepy?" "Yeah." "Me, too." "I feel sick." "Me, too.") It's a wonder we didn't die of carbon monoxide poisoning that day—or more violently, the day the brakes failed and the driver had to gingerly back down a Pocono mountainside in reverse.

My first start, my fingers still hadn't thawed out from that bus ride, but adrenaline was flowing like Irish whiskey at a McDermott family wedding. (This is no mere metaphor. At my sister's wedding, an alcohol-assisted donnybrook broke out and the cops had to escort the whole wedding party to the clink.) I flattened Utica 5–0 on five hits. My strikeout counts for what remained of the season were in impressive double digits, but there was a flip side to my dime. Wildness. I probably walked in more runs than opposing batters drove in. A few games later my arm scared the hell out of me by suddenly going dead, but it responded well to a month's worth of rest and heat and felt great again. But by the end of my short but wild and woolly season, I'd won five for the other guys (most by one run) and only two for our side.

Poor Elmer. His instructions from the farm team director didn't leave much room for managerial maneuvering: "Just let him throw. Sure, he's wild, but don't screw around with his mechanics. He's a dumb young kid. Give him too much to think about and he'll wind up confused. Leave him be. Eventually the talent will take over."

I'm afraid Elmer considered me a mixed-up blessing. "Morris," he implored (called to pitch—or to dinner—I answered to Maurice, Morris, or Mickey), "it's only 60 feet to home plate. How come your fastball gets lost on the way?" But he must have seen something besides wild pitches and hit batsmen. When the Scranton roster for '46 was posted, my name was on it.

Six months later, in the spring of '46, a rickety Red Sox bus that had already rounded up Bob Sperry in New Haven and Sam Dente in Jersey City collected me on a corner in downtown Elizabeth. We drove all that day and all night and woke up rumpled and stiff at a high school in Bennettsville, South Carolina, there to sign in and be assigned, two guys to a room, to—hell no, not hotels—local rooming houses.

Did Bennettsville have a hotel? I don't remember. Scranton's was a low-overhead operation. No meal money, but if you stretched a point you might say the meals were catered. Local housewives hand-delivered eggs, bacon, sausages, and grits to the schoolhouse where we ate breakfast, baseball-family style. Grits. One morning a nice old lady put them in front of me.

"What's that?" I asked suspiciously.

"It's good for you, son. You're thin as a weed. Need to gain some weight. Grits'll stick to your ribs."

"So will putty. My Uncle Eddie changes broken windowpanes. He could use some of this stuff." Yep, I was a wise guy even then.

I quickly appreciated my war-hardened teammates because it turned out the history books were wrong. South Carolina was still fighting the Civil War. ("Damn Yankees eatin' our food, screwin' our Southern belles . . .") There were battles between the North and the South every other night (the locals used the in-between nights to recover and regroup), and guys showed up at the ballpark with black eyes and beer-bottle-busted heads. We had a bunch of Johnny Rebs on our side, too. I didn't mind losing a few teeth, but I sure didn't want my pitching arm broken. Hanging out with teammates from the South seemed like a first-rate idea.

Red Sox buses finally finished the last roundup, and on the first official day of spring training I got a look at the competition, assembled on the field in one big Cecil B. DeMille mob scene. There were black windbreakers as far as the eye could see—150 in all, and 40 of them pitchers. Guys who'd played in the Red Sox farm system before they went in the army and played on some darned good service teams were back and determined to go all the way this time.

They were 22 and 24, with a scattering of die-hard 30-somethings. And at a game on July 4, as exploding fireworks illuminated the night sky, one of my teammates snapped. He'd been shell-shocked during the war in the Pacific. Now, seeing and hearing the bombs bursting in air, he suddenly flashed back to a disastrous landing on Okinawa. Spinning around, he grabbed first baseman Bob Sperry by the throat and would have throttled him if a bunch of guys hadn't pulled him off.

How was a skinny 16-year-old gonna stick in tough company like this? All I could do was give it the old St. Pat's High School try.

I sure must have looked high school. I was sitting on a bench on the sidelines waiting my turn to pitch when a foul ball bounced by. The guy next to me turned and said, "Hey, batboy. Get the ball." My indignant three-word reply would be unacceptable even to Triumph Books' sympathetic copy editors. (I'll let you figure out what the three words were.) But Mel Parnell—that's who the guy beside me was—still tells that story at baseball banquets.

Then he adds, "A few minutes later, I'm loosening up and this same skinny kid jumps up and hollers for a catcher. I have no idea why, but I pay no attention until I hear, 'Pop! Boom! Splat!' as his pitches explode in the catcher's glove. Afterward, I walk up to him and say, 'Sorry, kid. I guess you're not the batboy.'"

You knew where you were going, and it wasn't Boston, when a coach came up behind you and said, "The manager would like to see you." In a couple of weeks, we were down to 45 or 50, and, lo and behold, I was still there. But Scranton, which is the list my name was eventually posted on, wasn't exactly the Pearl of Pennsylvania.

About all I knew about it was that $2 could rent you a warm body—guaranteed, so 16-year-olds like me firmly believed, to miraculously rid you of adolescent pimples overnight. Sure, I'd heard that by the time you walked to the ballpark drifting smoke from the mines would turn your white shirt charcoal, and everybody walked around looking like Al Jolson in blackface, but still I was happy to be headed back north of the Mason-Dixon line. Not only no more grits. No more zits either.

What I wasn't counting on was that Red Sox management, fiercely protective of what they hoped would be my bright future, had arranged for a baby-sitter to protect me from carnal and other bad habits I would acquire and later indulge on my own.

With his cherry W. C. Fields nose, Mike Barrett seemed like a right guy. He drove me to the park, took me to dinner and the movies, regaled me with insider boxing stories—15-year-old Rocky Castellani, later to be world's welterweight champ, was in his stable—and kept me so busy that, alas, my zits remained intact. The only red lights I got to see were the ones when Mr. Barrett stopped his car at intersections.

Desperation and unrequited lust ensued in equal portions. Finally one night at dinner, I coughed discreetly and said as casually as I could manage, "The guys on the team say that this town has the world's biggest red-light district. And the way they tell it, they've been keeping the ladies pretty busy." I took a deep breath and squeaked, "How about getting me laid?"

Mike coughed out a thick morsel of T-bone steak he'd just tucked into his mouth. "Lord have mercy, Maurice," he sputtered. "Oh, no. It can't be done. Why, you could catch a disease and management would have me out the door in no time at all. Besides," he added, nodding his head wisely, "you're a growing lad. Boxers. Baseball players. It's all the same. Athletes need their sleep."

But, I wondered bitterly, did it have to be alone? I took refuge in another kind of gratification. Deep sleep. The sleep of the righteous. I was a young kid. I could sleep on a picket fence. There were no morning baseball games, so if I didn't mind missing breakfast I could snooze as late as I liked. The following Sunday I did. Right through a doubleheader.

It took a lot to turn my face red, but when, shamefaced, I walked into the locker room where the team was just changing back into civvies, the guys stood as one and applauded.

"I . . . overslept," I said lamely. Geez, they said, we thought you'd escaped home to Jersey. Eddie Popowski, the new manager, didn't make a speech. He just went shopping. Next day he presented me with a small gift-wrapped box. "Here's a little package for you, son. Take it back to your room and learn how to use it." I knew what it was without opening it. I hoped it would work. It would if I remembered to wind it.

On the mound, I continued to make Eddie's life interesting, first walking the bases loaded, then striking out the side—sometimes for real, occasionally just for the challenge of it. Early in the season, out of the opponent's dugout came a guy with one arm. I thought, what in the hell is this? Then: oh well, this should be easy. He cocked his bat, I threw a fastball, and he hit it over the right-center-field wall.

After the game, I phoned my father. "I'm coming home," I said. "How the hell am I going to get big leaguers out when I can't get the ball past a guy with only one arm?" My father laughed—very loud. "One arm? That must be Pete Gray. He played for the St. Louis Browns last year. And the year before that he batted .333 for Memphis. Led all the outfielders in the Southern Association in fielding percentage. Even got named MVP. How about that? Just one arm and he's the league's most valuable player."

OK. I felt better. And 30 years later they made a movie about Pete Gray's life. Not bad. He's one movie ahead of me.

We were in Utica, and the Blue Sox had a sturdy outfielder named Yogi Giamarco, built like a tall fireplug. My first pitch sailed and hit him right between the eyeballs—so hard that the ball rebounded halfway to second base. I was afraid I'd killed him, but he didn't even wince. He trotted to first base, looked up at big Walt Dropo, and said solemnly, "That kid is going to kill somebody one of these days."

Oh yes, my roomie and best buddy, Dropo. In Albany, there was a knock on the door. There stood the biggest SOB I'd ever seen in my life, wearing a green University of Connecticut sweater with stripes down to the elbow. He said, "I'm your new roommate, kid." I stared for a moment. I had to say something. "I get it," I said. "Ringling Brothers is in town.

They had a train wreck and Gargantua got off. OK, you take both beds. I'll sleep in the closet."

Walt had just been signed by the Red Sox with a Dropo-sized bonus. But he faced Mike Garcia—then of Wilkes-Barre, later a Cleveland Indian fireballer—in his first game. Mike struck him out three times. The third time he returned to the bench muttering, "I'm going home. They didn't throw like that in college."

He didn't go home. He adjusted. Not always successfully. One of our minor league umpires wore a hearing aid—which we all figured wasn't as bad as if he came to the park with a Seeing Eye dog. One day he called Dropo out on a pitch so far out of the strike zone it was practically across the street in traffic. Walter, noting that he wasn't wearing his hearing aid that day, exploded: "You stupid sonovabitch!"

"You're outta here," the ump said calmly.

Walt was stunned. "Hey, wait a minute," he said, "I thought you were deaf."

"I may be deaf," the ump shot back, "but I can read lips."

Walt just kept getting better and better. Later, in Boston, he was Rookie of the Year and led the league in RBIs. His amazing major league record for consecutive hits—12 in a row over a three-game period when he was traded to Detroit—may never be broken.

I wasn't the only one so awed by Walt's massive frame that, for lack of anything intelligent to say, I poked fun at it. Lefty Gomez, the great southpaw, notorious prankster, and my early idol, managed the New York Yankees farm club at Binghamton. The day we played his team, Dropo was the last man on ours to take batting practice. When Walt emerged from the clubhouse, Gomez waved at him. "Hey kid," he shouted, "Your breakfast's waiting for you in the batting cage. And so's your teething ring."

Gomez had suspended a tire from a rope. Beneath it sat a bale of hay and two bushels of apples. Everybody broke up. Everybody but Dropo. Our lovable Gargantua just gritted his teeth and drove the first two pitches out of the ballpark.

⊖   ⊖   ⊖

No more homework, no more books, just baseball, and I was having the time of my life. I wasn't exactly eating royally. Our road meal allowance was 75 cents a day, so we lived low on the hog, mostly (can you believe these prices?) on bags of three-for-a-dime White Castle hamburgers. I'm not complaining. Possibly the memory of their taste just improved with the years like good wine, but they were the tastiest patties I ever ate. Whatever the secret, alas, their corporate descendants seem to have lost it.

One night Mel Parnell and I splurged big-time at The Tiptoe Inn, familiarly known to our Scranton Miners as Tiptoe In and Stagger Out. The big attraction was a sale on lobster ("Lobster? Hmm, let's find out how the rich people live")—35 cents with a bowl of clam chowder. I'd never seen a lobster or one being eaten.

I spied a cup of water beside my plate, and thinking, "This is a real high-class joint!" I lifted it to my lips and scarfed it down—scalding the hell out of my unsuspecting tongue and gullet. Our waitress thought it was the funniest thing she'd ever seen. "That's not for drinking; it's hot water for greasy fingers," she hooted. Her tip suddenly shrank from a dime to a nickel.

⊖   ⊖   ⊖

I wasn't the only guy on the team with raunchy gonads running riot. Panty patrols scouted beneath the old wooden grandstands looking upward through knotholes. Periodically someone would report breathlessly back with, "Hey, I found one with no panties." The bench would empty. "I wanna see this!" one of our team members said, hurrying to the look-up post. It was his wife. "Hey up there," he shouted angrily. "Lucy, cut out the free show! Go home and put on a pair of panties!"

We got lucky at the old Bond Annex Hotel in Hartford when our Elmira team checked in to play Hartford. Returning to our rooms after the game, we heard the unmistakable cries of mounting ecstasy unbound as we trudged down the corridor past a room with its transom wide open to catch any possible breeze: "Oooh! Ah! Oh, Harry! Oh, darling! Oooh!" We stopped, exchanged glances, chose a lightweight infielder, and boosted him on a sturdy outfielder's shoulders so he could eye witness and quietly report the action to us. As he clambered up, his shoe collided loudly with the door. There was a sudden silence within. Hasty footsteps squeaked across the wood hotel room floor. We ran like hell, hooting and laughing and, I hate to admit it, leaving our unfortunate comrade dangling from the transom. As the door was unlocked and opened, our guy hit the floor and broke the record for the 60-yard dash, leaving the furious lover standing in the doorway shouting, "You c-sucker. You ever do that again, I'll shoot off your balls!" It's a good thing he didn't have a gun.

On the road, we'd don bathing suits and line up on the roof of whatever hotel we were staying at. Guys would pick blackheads out of each other's backs like monkeys at the zoo.

We had our own staff barber, Tommy Fine, an excellent right-handed pitcher who'd picked up barbering somewhere along the line, probably in the army. Tommy didn't bank the quarters we paid him. He socked them away in a big jar for a spectacular end-of-season beer bash at Irish Lannigan's saloon. Tommy, a great guy, had an amazing 20–1 record one year at Scranton. His big breaking curveball gave him an edge in the minors, but, despite everyone's great expectations, his inside fastball— the one pitch no pitcher can do without—didn't have the right stuff. He managed only 73 innings in the majors, for a combined 1–3 record with the Red Sox and the Browns.

Meanwhile, intoxicated in more ways than one by his success in selling me to the Red Sox, my old man decided two family members in the majors would be better than one. You'd have thought my $5,000 signing bonus would have been enough for him, but every other Friday, wherever we were on the road, I'd come back to my room and find him there waiting for me.

"Where's the check?"

"What check?"

"You've got four children to raise."

"What is this, the Immaculate Conception? Since when do I have four children?"

"You know what I mean. Hand it over."

He was too big to argue with. But if I was paying the bills, I felt like I needed some respect. I tried to get it the hard way once when he made a crack I didn't like at the kitchen table. I said, "OK, that does it. Step outside." My Uncle Eddie was there. He almost died laughing. "Who do you think you are?" he asked me. "Joe Louis?" We went outside anyway. I threw my best punch and my old man caught my fist in his big hand in midair. I said, "Forget it." So I no longer bothered to argue when he'd take my paycheck, cash it, keep $25 and give me $25 (either he was getting more generous, or I looked like I was getting stronger), and be on his way.

But he had bigger ideas, and a lot bigger thirst than $25 could handle. Besides, the cache of cases of ale in the McDermott cellar had dwindled alarmingly. The result was a phone call to the Red Sox about my cousin Vinnie—Vincent Gleason, 6'6" tall, who weighed in somewhere around 290 and had a strong right arm.

Vinnie joined us in mid-July—with my father $2,500 richer—and proceeded to get knocked out of the box early in the game. That happened regularly, with Vinnie hitting every bat in the league until he came back to the bench one day groaning, grimacing, and flexing his arm in apparent pain. "Geez, cousin," he said, "my arm. It's sore. It's killing me. I can't pitch no more."

Como Cotelli, a canny little veteran outfielder in his mid-thirties sitting beside him turned to Vinnie. "How high could you lift your arm before you hurt it?" he asked sympathetically. Vinnie fell for it like a ton of baseballs. "I could lift it up to here," he said, extending his right arm full length over his head. Como sniffed, laughed, and walked scornfully away. Vinnie lasted another week and then was gone.

I don't know what our trainer would have done for Vinnie's arm if it was really sore, but probably not much. When I pulled a muscle in my leg, he said, "No problem, I can fix that," and solemnly rolled a bat over it, leaning hard to flatten it out while I screamed. When I moved up to Triple A ball later on, my new trainer was much gentler. But if I dozed off on the training table, I'd wake up to find him working on the wrong arm. "Doc! Doc!" I'd have to say. "I'm left-handed. Remember?"

Trainer or no trainer, that left arm of mine kept getting stronger. Where my fastball had started at 86 or 88 mph in high school, it was up to 92 at Scranton. (By the time I made it to Triple A Louisville, I was closing in on 97.) That was plenty fast in a park where you could see the ball, but when Scranton played a night game at Utica it might as well have been 192. The lights there were so dim you felt like you were playing baseball in a London fog and any minute Jack the Ripper would loom up out of the soup and garrote you.

OK, I'm exaggerating, but our doughty outfielder Como Cotelli didn't appreciate having to chase fly balls in Utica's twilight zone when all it would take would be a few thousand bucks to upgrade the field's lighting system. "Waddawe gotta do," he asked, "pass the hat?"

Como's off-the-left-field-wall sense of humor took over when he realized we were scheduled to play three consecutive night games in that ridiculously underilluminated park. Before our bus headed north, he paid a quick visit to a mining equipment shop, and in Utica the following night, when the crack of the bat indicated the ball was headed his way, he slipped on the miner's helmet he'd bought in Scranton. He flicked a switch. A yellow beam of light probed the dark gray sky above him. The ball landed in Como's glove. Six thousand fans leaped to their feet and, guffawing and applauding, uproariously agreed with Cotelli's clear-as-daylight opinion of Utica's nickel-squeezing management.

Meanwhile, Pete Gray notwithstanding, my first full year in professional ball was turning out to be not half bad. My fastball remained just wild enough so that batters were afraid to dig in against me. Tino Barzie, who managed Tommy Dorsey's orchestra and loved baseball, came to the park whenever they were anywhere near where we happened to be playing. He sympathized with the hitters: "Geez, Mickey," he said, "you're all arms and legs out there, like a centipede in a baseball cap. How the hell can the poor guy holding a stick up there figure out where the baseball's coming from?"

My record was 16–6, and I struck out a pretty decent 136 in 175 innings, while continuing to wreak havoc with my manager's delicate stomach. Walking the bases loaded, pausing dramatically to remove a pebble from my shoe, and then whiffing two or three to close out the inning was not a tactic that appealed to him. The speech I heard most often from Popowski when I returned to the bench was, "Geezus, Morris, what are you doing? You'll make an old man out of me."

But after the game against the Albany Senators, I could do no wrong. As the final batter stepped to the plate in the last of the ninth, I had struck out eight and walked only four. I was, in a radio announcer's dramatic cliché, "one batter away from a no-hit no-run game!" But Rip Collins, a slugging first baseman who had been a member of the rough and tumble '34 World Series champion St. Louis Cardinals Gashouse Gang—Pepper Martin, Ducky Medwick, Frankie Frisch, Leo Durocher, 30-game winner Dizzy and brother Daffy Dean, and the rest—was the Cards' farm team's player/manager. And now, with my shot at my first no-hit game in the pros on the line, this rugged home-run hitter was at bat.

The crowd rose to its feet. I'd been lucky so far. My fastball wasn't taking off, but I'd had a good curveball and great support. In the eighth, a seeing-eye ground ball had found a hole in the infield. It was bounding through for the first hit when Al Kozar made an off-balance stab and a great falling-down toss to first to end the inning.

One more out to go. I toed the rubber and waited for the sign. And 25 or so years later, at an Old Timers' Game, Collins slapped me on the back and asked, "Mickey, remember your no-hitter in Albany? Well, I gotta tell you what was going through my mind."

"Tell away."

"I see a skinny little kid with a great arm on the mound throwing bullets," he said. "A 16-year-old kid pitching a no-hitter and us six runs behind. There's a pretty good little hitter coming up, so I put myself in to pinch hit. If one swing breaks up your no-hitter, it breaks your heart. Mine, too. So . . . I just take three down the middle."

I remembered then how, even as Collins' turn at bat was taking place, I'd been thinking, "What in hell is he up to?" The first strike, he never moved his bat off his shoulder. The second strike, he cocked his bat but never pulled the trigger. The last one he faked a half-swing.

I'd figured he'd put himself in to bust up my no-hitter. I mean, how many managers enjoy seeing their team humiliated? But the real question is, how many managers have Rip Collins' heart? Up there just to make sure my no-hitter didn't get away.

The Albany crowd knew it. And those home folks had heart, too. When the umpire called, "Strike three!" the people in that ballpark delivered a standing ovation. And it wasn't just for me. It was for Rip Collins, too.

CHAPTER 3

Ups and Downs

A Cup of Coffee in Boston

We did a lot of remarkable things in Scranton in 1946. Maybe the most remarkable was becoming the first team ever to have its batboy thrown out of a game. Yep, I said batboy.

Joey Mooney was a streetwise kid from South Boston. One day at Elmira, the umpire happened to turn around at the wrong moment and spotted Joey innocently standing behind him, not so innocently doing what comes naturally in baseball at all levels: his level best to steal Elmira's signs. The ump couldn't fine him. Joey was making about two cents a day. So he tossed him out of the park. But no evil deed goes unrewarded. A few years later, the Red Sox promoted Joey Mooney to Fenway Park and made him a groundskeeper. Not a bad move. He could make grass grow out of a rock.

This is how good our Scranton Red Sox (also known as the Miners) were that year: we had the Eastern League pennant won in July. And, with twelve thousand to thirteen thousand cheering customers a night, we outdrew the pitiful major league Washington Senators (about whom, unfortunately, more later). And, though I didn't find out about it for years (just as well, my head was too big for my baseball cap already), the Philadelphia Phillies offered Joe Cronin $250,000 for my $100-a-month contract. Unsuccessfully.

When the last out of the last game of that season landed in Sam Mele's glove, we had tangoed across the finish line 18½ games ahead of the pack. But then, why not? We had surefire future major leaguers like Mele, Mel Parnell, Walt Dropo, Al Kozar, and Sam Dente on our side.

At a clubhouse meeting after infield practice, just before the call of "play ball!" in the first game of the playoffs, we were all feeling pretty good about ourselves—but financially underappreciated. I don't remember who started the mutiny ("What is this bull? They rake in a fortune at the gate and pay us a lousy $100 a month?" "We deserve some extra dough." "Yeah, let's hold out. No bonus, no ballgame!"), but it took less than five minutes for the rest of us to join the revolution. When the owner walked in to give the traditional preseries speech ("I'm proud of you, boys! You got us to the playoffs. Now let's get out there and win it all!"), he was met by stony silence, followed by, "We want bonus money, or we ain't playing. And if that don't work we'll pitch McDermott, and then we'll be out there all night!"

Struck dumb and snakebit, with close to fifteen thousand people in the seats, he had no choice. We demanded $100 a man. He probably would have surrendered five. But with the promise of that extra C-note, we did go out there, and we did win it all.

The family had moved back to Poughkeepsie, and I went home successful, rich (only because my old man wasn't in the clubhouse during the mutiny), and happy. But pretty tired, too. I slept into the early afternoon every day for two weeks. Then one morning, an alarm clock I hadn't set woke me up at 7:00 A.M.

"Geez," I said, burying my head in the pillow, "somebody shut that damn thing off!"

A huge hand ripped off the covers. It was my old man's. "Up and at 'em, kid. I got you a job at Singer Sewing Machine. You start this morning."

"What! I'm a professional baseball player. I don't sew dresses."

"You do in the winter," he said. "Up! Now!"

At the Singer plant, I buried my face in my hands and, falling asleep sitting up, heard my father talking about somebody else: "hard worker . . . strong . . . reliable . . . punctual . . ."

"Is your son mute?" the interviewer asked, "or is he just too tired to work?" But my father was, after all, a cop. Mr. Singer's proxy agreed to try me out in the department that made nuts and bolts for the sewing machines. He took me to the foreman, a huge German with close-cropped hair who looked like he'd commanded a squad at the siege of Stalingrad. When he ordered me down to a room in the basement, I half expected him to say "*Achtung!*" Instead, he pointed at a metal chest labeled "Iron" and said, "Pick it up undt follow me." I eyed the chest suspiciously. If it contained only feathers, it would weigh a ton.

"You pick it up," I replied. "I'm leaving."

I spent the rest of the day at the burlesque theater studying Anatomy 101 and laughing every time the guy who sold Eskimo Pies (if they're still in business, I want one right now) strolled down the aisle, calling, "Get your ice-cold ice-cream pops! If you have the lucky number, you win a 1947 Cadillac [pause for effect] windshield wiper!"

That night I had it out with my old man. "I'm a professional pitcher now," I said. "Another couple of years and I'll be in the big leagues. You want me to blow out my arm picking up boxes of iron?"

My father chewed on that disturbing thought for a moment. He appeared to be recalling the fable about the man who killed the goose that laid golden eggs. I followed up my advantage. "From now on," I said, "I'm only working in the summer."

But playing was something else. I played a lot of basketball that winter. I'd been an all-state forward as a high school sophomore, good enough that Canisius College offered me a letter of intent to sign, with the promise of a basketball scholarship. But my old man still made the decisions. Red Sox signing money—and the chance to have his son live the father's dream—trumped Canisius' piece of paper. Basketball was out. That was fine with me. I could go either way. Just no iron chests. Please.

A Funny Thing Happened on the Way to Cooperstown

Early in March '47, promoted to Louisville's Triple A roster with a 50 percent pay hike to a royal $150 a month, I left the frozen north and my galoshes and long johns behind, and with a silly smile on my face reported to sunny Bradenton, Florida, for spring training. The Boston Red Sox trained in Sarasota, only seven miles away, and at Bradenton I got good news. Our camp wasn't open yet, and second baseman Chuck Koney, right-handed pitcher Willard Nixon, and I were to spend the next month with the parent club. They would get a good look at us, and we would see up close how the big guys played the game.

Pitching batting practice was my big moment, and I gave it all I had. Ted Williams watched from behind the cage as bullets whistled over and behind batters' heads and, for the first time anyone could remember, prudently declined to take BP—anyway, not 'til he'd had a man-to-boy talk with me. "Bush," he said (the great man called everyone that, and compared to him we all were), "take it easy. Batting practice pitchers come and go. Making it in the game is what counts."

I got it. I was wearing a Red Sox uniform and that felt great, but the odds that I'd be wearing it when the season started were about the same as the odds I'd be hit by a flying saucer. A kid my age? Hell, I was lucky to be a Louisville Colonel.

But even that wasn't for long. All the king's horses and all Louisville's coaches couldn't tame my wildness. They praised my fastball's movement and velocity, but they weren't too crazy about where it was going.

Neither were the guys, Louisville Sluggers in hand, on the endangered species list at home plate. Nick Etten, a big Phillies first baseman who was on the way down, took me aside and put it to me this way: "Don't hit me, kid. I got a wife and three children. McDermott, when your fastball starts to sail, you got guys ducking for dear life. I wish you could hit against yourself, so you'd know how we feel."

The trouble was there were more balls than strikes. When the season started, I dispensed gift-wrapped walks as though it was Christmas and I was Santa Claus. I gave up 32 passes in 27 innings—well, it could've been worse—and five games into the season, my new manager phoned Boston.

It happened on a day when I had walked the bases loaded in four different innings and then pulled myself together and struck out the side. "Please," my manager implored, "I know this kid is going to make the big leagues, but right now he's f'g killing me. He's got me pulling out my hair, and I'm bald enough already. He needs more experience. Give him some more innings at Scranton."

My inattention to my catcher's signs probably had something to do with it, too. We used scoreboard signs, which worked—well, were supposed to work—this way: when the catcher tossed the ball back, the pitcher turned to check the count on the scoreboard. Say the count is 1 and 0. That's an odd number, so you nod at your catcher's first sign. OK, now the scoreboard reads 1 and 1. That's an even number. So you execute the catcher's second sign.

Fine. But I'm a school dropout. I count like a broken adding machine. So when a redheaded stunner stands up in the first row, I lose my concentration. I know that when Eddie McGah calls for the first pitch, the count will be 1 and 0, which is odd. But I'm thinking, "I better get that redhead's phone number between innings," and I miss Eddie's initial sign. It was a call for a curve, but I never saw it. So I take my cue from his second sign, which I think is his first sign, and throw smoke.

Eddie is taken by surprise. Before he can raise his glove, the baseball smashes into his throat, slightly grazing the bottom of his facemask, which lacks the protective wire tail that would come along a few years later. (Better padded chest protectors would come along, too. With what catchers had then, they might as well have worn a window shade.)

The ball barely misses the spot where karate chops kill people. It could have blown Eddie's Adam's apple right through his brain. Eddie and I are lucky, but he doesn't feel lucky. He comes up gasping and coughing and takes off after me, chasing me in circles with nothing on his mind but blind revenge. I run like hell toward the clubhouse, and our manager runs like hell after Eddie. He shouts, "McGah, stop! McGah, stop! He's only a kid. He can't count. He's only a kid!"

McGah, who had to be pretty damn tough or he wouldn't have survived that pitch, pants, "I'll give you a kid! A dead kid! I'm gonna kill you, kid!" My legs are longer than his, and as I run, I'm thinking, where is the nice, clean-cut kid who came into camp in a yellow convertible with his tennis racket, golf clubs, and a blonde knockout beside him? Fortunately for me, underneath the understandable anger, that's who he still is, and before he can commit the homicide that lurks in his bloodshot eyes, the manager catches him and calms him down.

The game continues. The redhead in the first row is still there, but this time I focus on my catcher's signs instead of her short skirt and crossed legs. Eddie McGah played a couple more years in the minors and had a couple of short stints with the Red Sox, after which his father invited him to come home, take over the family business, and make some real dough. He probably married the blonde and lived happily ever after—without McDermott.

Louisville, too, would now live without McDermott. I was sent down to Scranton, but I was too young and stupid to be depressed. I was 17 going on 18 and playing pro ball, and I didn't care where. Endless bus rides notwithstanding, it was a wonderful life and it beat the hell out of the Singer Sewing Machine Company. I was still pitching, and that was all I cared about. And, all of a sudden at Scranton, everything seemed to fall into place.

I went 12–4 with four shutouts and averaged a strikeout per inning and only one walk for every two Ks, which, for me, was like pulling two rabbits out of a hat. I was primed, ready, and feeling like Superman when we met Utica at home in the playoffs, and I was a human lawnmower as I cut them down inning after inning. Nobody in the dugout said anything, but it was beginning to look like another—well, you know.

In the first of the ninth, Richie Ashburn walked, moved to second on a ground ball, and got to third on a fly. Two outs, one to go, and the catcher called for a curve. I misread the sign one more time, and my best fastball became a passed ball. Ashburn cruised home, and we were behind 1–0. I struck out the last man for my 15th K, and we failed to score in the last of the ninth. I had my second Eastern League no-hitter, but it wasn't a no-runner. We lost 1–0.

On the bus, headed to our next playoff game, Mike Ryba got on me, riding me like a camel driver. He was a nice man, but hard-nosed. He pitched for the rough and rowdy St. Louis Cards' Gashouse Gang, and, in his first season managing Scranton, he wanted that Eastern League pennant bad. "How in the hell could you miss the sign in a situation like that?" he ranted. "How could you be so almighty stupid?" he raved. "When are you gonna learn to play with your head instead of your ass?" he raged.

Ryba's temper tantrum continued. I sat there sinking lower and lower in my seat. I wanted to say, "Why are you riding me? How about the catcher? If you're in the profession, you gotta stop the ball some way or other." But I kept that thought, which would not increase my popularity and would only encourage him to shout longer and louder, to myself. When I had shrunk to about three feet, en route to Tom Thumb, an angry voice from the rear of the bus came to my rescue. It was Molly Craft, a veteran outfielder who had heard enough. "Leave that young boy alone," he said fiercely, "or I'll put out your lights!" Ryba glared at him, but Craft was a pretty big guy. Our manager shut up. A couple of days later, he apologized —kind of. And with the season over, once more I was assigned to Louisville.

It was spring training with the Bosox again in '48. I was warming up to pitch for the B team and firing my best bullets. I saw a guy who was hard not to notice standing behind the batting cage. He was in civvies, tall and slender—about as long as my 6'5" old man—and he looked familiar. I fired a pitch that knocked my catcher on his back. While he was dusting himself off, the tall guy came out and introduced himself.

Now I knew why his long triangular face and the jug ears almost as big as mine looked familiar. I read the sports pages avidly, and last season his face was all over them, particularly when, against the Dodgers, he came up just two outs short of matching the legendary Johnny Vander Meer's pair of consecutive no-hit games. With a sidearm fastball that approached 100 miles an hour, he'd pitched 16 straight victories for Cincinnati and ended the season at 22–8—on a fifth-place ballclub. Pittsburgh Pirate home-run king Ralph Kiner had declared, "He's a scary pitcher. Your knees shake when you try to dig in against him." (Well sure, in 10 years in the majors he led the league in hit batsmen six times. And in those days, guys didn't wear batting helmets.)

Ewell Blackwell extended his hand and confirmed that that's who he was. And then he said, "We heard about you. Yep, you can throw the ball." Suddenly I was 6'5", too.

I felt even taller when I found the ball in my shoe when I reported to the locker room to suit up for our first exhibition game, which happened to be against Blackwell's team. Boston's kindly new manager, Joe McCarthy—"Marse Joe" as the sportswriters had tagged him when he ran the Yankees—gave me a few final words of advice on the sidelines. My fastball had so much natural movement that nobody could be sure where it was going. Especially me. "Now Morris," McCarthy counseled, "all you have to do is aim the ball at the middle of the plate and they'll all jump in the barrel." English translation: aim for the middle and maybe you'll catch one of the corners. Actually, that sounded like a good idea.

That's where I aimed. But in my first start, I was all nerves, and with rugged Clyde Vollmer up at bat, this is what happened—and I quote word for word from a tape the radio announcer of that game of the day ("the Old Scotchman" is what Gordon McLendon called himself) kindly sent me 20 years ago: "Ladies and gentlemen, spring training is about to officially open on a beautiful sunny day here in Sarasota, Florida. A young left-hander named Maurice McDermott is on the mound for the Boston Red Sox, and here comes his first pitch. [Pause.] Ohmigod!"

This was my big moment. I wound up and threw as hard as I could. The ball whistled through the air so high above Vollmer's head that he'd have needed a fireman's aerial ladder to reach it. It tore through the protective wire mesh in the broadcast booth far above home plate and damn near killed McLendon, who, hastily ducking for shelter, knocked over his mike and probably had to be promised an Easter bonus to get him back to the booth. McCarthy and a dozen players on both teams fell off the bench laughing, and I gathered my dignity around me as best I could and got ready to throw the ball in the general direction of the plate again. Preferably at an altitude that wouldn't knock a passing Delta airliner out of the sky.

Once more success did not crown my efforts. This time my efforts crowned Vollmer. It was another smoking fastball, and as it speared poor Clyde in the small of the back, he leaped and gasped for air like one of McCarthy's fish in the barrel. The powerfully built Vollmer was one tough ballplayer. With the slave-labor ballplayer paychecks of that era, he worked winters as a butcher, lugging sides of beef to keep his family in hamburger. Now, with a dazed look on his face, he started an automatic jog toward first. But the wind had been knocked out of him. As he ran, his knees buckled slowly. Then, looking like Buster Keaton disappearing down a flight of cellar stairs in a one-reel silent comedy, before he reached first base, he was out cold.

Several years later, with the pain long gone, Vollmer was traded to the Red Sox. "Do you remember when you hit me in the back?" he asked me, grinning. Now he could grin. "I didn't see the ball. I couldn't believe how hard it hit me. My knees felt like the joints were made of jelly beans."

So with me on the mound, players continued to feel they deserved combat pay every time they went up to the plate. During one exhibition game of the A team against my Bs, with Louisville's manager Mike Ryba umpiring, one of the A-team players claimed he'd been grazed by my fastball. Ryba wasn't buying it. "Get back in there," he growled. "If that guy hit you, you wouldn't be able to walk to first base."

Birdie Tebbetts came out to the mound and instructed me to go easy on veteran outfielder George Case. Case was in his early thirties. He'd had a fine career, mostly with Washington, was a lifetime .282 hitter, and was one of the fastest men in baseball. He made the newspapers once with a crazy stunt in which he raced a horse. All he needed was to beat the horse and they'd have thrown a saddle on him and run him in the Kentucky Derby. He claimed he lost because the horse had two extra legs. Birdie explained: "The Senators released him. He's a great guy and he's trying to make the team. It'll fatten his pension a little. Give him an easy one down the middle." I did, but he popped it up.

I had a good spring. My arm strength continued to grow. Cocky as ever, I felt I'd served my apprenticeship and was ready to play with the big boys. As the camp prepared to break up, McCarthy invited me into his office for a one-on-one. This is it, I thought, my one-way ticket to Boston.

It turned out to be a two-way ticket. McCarthy had 22 pitchers to choose from and, when he made his choices, I'd made the team, but I was the tail end's tail end. I made the team not because he thought I was ready, but because he was under heavy media pressure from reporters and impatient fans who demanded a "youth movement" to get the Sox in contention.

I was semifamous—or maybe the word is notorious—when I showed up in Boston. Back at Sarasota, a freelance photographer had snapped a shot of me with a big silly grin on my face while the trainer rubbed ointment on my fiery sun-reddened neck. (From then on, my teammates called me Turkey Neck. But with the wingspread of my ears in that photo, they could have called me C-47.) The photog sold it to *Life* magazine (for $5,000, somebody told me—I would have paid him $5,001 to burn it), and they ran a full-page glossy picture with a caption describing: "The baseball rookie, his face reflecting the eternal glow of optimism . . . a far more reliable harbinger of spring in the U.S. than the first robin . . ." Man, what a dumb-looking shot. I couldn't get a date for a month.

Norman Rockwell must have had a subscription to *Life*. He painted Ted Williams, Dom DiMaggio, Jackie Jensen, and Billy Goodman in the locker room skeptically staring at a gawky freckle-faced newcomer with teacup ears in an ill-fitting sports jacket clutching a battered suitcase cinched with a leather trousers belt. Me again, or at least everyone assumed it was. Titled "The Rookie," it became a *Saturday Evening Post* cover.

I even had fan clubs. Well, they had started in Scranton. All girls. How about that? I'd get letters in the mail addressed to me in Poughkeepsie or care of the Boston Red Sox, and at first I answered them myself. After a while, there were too many. I sent them to my old man and he did that job for me. Well, he had better handwriting. The first time

I was sent down, one of the girls sent me a song she'd written. The chorus was something like, "The Red Sox will soon see their lack. Mickey, we know you'll be back." Once I went to a fan club meeting, but I kept my distance. These were 13- and 14-year-olds. I didn't want to pitch for Alcatraz.

Every team has its groupies, of course. They were everywhere. Some preferred pitchers. Some preferred big rangy outfielders. Most were equal opportunity givers. The bigger the name, the bigger the following. My old pal Eddie Fisher, the once-superstar singer, came home one night to his hotel to find a nymphet crouched in his laundry hamper. And Mickey Mantle once pulled into his driveway and heard a steady rapping noise from the back of his car. He opened his trunk just as his wife came out to greet him. "Oh," she said caustically, as, to Mickey's astonishment, two teenyboppers crawled out of the trunk, "so now you're hiding them in there." Mickey was pretty glib, but that one was a little hard to explain.

In the bigs at last, I became Mickey McDermott, Finisher of Lost Games. Also Bullpen Hot Dog Gopher. In Detroit, home and visitor pitchers shared the same bullpen, and guys got real bored out there. I was 19, and they were hungry. Both teams took up a collection, looked around, and said, "Here, kid. You get the hot dogs." They rolled my pants up to the knees, put my cap on backward, hung my glove on my belt the way kids carry them, and sent me through the gate leading up the ramp to the center-field bleachers and the concession stand. I came back incognito with 25 hot dogs, feeling grateful that they weren't thirsty, too.

I wasn't as incognito as I hoped. Boston GM Joe Cronin came by just as I arrived at the bullpen gate. He tapped me on the shoulder. "Morris," he said sarcastically, "why don't you just get a scorecard and a pencil and sit in the stands?"

Sitting in the pen or in dugout heat day after day, dozing off was easier than focusing on the game. But McCarthy wasn't having it. The first time he caught me napping, he asked as innocently as though he'd lost it, "Maurice, what's the count?" If you said, "I don't know," he'd tell you, "Now you've got to get in the ballgame. Gotta watch the hitters. Gotta remember what they hit and what they can't." Now there's a manager for you.

There were some pitching moments to remember, too—like my first appearance for Boston in a game against the Yanks in which I struck out Charlie "King Kong" Keller twice. The second time he went down on a curve, swinging so hard he fell down. Old pals McCarthy and Keller got together after the game. "If you got any more rookies like that one," Keller said, "I'm going back to my ranch to raise horses. I've seen some curveballs in my time, but that one I'll never forget. It was awesome."

"My kid," mused my manager, "is still two years away from the big leagues." Grunted Keller, "I wish he was 10 years away."

Nice. I could get Keller out. But that was small comfort one particularly harrowing day when, relieving Mickey Harris in a game at Municipal Stadium in Cleveland, I couldn't get anyone out. Harris had already walked seven men. I should have insisted that the umpire boil the remaining baseballs because they turned out to be contagious. In no time at all, I had walked 11 more. By the time we were finished with our day's work, we had equaled an American League mark unchallenged in 32 years. I think the two Mickeys still share that record. Who else would want it?

A lot of years later, I faced Charlie Keller again when the Yanks and Red Sox played a seven-inning Old Timers' Game. Because I'd played in a Yankees uniform after my Red Sox years, I assumed that their dugout was where I belonged, but when I got there I found that after all those years I was still Wrong Way McDermott.

Yankees executive Art Richman grinned and, to a background chorus of hoots and laughter, announced loudly, "Sorry, Mac, you're playing with the Red Sox. You've been traded again." What a distinction. The only guy ever to get traded in an Old Timers' Game. I had to go back to the clubhouse and change uniforms.

I made them regret it. I pitched a scoreless inning. They didn't radar me, but if I lobbed any balloons over 70 miles an hour, I think my arm would have fallen off. It's like Lefty Gomez said near the end of his career, "I throw as hard as I ever did. The ball just don't get there anymore."

My revenge came when I hit a home run to win it for the Sox. Broadcaster Mel Allen was announcing the game from the field on a loud-speaker: "There it goes, folks. Going, going, gone. Over the fence for a home run. Pitcher Mickey McDermott. How about that? Mickey's on his way to first. Now he's chugging to second. He's huffing and puffing his way to third. I do believe he's gonna make it. No. No. He's tottering halfway between third and home. Hold your breath, folks. Will McDermott make it, or will we have to call an ambulance? He stops. He's catching his breath. He's on his way again.

"How about that? McDermott has touched home plate. And—let me have a look at my watch—rounding the bases only took him three hours and 22 minutes. Now wait, folks. Will he have enough strength to tip his cap to the crowd? Yes, he's done it. Hats off to Mickey McDermott!" Well, it went something like that. I was breathing too hard to hear it all.

Old Timers' Games turned me into Mickey the Menace. When we played at Shea Stadium, no one could argue that I had ever been a Met, so I suited up as a Yankee. When Mantle's turn at bat came up, his legs were hurting, so I grabbed a bat and became the only guy ever to pinch hit for Mickey Mantle. He couldn't have done better himself. I hit another home run.

Now back to Boston. I don't think my manager was pleased by my walkathons. Early in July, with no wins, no losses, a ratio of two walks to every strikeout, a grand total of 23 innings pitched to show for two months' work, and immediately after issuing five passes in two-thirds of an inning against the hapless Philadelphia A's, I was called in to my manager's office. Not, I was pretty sure, to be congratulated.

Marse Joe put it to me straight. "Morris," he said, "I'm sending you to Scranton." He saw the look of indignation on my face. "Now, now. Don't get excited. I'm doing this for your own good. Your arm's not getting enough work up here to be consistent. You need regular innings. Scranton's shorthanded, and you'll get a lot of work there. In time, I expect you to be one of the great ones."

"In time?" I demanded, grabbing my insulted left arm. "I'm the best pitcher you got on this f'g club!"

"Now, Morris. Take it easy. The hardest-throwing, yes. The best, not yet. And I've seen too many strong young arms rushed up and ruined in the majors. I know where Scranton is. It's not Africa. Go do your thing. I'll be watching, and we'll have you back before you know it."

McCarthy was right, of course. In the minors, inexperienced hitters will swing at a fastball a foot over their heads or at a curve in the dirt. Major leaguers are patient. They sit on the curve and wait for a fastball over the plate they can bash back as hard as I threw it. Or they let the umpire do the job for them—keep the bat on their shoulders and cheerfully accept a base on balls. They'd been doing both to me for two months.

But I was a slow learner. I had to learn it all over again in the next chapter.

CHAPTER 4

Second Chances

Sitting on Top of the Triple A World

So, in the second half of the '48 season, it was back to the coal mines. "When do I stop commuting?" I wondered. If they keep this up much longer, I'll be registering to vote in Scranton.

But with plenty of time to think on our 200-mile bus rides, I chewed over my fighting words in Joe McCarthy's office. Yeah, they were going to miss me, all right. Maybe they wouldn't miss my pitching, but they'd miss my harmonica playing. But if I had the best left arm in Boston, how come my numbers there didn't add up to awesome? And now? Now if you judged me solely by my record of three games won and six lost, even Eastern League batters didn't appear to be jumping in the barrel for me.

Look further, though, and I looked a lot better. Some of Scranton's best hitters had moved onward and upward and hadn't been replaced. My teammates swung their bats as though they were afraid opposing pitchers were lobbing hand grenades with the pins removed. I lost three games by 1–0 scores and one by 3–1. One loss was a one-hitter. I averaged 13 Ks a game, and my control was coming along. In one game, much to my surprise, I rang up 18 Ks accompanied by only three walks. And in 10 of the 11 games I started, the scouting reports (yes, McCarthy was watching) read, "Great stuff." Some of them with an exclamation mark! The season's highlight for me came when the regular season was over. In the playoffs, I pitched my third no-hitter, this one the real McCoy with no runs allowed either, beating Utica 8–0.

I'm sure that, back in Boston, McCarthy was pleased that I was making progress. But he had made up his mind about me in mid-'48, and his thought waves read, "Slow and steady wins the pennant." Obviously he'd written my name down in his little black book under the heading, "Needs aging. Do not open this bottle until 1950."

Brilliant as he was at managing, McCarthy didn't—no manager could—make *all* the right moves. And it was his distrust of rookies or, at any rate, his belief that experience trumped youthful promise, that contributed to his biggest mistake of a great 1948 season.

I witnessed that one. Jimmy Piersall, Willard Nixon, and I had been brought up after our season ended in the usual expansion of the parent club's September roster. The Red Sox had been chasing the Indians for weeks and, improbably, by winning our final game of the season (against the Yankees) while Cleveland lost theirs (to Detroit), we finally caught them. Boston went wild. It was his turn in the rotation, and we were all sure that our buddy, hard-working Mel Parnell, who had had a sensational rookie season, was 15–8 with the team's lowest ERA, and had been red-hot in the last half, would start the winner-take-all one-game playoff.

But Marvelous Mel, which is what we began to call him after Dave the "Colonel" Egan dubbed him that in his column in William Randolph Hearst's *Boston American*, made a painful discovery when he arrived in the clubhouse. It had been a tough call for McCarthy, but in the end he had chosen experience over youth. The game ball was in 36-year-old Denny Galehouse's hand.

Denny had had a fine career, but not lately. Experience turned out to be the worst teacher. With a so-so record—he'd won only eight games all season and his ERA was 4.01—Galehouse, well past his prime, was cuffed around by Cleveland batters from, "Play ball!" on. We lost the game, the pennant, and a place in the World Series by a lopsided score of 8–3. McCarthy never forgave himself. And how did Cleveland player-manager Lou Boudreau beat us? By pitching his own prize rookie: 20-game winner Gene Bearden.

But there's always next year, and I was desperate to be a part of it. In the winter of '48, I traveled from Poughkeepsie to Boston to sign my contract and find out how many new suits I could afford. Happy-go-lucky John "Windy" McCall, a fellow rookie but three years older, a gutsy decorated ex-marine who'd seen lots of action, was sitting in GM Joe Cronin's outer office quietly whistling a happy tune.

He went in first and came out smiling. "I just got five grand," he said. "I'll wait for you. When you come out, we can go for some java and doughnuts."

"What'd you get?" he asked when I emerged.

"Four." I didn't plan to hold out. All I wanted to do was play baseball. Hell, four thousand clams a year? I was rich.

"No, no. That's wrong. Wait here." Without knocking, he stormed back into Cronin's office. He emerged five minutes later. "You got another thousand," he said cheerfully.

"Gee, thanks," I said. "Wanna be my manager?"

"Anytime, Mac," he said. "But hey, never be afraid of owners. They're not shooting machine guns. The worst they can do is say no."

In the contest for fun-loving team character, Windy beat even me out. I roomed with him in Sarasota in the spring of '49. I had no toothpaste and asked to use his. He obliged, then said, "Come on, we're going to breakfast." There was a shop in the lobby. He took me by the hand and led me inside. "Give the kid a tube of toothpaste," he said. He wasn't afraid of rookies either. He made me buy my own.

A week or so later, as the team bus left the hotel in Sarasota en route to play the Cards, McCarthy walked down the aisle counting heads.

"Where the hell is that kid McCall now?" he asked wearily.

He was my roomie, but I didn't have a clue. As the bus chugged onto the highway, we heard a car horn toot enthusiastically. A convertible with its top down and three good-looking broads with their hair blowing in the wind pulled alongside.

"Hey, guys! How the hell are you?" shouted the ballplayer behind the wheel. McCarthy just shook his head resignedly as the car, with a farewell toot, accelerated and left us behind. It was McCall, just being McCall.

If you'd read the headlines in pennant-starved lusting-for-revenge Boston papers the morning after I signed my contract in the winter of '48, you'd have thought I'd signed the Declaration of Independence. And the first to do it, risking King George III's gallows, at that.

"McDermott Stardom Seen," said Burt Whitman's two-column story, with a subhead of, "Hose Sign Colorful Youngster and Kinder." Another was headlined: "McDermott Signs, Has Great Future," with the subhead, "Young Southpaw Has Stuff to Be 20-Game Winner if He Masters Control; Kinder Signs." Ellis Kinder, who had won 10 games for the Red Sox the year before and could have been forgiven if he hated me on sight, was old news. I was fresh flesh, especially when the lead could quote GM Joe Cronin burbling (with one eye on the gate), "Why, McDermott's just a baby, but he has all the natural requisites to become an outstanding and a most popular star. . . . It's our belief that McDermott has a fine chance to come close to both Lefty Grove and Lefty Gomez when they were tops, and that stardom may catch up with Maurice overnight."

Some writers were more realistic. When he profiled me in *Sport* in a pre–spring training piece, Al Hirshberg did write a lot of nice things. For one thing, he quoted Yankee Tommy Henrich saying, "Sure, he's a bit wild. But that makes him all the more dangerous. He's as fast as anyone I ever faced—and boy, what a curve!" But Hirshberg led off the profile with a bit of doggerel:

> There was a young man named Mac
> Who used to wind up and rear back.
> He'd throw the ball high and then say, "Oh, my!"
> And his pitch would go far off the track.

Well, I was just as likely to be on the wrong track as the right one. So I made news again ("McDermott Misses Train") when the big day I'd been waiting for all winter finally arrived and, suitcases in hand and with only moments to spare, I hurried to board the Florida Flier—or whatever they called it at the time—at Grand Central. On the right side of the platform sat the Red Sox train. But, being a southpaw, I turned left. I walked forward through the train with the shoulders of the debonair zoot suit I'd just bought at Isenberg & Isenberg knocking spectacles off passengers' noses on both sides of the aisle.

Finally I reached the dining car. Four large men were playing cards at a table at the other end. They had to be baseball players. And the one facing me scanning the cards in his hand . . . it was, no, it couldn't be. Joltin' Joe. Why was he on the Red Sox train? My zoot suit kept on walking, taking me with it, and, as DiMaggio pointed and laughed, they all looked back at me. Charlie Keller? Tommy Henrich? What in the hell were they doing here?

Trigger-quick pitcher Frank Shea spoke first. "Hey, kid," he asked, "did you get traded?" After the laughter died down, he zinged again, "Oh, and next time you leave the house, don't forget to take the hanger out of your jacket."

I made the best of it. I reported to the traveling secretary, who said, "Welcome to the Yankees"—seven years early as it turned out—and found me an empty bunk in the sleeping car, for which, I'm sure, he sent the bill to Boston. "This train goes to St. Pete," he said. "You'll have to figure out a way to get to Sarasota from there." I did. It was the next stop.

When the laughter had died down in Sarasota ("Geez, you southpaws are all cuckoos"), veteran catcher Birdie Tebbetts, obtained in a trade with Detroit, made a special project out of me, putting in extra time behind the plate, trying every trick in the books to cure my wildness. Nothing worked. "Talk to Harold," he said when we played exhibition games against Detroit, "he's a swell guy. Get some advice from him." The first couple of times I was too shy to do it. (Me, too shy? It must have been Florida sunstroke.) But finally when I saw him sitting alone, I introduced myself to the brilliant lefty Hal "Prince" Newhouser and bemoaned my chronic wildness.

"When am I ever going to learn?" I asked wearily.

"Don't worry about learning," said Prince Hal. "You're a baby yet. You learn from experience, not from books or advice. And you gotta pitch to learn. Some one of these days you're gonna wake up on a morning that seems like just another day. That afternoon, you'll walk onto the mound and you'll own it."

I continued to pay rent. But it was heartening—though a little worrisome—to read those spring training press clippings predicting future greatness for me. They made good copy and someday would sell a bunch of curiosity tickets, but once more when spring training camp closed in '49, my ticket read Louisville.

This time Triple A Louisville was a whole different ballgame. I drew the Opening Day assignment against the Minneapolis Millers, owned the mound for the day, and pulled out my favorite letters of the alphabet: a W and 17 Ks. Plus I hit 2 for 4 with a double and a single. The results of my next four starts were promising but not world-beating. I fanned 15, 12, 9, and 12, but though three were only one-run margins—1–0, 2–1, and 3–2— all four went in the books as losses.

Then things started looking up. Toward Boston. May 24, 1949, definitely wasn't third baseman Spider Jorgensen's favorite career moment, it being the day the Brooklyn Dodgers sent him down to St. Paul. But that night's Louisville–St. Paul contest is definitely in my top 10. And 20-something years later it climbed a couple of rungs higher when I was scouting for Billy Martin's Oakland A's and Jorgy, scouting for Kansas City, gave me a Spider's-eye view of that game.

On that enchanted evening, I was in top form. While I was out there taking it one batter at a time, Jorgy's plane deposited him at the Twin Cities airport earlier than he'd expected. He thought, "Hmm, why check into a dreary hotel room to watch the game on TV? I'll show up at the ballpark. Hey, with a little luck, I get a pinch-hit at-bat and whack the ball over the fence. Just to show them back in Brooklyn."

Spider cabbed to the ballpark, dropped his suitcases in the clubhouse, and, about to suit up, stopped in his tracks and—well, let him tell you what he told me: "Through the open windows, I hear this awesome 'pow' as a ball smacks into the catcher's mitt. I hear the crowd roar: '13.' Then another 'pow.' And another. I start to walk down the stairs toward the St. Paul dugout. There's a fourth 'pow' and another roar from the crowd: '14.' What the hell is going on? I hang back just out of sight of the dugout and watch the game. I see you out there, a skinny kid throwing rockets. I don't see the pitches. I just hear them explode into the mitt. The crowd shouts: '15.' By now I've got it figured out. Fifteen Ks. The crowd's keeping count, but that's high enough for me. I think, 'Who's gonna hit against that? I got a wife and kids. No point in getting killed.' I turn around, grab my suitcase, and head to the hotel."

Jorgensen had arrived on what, for me, too, was a night to remember —a night in which I struck out 20 batters and broke an American Association single-game strikeout record while fanning the side in the final three innings. It's a record that still stands, though a few years later Herb Score, then pitching for Indianapolis but later a Cleveland strikeout king, was on a pace to take it away. Amazingly, with three full innings still to go, Score had already struck out 17 of 18 batters. Suddenly, the curse of the fastball pitcher (how well I know it) struck. He walked one batter, then another, and a third. After the fifth gift walk, his manager yanked him and my record was safe—forever, I guess, because the American Association has since gone out of business. But Herb gets the consolation prize: most Ks in six innings.

After that St. Paul game, I was sitting on top of the Triple A world. Radar guns weren't used in the minors yet, but somebody in the stands who claimed to be able to clock pitches told me mine had ranged from 95 to an even-I-was-impressed 101 miles an hour. Tex Aulds, who caught me then and had caught me at Scranton, didn't need a radar gun to tell him that. After every game, the meat of his catching hand was red and swollen.

Catchers are used to being beat up. It goes with the territory. But a couple of years later, catching me in Boston, Sammy White decided it was time to do something about it. Bright idea. He went to Filene's Basement. There he found just what he needed to protect his palm from my heat.

And what, I wonder, was the cashier thinking when she rang up Sammy's purchase of a pair of falsies?

One afternoon when my fastball wasn't fooling anyone but me and the traffic at home plate got unusually heavy, Sammy's gloved hand tagged the first man crossing home plate. But then, before he could set himself, a second runner came flying through. Sammy's mitt took a hard hit. He got the double play, but high into the air flew mitt and falsies. They landed on the mound with the red nipples Sammy had painted on them for locker room laughs exposed for all the world to see. The crowd roared, and the next day anyone who hadn't seen the game roared, too— at the graphic cartoon starring Sammy and his falsies on a *Boston Globe* sports page.

Meanwhile, not yet at Boston, I loved (and you can bet I saved) the Associated Press piece in the papers headlined, "Fanning 20 Batters Old Stuff to Sox Farmhand McDermott." Datelined May 25, it said: "The slim 20-year-old set an American Association strikeout record against St. Paul last night, but he's been doing it since he was a kid of 15 in high school." (Who says the media doesn't get anything right?) It continued with words that must have made a happy woman out of my mom, and I could just see my old man proudly waving that clipping, wrapped around a bottle, in the saloon that night. I knew how proud he was of me when my mom told me that for years when he knew I was pitching he'd take a radio up to the top of College Hill where the reception was so good that he could pick up games broadcast from Albany, Chicago, or just about anywhere.

I'd made a little piece of history, itched to make more, and now my streak of pitching K-ball continued. In my next four games, having a wonderful time trying to break my own record, I struck out 19, 18, 17, and 19 and in the process compiled another one of those bizarre records that baseball statisticians love to come up with and color broadcasters love to quote—the record for most batters struck out in five consecutive games: 93. But that was in the minors. The majors was where I wanted it to happen.

Because of circumstances beyond McCarthy's control, I was about to get my shot—but not before a very tragic event. My buddy Chuck Koney and I were both sure that it was just a matter of time before we were playing in Fenway Park. Chuck was smart, a sweet hitter, and an acrobat at second base who could have been as good as or better than (and I'm not knocking one of the greatest) our parent team's Bobby Doerr. And with his warm, infectious laugh (he even laughed at *my* jokes), he was great fun to be around.

A three-game series in Milwaukee with the Brewers was coming up, and Chicago, where he lived, was only an hour or so south on the lake shore. Chuck got permission to spend the night home before the series started.

"What's your rush?" I asked. "We've got two off-days after the series. Why not wait 'til then?"

"No. My wife's about to have a baby. She needs me."

Chuck went home. That night, he went down the basement stairs to light a gas furnace. There must have been a leak in the system. When he lit the match, an explosion threw him to the concrete floor, mangling his leg. He was a young ballplayer who could do it all, on the verge of making the big time, and suddenly one-legged. It would have been easy for Chuck to slide into self-pity, heavy drinking, and chronic depression. Not this ballplayer.

He got fitted for an artificial leg, his teammates threw a benefit for him that brought in more than $5,000 (equivalent then to a major league salary), and the Sox gave him a lifetime job as a scout. I see him now and then. He's still the same old cheerful Chuck. And, of course, I've never said, "You should have listened to me instead of going home." If I did, he'd probably smile and say, "Ah, it was worth it. Before the explosion, I got to kiss my wife."

On June 13, I beat Indianapolis 1–0 at Parkway Field in Louisville, bringing my K total to (but who's counting?) 116 in 68 innings. The season was young, but the Red Sox were already 11 games out of first place, and Boston's impatient sportswriters were at it again, agitating for an early burial of the current pitching staff. They were in full cry with, "Stop trading for arm-weary old veterans. Bring up the farmhands!" I wasn't complaining. That was me. Fresh meat.

Next day, I was back in our Louisville locker room changing when the club president and Red Sox chief scout Larry Woodall entered wreathed in smiles. "Nice going, kid," said Woodall. "Mr. McCarthy has ordered you back to Boston. He's leaning too hard on Parnell. They need another lefty. You fly to Boston in the morning."

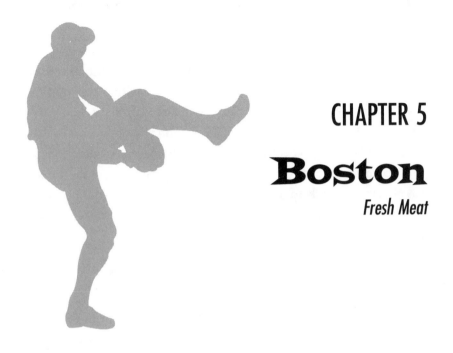

CHAPTER 5

Boston

Fresh Meat

Al Lopez—who later managed the parent club in Cleveland—was the Indianapolis Indians manager who watched me shut out his team with 19 strikeouts.

"The Bostons made a mistake bringing you back up ahead of schedule," he told me years later. "I wish I could have told you at the time, but it would've been called tampering. You were still learning how to pitch. Sure, you were finally getting the ball over the plate, but you were too much in love with your fastball to set it up with a change and keep hitters off balance."

After shutting out his team, would I have listened to Lopez? No way. And the sportswriters whose columns—about Red Sox players who belonged in nursing homes—helped get me up there? If I'd had the money, I'd have bought them each a case of 12-year-old Scotch.

I realized how many cases I'd have had to spring for when we landed at Logan Airport and I found myself surrounded by reporters and photographers. They had demanded that owner Tom Yawkey stop buying "used-up big leaguers from second division clubs" and bring up the kids. Here, at last, was a real kid, a gawky 20-year-old string bean, the only Eastern League player ever to throw three no-hitters, and with a bunch of strike-out records (let's not talk about the bases-on-balls records) in the American Association behind him. They didn't want much—just that I close the 11-game gap between Boston and the league-leading Yankees.

McCarthy, forced to pick a minor league plum before he thought it was ripe, wasn't ready to start me. But since I was just 20, and the youngest member of the team, he seemed ready to adopt and protect me—even keep me chaste. One day he called me into his office.

"Morris," he asked, "do you have a girlfriend?"

"Yes, sir," I replied.

"Morris, did you ever hear of a pitcher named Lefty Gomez?"

"Yes, sir. He was my idol as a kid." (I didn't think this was the time to tell him that when the Yankees farm team Gomez was managing came to Scranton, I'd infuriated my "idol" by shouting, "There's the guy who took 10 years off Johnny Murphy's arm." Murphy, of course, was the ace Yankees relief pitcher who frequently had to bail out the strikeout king.)

"Well, a word of warning, Morris," McCarthy continued solemnly. "Lefty Gomez left his fastball in the sheets."

The clubhouse door was open, and not a few pitching arms and ribs were put in jeopardy as guys pounded one another on the back, hooting fit to split their undershorts.

I think McCarthy firmly believed, as boxing trainers probably still do, that sex drains an athlete's vitality. Enjoying newfound celebrity that attracted young women like a patented love potion (and, yes, as so often happens, led to a break up with my shy high school sweetheart), I was not eager to believe that. I still don't. One winter, convinced that I should put a few more pounds on my bones, the club sent me to Grossinger's, a legendary Catskills resort famous, among other things, for its food. In the first few weeks, I discovered to my delight that sex, too—lots of it, with a new crop of chicks checking in every Sunday after-noon—was on the menu.

The Swedish heavyweight, Ingemar Johansson, happened to be training there. He ran, he went a half-dozen rounds, he hit the light and heavy bags, and then he hit the sack with his beautiful blonde fiancée, Birgit. That performance didn't seem to affect his ring performance one bit. In fact, he won the world heavyweight championship.

Nevertheless, McCarthy did his best—very unsuccessfully—to field a team of virgins. In my second Red Sox spring training in '48, I reported to Sarasota, which as far as the eye could see in those condo-free days was nothing but playing field, palm trees, and sand. At 3:00 or 4:00 A.M., through my open window I heard a woman's plaintive wail from outside on the beach, "Oh, Junior, don't leave me, honey!"

The next voice I heard was Junior's—Vern "Junior" Stephens, our shortstop—and it was clear that in his first night game of the season he had not struck out. "Enough! Go home, woman," he shouted. "I gotta play ball in a few hours."

Next morning, McCarthy strode through the locker room, a little cigar thrust in his mouth. We all had to be suited up before he arrived, but we couldn't hit the playing field until Marse Joe, who demanded and commanded respect as the winningest manager in New York Yankees history, made his late and dramatic entrance.

The room fell silent as he walked through. He spoke suddenly in a shrill voice: "Oh, Junior, don't leave me, honey!" There was a moment of stunned silence, and then the clubhouse exploded with laughter. Marse Joe just kept on walking. He'd made his point. Stephens turned redder than a hooker who's been stiffed.

When I first joined the team in spring training, I was so skinny my bat cast a fatter shadow than I did. But I sprinted around the outfield like a yearling colt, and I loved to showboat—to haul off and throw from deep center to home plate on the fly. McCarthy watched for a while and then waved me in.

"Morris," he said paternally, "sit down next to me. I don't want you running like that. Go back to the hotel. Have a glass of milk and a sandwich, and take a nap."

Walt Dropo, my ex-Scranton roomie and fellow rookie, was standing nearby. "Geez," he complained when I left the bench, "you are McCarthy's little Bobo. He's giving you milk and cookies, and he hasn't even talked to me yet."

McCarthy's coddling included rooming me on the road with my buddy Mel Parnell, a serious lefty with a sparkling rookie year already to his credit. "Mr. Parnell," he said, "you've been in the army. You're six years older than Morris. I want you to be a father to this young man. And I want you two to talk a lot of baseball."

Mel tried. In the end he had to tell our manager, "I can't keep up with Mickey. He's a night person. How can we talk baseball? When he comes in, I've been asleep for hours." He did talk to me about the short left-field wall. "For a lefty to win at Fenway," he counseled, "you've got to work on the inside of the plate." He did it so successfully that in his sophomore year he won 25 games. Never very good at taking advice, I didn't do it enough.

Poor Mel. I'd come in late and wake him up to tell stories and talk— about celebrities I'd met at Toots Shor's but rarely about baseball. Finally he'd implore, "Please, Mickey, please—let's go to bed. I'm pitching tomorrow." In despair, he went to the skipper and begged for a change of venue. "Please, Mr. McCarthy," he said. "I can't room with McDermott anymore. All I see are his suitcases. You asked me to help him. Help him? If this keeps up, he's gonna take five years off my career and I'll be back in the minors."

Parnell got his wish, but not 'til the end of the season. For my remaining years with the Red Sox, I bounced from roomie to roomie like a chrome ball in a pinball machine. There was, I heard, some talk of renting a park bench for me. Unfortunately, I did take five years off Mel's career. But that's another story. Later.

As part of his rookie education project, McCarthy would sit next to me on the airplane and point out negative role models. "Don't get like him," he'd say. One of the "hims" at the time was noted ladies' man Junior Stephens. Another was Handsome Jack Kramer who had a movie star's wardrobe and wore a different outfit at every meal. (OK, once in a while a breakfast outfit was repeated at lunch.) A few years later, I was probably one of the "hims."

Someone McCarthy didn't finger—and this undermined his arguments against both whiskey and women—was Ellis Kinder, who led the club in booze and broads while winning 23 games and exhaling whiskey fumes instead of carbon dioxide. But then, how could he not want me to be like this uniquely iron-armed, iron-stomached pitcher?

He never asked Kinder where he'd been and what he'd done the night before. He always knew where Kinder was—in bed with a bottle and a blonde. And, after a failed experiment when he'd persuaded Kinder to pitch a game without drinking the night before only to see him knocked out of the box, he knew better than to order him to attend an AA meeting. Ellis may have had two hollow legs, but his pitching arm was solid.

The rest of us were treated differently, and we were all convinced that he either had spies in every saloon in town or eyes in the back of his head. He'd say, "Mr. Kramer, did you have a nice time last night?" Handsome Jack, looking as beatifically innocent as Saint Peter, would shrug: "Geez, no, Joe. I was in bed at 11:00." McCarthy would ask, "Mr. Kramer, do you have a twin brother?" His mystified victim would deny that he did. "That's odd," McCarthy would say, "I could have sworn that was your twin brother I saw at Blinstrub's about 2:00 this morning." We finally figured out that he went through our civvies in the locker room before we came off the field after batting practice. The matchbook covers in our pockets gave us away.

McCarthy was a student of human nature—a psychologist without a Ph.D. If he caught you in the hotel barber shop getting a shave, you might as well pack your bags. Any man who was too lazy to shave himself was too complacent to hustle on the field. And to McCarthy, complacency was private enemy number one. "Give me 100 percent on the field," he'd say. "That's all I want—100 percent." And that meant no fraternizing with the enemy on the field. His position was, "I don't care what you do after the game, but never talk to the other team while you play the game."

McCarthy distrusted anyone who drank from a bottle labeled in ounces instead of proof. "Never trust a Coca-Cola drinker," he'd say. "A drunk? You always know where to find him. In the nearest bar. But a Coca-Cola drinker? He might be at your house screwing your wife."

We were in Detroit when he stopped me as I was walking through our hotel lobby. "Come with me, Morris," he said. "Do you see that gentleman over there?" He indicated our first baseman and utility outfielder, Billy Hitchcock. "He's smoking a pipe. People who smoke pipes are happy and complacent." He led me to Hitchcock. "Son," he asked, "what are you hitting?" He knew, of course, to the last decimal point. "Oh," said Billy, "I'm getting there, Joe. I'm up to .239." McCarthy smiled. "Really? You're going to love Washington, Mr. Hitchcock."

The often-cellar-dwelling Washington Senators team, where I later served time myself, was a combination penal colony and purgatory. Hitchcock managed to escape that fate by coaxing his average up to .298 (I guess he ditched his pipe), but Sam Mele wasn't as fortunate. When Sam missed an easy fly ball and came into the dugout moaning, "I lost the ball in the sun," McCarthy, who hated excuses and was not thrilled with Sam's .233 batting average, was ready. "They play a lot of night games in Washington, Mr. Mele," he said sardonically. "But be careful there in the outfield. The moon might get in your eyes."

I was manager's pet for a while, but he didn't spare the sarcasm when I screwed up. One day, Joe DiMaggio hit a home run off me in the tenth inning to win the game. I was furious at him but angrier at myself. I stormed into the clubhouse, throwing bats and pop bottles across the room and endangering life and limb. McCarthy entered. "Morris," he said quietly, "come into my office." I followed meekly.

"Do you know the name of the gentleman who hit that ball into the bleachers?"

"Yes," I said, playing my bit part. "Joe DiMaggio. But I don't give a rap. I had two strikes on him."

"Morris," he said, "when a pitcher has got two strikes on a batter, that is not the time to feel proud of himself. When you're pitching to hitters like Mr. DiMaggio, the third strike is the only one that counts." He paused for effect. "Beside that, Morris, Mr. DiMaggio has hit home runs off better pitchers than you'll ever be." With a few well-chosen sentences, McCarthy had made two important points. The second one dropped me to my knees, where I belonged.

Sportswriters knew McCarthy ran a tight ship, insisting, for example, on something no manager could get away with in running today's millionaire-ballplayer clubs—that his team appear in public in jackets and ties. But common sense prevailed. When a sportswriter challenged him with, "How come you let Williams get away with breaking your dress code?" McCarthy answered the question with a question: "Hmm, what is Mr. Williams hitting?"

"About .390," the writer volunteered.

"Well," asked McCarthy innocently, "what would you say to Mr. Williams?"

The writer squirmed. McCarthy smiled. "I want to be fair. Any other gentleman on this club hits .390, he won't have to wear a necktie either."

As much as McCarthy thought of me as a son, I thought of him as a second father (made easier by the fact that he was no slouch at drinking and often matched Kinder shot for shot), and he often acted like a proud father. Like the time early on when a photographer asked him to call me in from the outfield where I was shagging flies so he could shoot some pictures. McCarthy shouted, "Hey, Gomez, come on in here." Then he added, "Sorry, it's those bullets he throws. I keep confusing him with Lefty Gomez."

But my manager knew I needed steady work or I'd be firing blanks. I would be wilder than (take your choice from a few of Boston writers' colorful metaphors from my first short season) "a prairie flower," "a South African bushman," "a soapbox orator," or "an unmowed lawn." So he put me in the bullpen for spot and long relief. If it hadn't been for the one occasion in which Kinder outdid himself, I might have stayed there for the rest of the summer. As it was, Ellis thoughtfully gave me my first big-league "start" against the Chicago White Sox.

My locker was next to Kinder's. When I ambled in late one afternoon for practice before a Friday night game, it was immediately clear that he had had a very busy night extending into a very busy day. He looked like a Cherokee brave ready to go to war, but the war paint daubed on his face and neck was lipstick, and when he reached out to don his spikes, they fell from his hand. He was sloshed, so sloshed that I wondered if he'd be able to find the pitching mound without a guide dog. I looked around at the other players changing into their uniforms. Nobody else seemed concerned. OK, everybody knew Kinder pitched better drunk than he did sober. So who was I, a mere rookie, to poke my Irish nose into what was clearly none of my business?

The game started. I loosened up with a few warm-ups and then watched from the bullpen as Kinder wound up and let go. The ball sailed over the press box. The umpire—as if he had to—threw up his left arm. John Schulte, the bullpen coach, had not been blind to Kinder's condition in the locker room but wasn't going to be the one to rat on him. He said, "Uh-oh." Kinder threw another pitch, closely resembling the first. The bullpen phone jangled. The coach picked it up. As he did, a third pitch whizzed to parts unknown. McCarthy hurriedly abandoned the bench and jogged out to the mound. Schulte told me, "Get loose quick. Joe wants you out there."

Waved in by McCarthy, the infielders surrounded the mound, attempting to hide Kinder from public view. McCarthy, who was a very smart man, urgently whispered in his pitcher's ear. Kinder nodded and slowly lifted his left arm over his head, shook it, and obligingly winced. Oops. He was a right-hander. McCarthy turned and beckoned me in. As I trotted toward the mound, Kinder reflexively reached down for the rosin bag, missed it by a foot and, unable to stop himself, stumbled toward second base. As we passed, he mumbled, "Go get 'em, kid."

A couple of coaches helped Kinder off the field, locked the door to keep out eye-witness sports reporters, and for the next several hours alternated cold showers with black coffee IVs, so that when the sportswriters filed in for postgame interviews Kinder would be as sober as a Supreme Court judge. Which, eventually, if temporarily, he was.

Meanwhile, I was doing OK out there. Well, OK enough to win. I made it into the eighth inning, fanning five and giving up only three hits. That's the good news. The not-so-good news is I threw 36 pitches in the second inning and 28 in the sixth. I walked nine (most of them late in the game) and hit one batter, enabling the White Sox to piece together five runs. Fortunately, my teammates were having a real good hitting day and we had twice as many runs. The final score was a ragged 10–8, but who cares? Next morning's headline read: "Sox Rookie Pitcher Wins in Debut."

Actually, I did care. I fervently wished I'd been allowed to finish. Sure, nine walks looked bad, but I wasn't missing the corners by much. A veteran would have gotten a lot of the close calls, but this was the majors. No umpire gives the corners to a rookie, especially one with a reputation for wildness. Anyway, the game built up my confidence. It wasn't like the year before when I just threw the ball as hard as I could and prayed it to the plate. (But I did keep Mr. Yawkey awake nights worrying about the lawsuits if one of my wild pitches sank a Harvard crew rowing a shell three blocks away on the Charles River.)

My second start? Well, legendary McDermott modesty prevents me from telling it like it was, so I'll let sportswriter Jack Malaney do it for me. With a box score headed, "The Kid Is There," Malaney wrote, "Come what may during the remainder of the season, Maurice 'Slats' McDermott was proclaimed a major league pitcher deluxe last night at Fenway Park by the 28,080 fans who watched him start and finish his second major league pitching chore. . . . The 20-year-old southpaw marvel, recalled only last week from Louisville, limited St. Louis Browns to three hits and shut them out. . . . Facing only 28 batters, young McDermott was as near letter-perfect as Marse Joe McCarthy and his severest critics could ask." (Malaney did taint my triumph just a tad when he added that, with two key players out of the lineup with injuries, the weak-hitting Browns were even weaker than usual. Writers! What a bunch of cynics.) Nevertheless and notwithstanding, I was suddenly the cinnamon toast of Boston—the new Lefty Grove, the new Herb Pennock, the new this and the new that. The new messiah who would lead the Red Sox not just to the pennant but to the World Series as well. And the best omen: I'd walked only two.

I paced the bullpen for the next 10 days, but then came the moment I'd lived for. On June 27, McCarthy announced to the press that when the Yankees came to town the next day, I would be his starter. Well, if you read my Foreword (on pg. ix), you know what happened. I struck out nine and gave up only three walks. But Joe DiMaggio, coming back full of fire after being out for two months with a painful heel spur, singled and then homered with a man on base, after Hank Bauer—who had my number throughout my career—started me off with a three-run homer. We lost 5–4.

One of the sportswriters summed it up this way: "What the big guy did to McDermott stock shouldn't happen to Casey Stengel's oil investments. . . . But aside from two devastating socks, the Bombers didn't do much with the young fireballer's slants, no less than nine going down on K's and admitting the elongated McDermott was the fastest pitcher they'd looked at this season."

The Big Dago (yes, that's what we all called him in those ethnically incorrect days) put another small bandage on my bruised ego when a reporter asked him what he thought of Boston's rookie southpaw. Said the great man, "He can't miss." Well, I sure didn't miss his bat.

Eight days later I got another shot, this time in Yankee Stadium. After my 5–4 loss, we'd dropped seven games in a row, and I was not about to let it be eight—not with all my pals from Elizabeth and Poughkeepsie in the stands rooting for me. This time I went all the way to a 4–2 victory, striking out eight and allowing only five hits.

It was a game that almost got away when Big Joe stepped into a nickel curve that failed to spin. When I heard the crack of his bat, all I could say was, "Oops!" But, the luck of the Irish, a leprechaun must have been riding the ball that day. Steering it just inches to the left of the left-field foul pole, the little fella turned what looked like a certain home run into just another strike. After that I just poured the ball in and away from DiMaggio—hard enough so my back and shoulder felt sore the last few innings and I missed my next turn, but that was OK. It was the start of an eight-game Boston winning streak from a dozen games back that began a dramatic 36–10 pace and overtook the Yankees in the waning days of what David Halberstam famously called the "Summer of '49."

Parnell, Kinder, Kramer, Stobbs—it didn't seem to matter who pitched, the team was hotter than July 4 at the equator. I pitched three consecutive solid games, losing one to Cleveland's Mike Garcia 1–0 ("the Sox let down one of their finest young pitchers, who pitched his heart out to win and didn't even get a run to help him"), beating the White Sox 11–2 on a 7-K six-hitter (I had two hits), and then getting even with Cleveland in a shutout (a no-hitter for the first six innings) in which only one batter reached third base.

The second Cleveland game made me a popular hero in Boston almost as big as the Dutch boy who saved Holland by sticking his finger in the dike. I pitched the game with a blister on my middle finger, but from the newspaper stories next morning, you'd have thought I'd done it while fighting off a pack of snarling wolves.

Here's what John Drohan wrote (yes, I saved all my clippings—anything wrong with that?): "As the tall skinny kid came steaming into the room, McCarthy shook his hand, 'Kid, you've got heart. That's what counts in this game.'" And Steve O'Leary (in Boston all the sportswriters were Irish) wrote, "The kid is not only well on his way to pitching greatness, but he has the heart of a lion. . . . Mac didn't mention it after the game, but he pitched the entire affair with a broken blister on the middle finger of his throwing hand that grew more raw as the game progressed. Catcher Matt Batts enthused, 'That kid may be a skinny little guy, but he has the heart of an elephant.'" (Oh, shucks.) I didn't mind what Jack Malaney said either (I was already a lion and an elephant): "Maurice McDermott advanced one notch nearer to greatness yesterday afternoon when he shut out the high-flying Indians, 3–0, in his second shutout of his short season."

Apparently none of the writers had any idea what a leaky blister could do for a pitcher's effectiveness. I didn't realize it either until the day trainer Eddie Froelich came up to me in Philadelphia and said, "It's the skipper's birthday. He wants to know if you can pitch against the A's tonight."

"The blister's not all healed yet," I said, "but I'll give it a shot."

"I can try painting it with that new stuff," Eddie said. "NuSkin, it's called. I'll give the blister a couple of coats. When it dries, it's supposed to fuse with the skin to protect it."

But baseballs have seams, and it didn't take long for them to blow my fuse. I didn't have my good fastball because the seams—a fastball pitcher goes across the seams to make the ball rise—would tear the skin immediately. I threw between the seams, which makes the ball sink. In the second inning, Sammy White lobbed the ball back to me and I saw blood on it. The next pitch I threw, the ball fell off the table. The batter missed it by a foot.

Sammy came out to the mound. "What the hell was that?" he asked. "Whatever it was, keep doing it."

I showed him my bloody finger. He grinned. "They'll never hit you today. You've got a natural spitter." With the adrenaline flowing, I didn't feel any pain, but by the end of the game the finger was red and raw. McCarthy told the press corps he was gonna stop calling me Morris and start calling me Moxie. And by my next pitching turn five or six days later, the finger had healed.

As sportswriters desperate to fill their daily quota of newsprint wrote about me, someone, dipping into my life before Boston, implied that when I signed with the Sox, the club's filthy lucre—the $5,000 dangled before my innocent father's eyes—had forced me to sacrifice my last two years of high school education. Of course, to a student whose favorite subject was baseball, it was a sacrifice eagerly accepted. The writer failed to point out that my favorite lyric belonged to a song traditionally chanted on the last day of school, one that no doubt danced through my head when I signed the Boston contract: "No more homework, no more books, no more teachers' dirty looks."

Still, the burden of guilt this revelation carried was apparently too much for owner Tom Yawkey to bear. Yawkey spoke to McCarthy, who spoke to Boston's popular Cardinal Cushing, and, much to my surprise—my closest involvement with the Church on Sunday mornings had been to pass it by on the way to sandlot games—I was invited to drop in on His Excellency.

The phone beside my bed at the hotel disturbed my sleep one morning with an unexpected ring. It was my manager.

"What did I do now?"

"The boss wants to see you."

"You mean Mr. Cronin?"

"No, Cardinal Cushing."

"What does he want with me?"

"The appointment is 10:00 A.M. tomorrow. Don't oversleep. And don't call him Father. Genuflect and kiss his ring."

"I know that. I was an altar boy. Well, not for long. I knocked a 30-pound missal over on the priest's foot. He screamed and dropped everything, including the chalice. It rained wine. They traded me to another church."

"Well, don't drop a missal on the cardinal."

The next day I was at the archdiocese on time, sinking into a red rug so thick you needed a machete to walk through it. Two bishops came out and took me by the arm. "Well, lad, how are you?" They led me into the cardinal's office where he was seated—all 6'3" and 200-plus authoritative pounds of him—behind a huge mahogany desk.

"Morris lad," he said, "I hear through the grapevine you don't have your high school diploma."

"Your Excellency," I start to say.

"Off your knees, my boy" he said. (I had no idea I was on them.) "Sit down. You're an Irish lad and this is Boston. We can't have this. Your high school principal is waiting for you in a room down the hall. You're a good lad. We'll help you here. Keep going to church."

The audience was over. It's just as well that I didn't get a chance to say, "I do most of my praying when Joe DiMaggio is up at the plate." A bishop turned me around and led me to a room where my favorite principal, Sister Teresa, was waiting.

"You big sonovabitch," she said amiably, amazing and delighting me with words I'd never heard from her before. (But, then, soon after—and I hope I didn't drive her out—she left the Church and went to work for an oil company.) "Looks like you conned the cardinal. Here's your high school diploma. Amazing—you got it without doing a day's work." And she gave me a hug.

Back at the hotel there was a message waiting for me: "Joe Cronin called. See him at his office." Later that day I paid him a visit full of my usual boyish charm.

"How did it go?"

"The cardinal gave me a high school diploma, sir." Pause for effect. "I thought about refusing it."

Cronin was alarmed. "Sonovabitch. You didn't, did you?"

"Not exactly, sir. What I said was, 'Shove it. I want one from Harvard.'"

Cronin almost swallowed a chunk of his Havana cigar. "You didn't," he accused. "Did you?"

"No, sir. But could Mr. Yawkey speak to the president of Harvard? I can't wait to see the proud and happy look on my mom's face when I unroll an honorary degree from Harvard."

Cronin threw me out of his office. The look on his face wasn't proud and happy.

CHAPTER 6

The Wintry Summer of '49

A Run for the Pennant

The look on Ted Williams' face was pained but amused when someone showed him the headline, "McDermott Wins Fans, Outshines Williams." The article was written by a writer who, like most of them, embraced every possible opportunity to rub Ted the wrong way. With sandpaper.

This time the writer stated, "Bigger and better in the estimation of fans, Mickey McDermott has become the most popular player on the Red Sox and bids fair to become the most popular player in the American League before the season is ended. It's been just six weeks since McDermott came home and in that short space of time he's already become Boston's greatest baseball figure. The slim southpaw with the buggywhip arm has surpassed in popularity Ted Williams, Vern Stephens, Johnny Sain and the other established Boston stars . . . Boston fans have been seeking some athlete to worship since the late Babe Ruth left here for New York back in 1918. . . . Ted was never really popular after that first season. . . . A kid who set attendance records in nearly every

American Association park during his brief stay with Louisville has arrived. He'll be the game's greatest attraction and as long as he keeps his sunny disposition, his popularity will grow. He's out-statured Williams already. And maybe it's a good thing. Ted didn't appreciate his chance. McDermott may."

Of course, I got a kick out of reading that. Who wouldn't? But as a prediction ("the game's greatest attraction"), it was about as credible as, "Buy Enron and you'll be on Easy Street for life." As I read, icicles formed on my spine. "Uh-oh," I thought, "how's Ted going to take this?"

It was insulting to the purest and most passionate ballplayer in baseball and ridiculously early in the game to even imagine about me. Ted was suiting up for BP when I came in, and when he'd finished tying his shoelaces, he beckoned me to join him with a stern look on his face. "Well," I thought, "here it comes!"

"Bush," he said, "don't let that write-up go to your head. You're not the star here. I am."

"Ted," I said, wondering if sinking to my knees and groveling might be a good idea, "I know that. But hell, I didn't say it. I didn't write it. I had nothing to do with it. I don't know where he got a crazy idea like that. But you know how writers are."

If anyone knew that, Ted did. He'd been assaulted by a handful of crusty sportswriters on a daily basis no matter how many games he won in the last of the ninth, no matter how often he made a game-saving catch or won the Triple Crown—all because he refused to tip his cap or take curtain calls after a homer, and, perhaps the biggest sin of all, because he thumbed his nose at the press. Anything he said went, and what he had said to management was, "No press in the locker room until an hour after the game." That gave him time to shower and get out of there. The sportswriters never forgave him. It delayed their cocktail hour.

Where there was no fault, they'd invent it. And if they could use me to get at him, well, why not? So he did know how writers—at least, some of them—are. But a week or so later, he didn't know why I was wearing his custom uniform pants.

Ted's uniforms were made to order. The shirts were especially important. They had to have wide sleeves and be loose in the arms to offer complete freedom for that incredibly free-and-easy swing of his. So that day, I was about to pull up my regulation wool pants (Can you imagine what wearing all-wool shirts and pants was like on a humid August afternoon, collecting five pounds of sweat that felt like 20?) when I heard my name called again: "Bush!" That had to be Ted. I looked toward him. With a disgusted look on his face, he held a pair of pants in his hand.

"What, Ted?"

"Come here, Bush. Don't make me tell you again. Hand over those pants. *I'm* the star."

I looked down at the trousers. Inside the waistband was a circle of stars. His tailor's idea? Ted's idea? I had no idea. All I knew was that Johnny Orlando, our clubhouse guy, had given me the wrong pair of pants. And because we all had name tapes sewn inside, Ted didn't have to be Sherlock Holmes' younger brother to figure out that the pants he was holding were mine and I was the rascal who had his.

I didn't want Ted's clothes. I didn't have stars embroidered into mine, but in civvies I was a pretty hot dresser myself. When we were in New York, I'd drop in at Isenberg & Isenberg's to outfit myself in New York's finest. I'd be standing there in front of the three-way mirror with a spiffy new sharkskin suit on, and I'd say, "Looks great, huh?" And Joe, the tailor, the owner, and the sweeper, would say, "Yes, Moishe, and for you this suit is perfect. Two pairs of pants. You get a cigarette burn, you still got a spare." I usually burned the jacket.

I fell in love with a gleaming black mohair suit Nat King Cole wore onstage. "Joe," I asked, "you got any mohair suits?"

"For you, Moishe, anything."

It took him a couple of days to get my size, but when he'd made a few alterations, I was proud as a Poughkeepsie peacock. Next day, clad in my new suit, I stepped out from under the canopy of the Commodore, an elegant hotel that Tom Yawkey owned at 42nd and Lex in Manhattan. In the off-season, ballplayers could stay there for $5 a room. It was raining hard, but who needed an umbrella? It wasn't more than a dozen steps to the game bus that would take us to the Bronx to face the Yanks.

We were rolling along the East Side Drive toward Yankee Stadium when Parnell stared at me funny.

"What?" I asked.

"Mac," he said, "look at your suit."

I looked down. The cuffs of my suit jacket had started to climb precipitously toward my elbows. My trouser cuffs were headed north toward my knees. "What in the hell is this?" I asked. "Where did Joe Schneider get the material for this suit—from Houdini?"

Next day, I ambled into his store with the suit on a hanger. He was all smiles. I put on the suit and stood there feeling like I was wearing my little brother's clothes. Joe's face was still wreathed in smiles. He said with fatherly pride, "Moishe, look how you've grown!"

P.S.: He took the suit back.

My first year with the Red Sox, Johnny Pesky and his sweetheart of a wife, Ruthie, had adopted me and I boarded with them. I didn't want anything to do with laundry, so I'd buy a shirt (and I did not wear $2 shirts), wear it once, and then toss it in a corner.

At hotels, there'd be a pile left behind and sometimes a sports jacket I'd gotten tired of, too. I'd give the bellhop a couple of bucks and say, "By the way, I left some stuff for you in the closet." When I called down to the service desk for a bellhop, there were small wars for a shot at McDermott's abandoned wardrobe. When I roomed on the road with Parnell, for a while he thought I was just absentminded. He good-naturedly stuffed my leftovers in his bag to take to the next town. Then he got the picture, and it didn't take long for him to get tired of playing Road Mama.

Ruth Pesky wasn't about to let me throw away "perfectly good shirts," so she'd pick them up and wash and press them. What could I do? I wore them again—at least until we went on the road and I could leave them for the bellhops. Ruthie made a great meatloaf and did her best to fatten me up. A couple of years later, I married Barbara Riley (my first wife—you better keep a scorecard) out of the Pesky house. But my days there were numbered.

There was a good reason. Johnny cheerfully lent me his car for dates and didn't flinch when I asked to borrow the handsome new blue Lincoln presented to him at Fenway on Johnny Pesky Day. But when I brought it back with a rear window kicked out, the direct result of extraordinary horizontal activity in the backseat, my adoption papers were revoked. I was a big boy now. Making volcanic love on the creamy leather seats of his showroom-new Lincoln was not an exceptionally good idea. In Johnny's opinion, stated eloquently to Ruthie: "Mickey's gotta go."

I moved into a place of my own on Kenmore Square, two blocks from Fenway Park—with a lot of closets. One of them stored the tripod and telescope of my new roomie, pitcher Walter Masterson. It was out of the closet more than in it because our pad was across the street from a Boston College girls' dorm in what had once been the elegant Somerset Hotel. Figure it out. It's not generally known, but scouting the horizon for babes in various forms of undress is (or, at least was then) a significant part ("Dammit—she pulled down the shades!") of ballplayers' recreation at home and on the road.

Walt's interest in heavenly bodies kept him semiglued to the lens of his telescope for hours at a time, and if I said that I didn't take my turn on watch, I'd be in danger of tripling the size of my nose. I reported to the clubhouse one afternoon to be greeted by Walt Dropo with, "What's wrong with your eye? You look like Buster Brown's dog." I looked in the mirror. Yep, just like the comic strip canine, I had a black circle around my left eye. I had stared so long and hard through the lens the humid night before that telltale paint from the telescope's eyepiece had stuck to my skin.

But all of that was secondary to the headlong pursuit of pennant happiness that was on our minds night and day now that our suddenly winning ways had given us a chance to take it all. One reporter, thirsting for a miracle finish, went biblical after my four-hitter against the Yanks on July 5, writing ". . . and a little child shall lead them." That began an 8-game winning streak which, in turn, ignited a 36–10 tear. In one of those games, we scored 17 runs against the Philadelphia A's in one inning (where were those runs when I needed them?), and Mel Parnell's four-hitter put us dead even with the Yanks on September 26 as the season neared its end. We had six games left to play, the first and the last two against New York. Each team had won 93. Each had lost 55.

When our train pulled into Grand Central the night before the first New York game, I was mobbed by women fans clamoring for the autograph of the pitcher who'd been named to a game so crucial that the following morning's *New York Daily News* had nothing on its front page but baseball. A "War Declared!"–sized headline announced "McDermott Set to Face Yanks." A six-column half-page photo, captioned, "Sox Pitcher Mobbed by Lady Fans," filled the rest of the page.

I was in heaven. I'd been out for a month, since August 25. In Chicago in my previous turn, I'd caught my cleats on the rubber as I delivered the ball. I pitched through the sudden pain under my left shoulder blade, but it caught up to me in Philadelphia. After only five pitches, I felt something pop. Not just felt. Heard. Not as loud as the sound when Parnell broke his arm pitching a few years later, but loud enough so I tossed the ball in the air, mumbled, "Welcome to the big leagues," and walked off the mound.

In those days, we didn't have doctors on tap the way they do now. We know now that cold encourages blood circulation around injuries. Heat coagulates. But trainers didn't ice injuries then. They smeared on red-hot horse liniment and then mummified the area. With his osteomyelitis, after a game Mickey Mantle used to look like King Tut ready for the big sleep. My injury turned out to be a pulled muscle in my back. Heat, rest, and daily throwing after the first week had gotten me back into decent shape, and I was sure I was ready for the damned Yankees. Ready to be a hero.

But Ted was ready for me to be a hit man. "Bush," he said as we trotted onto the field, "the first pitch to DiMaggio, break his arm."

"You're crazy, Ted," I said. "I wanna get out of this stadium alive. He knows every mobster in town. I'll be so full of holes, I'll look like a fishing net." Ted laughed. "Now you're getting smart, Bush," he said. "But don't start thinking. When you think, you get into trouble. Just hold 'em. Byrne's gonna give me my pitch, and we're gonna score a bunch of runs."

Tommy Byrne was the Yankees pitcher, but not for long. Byrne, another eccentric lefty, owned a reputation for wildness that equaled or exceeded mine. Like me, he wanted to strike out the side. Like me, sometimes he walked it. This time he got no one out in the first, and we jumped out to a three-run lead.

If it had been a three-inning game, they would have made me governor of Massachusetts. I felt invincible. Something like Warren Spahn—with more than 300 wins, he really was invincible. When a sportswriter asked if anybody he faced ever put the fear in him, Spahn shrugged. "Only Hank Aaron," he said, "and he's on my side. I got shot at with real bullets for three years. Here all they've got is a bat." He grinned. "I've got the ball. They're the ones who need to be afraid."

(I hate to interrupt this exciting story, but I've gotta tell you why I empathized completely with Spahn about Hank the Hammer. We were playing the Braves in Bradenton during spring training early in the fifties when this muscular young nonroster kid came out of the dugout and Birdie Tebbetts took a moment to tell me, "I don't know anything about him. Throw him your best stuff." I did exactly that, and Hank Aaron lined it so hard over the left-field fence that nails and shingles popped off the roof of the YMCA across the street. I said, "Well, we found out about him, didn't we, Birdie?")

OK, back to Yankee Stadium—65,156 people to strut my stuff for. And how could I have missed when I was wearing the same dirty lucky sweatshirt I'd worn the night I beat the Yanks to end our eight-game slide? In the top of the first, I already had a three-run cushion. I zipped through the Yankees lineup and gave them nada—well, except for a bad moment in the second when I walked Johnson and Bauer. Al Zarilla, our acrobatic outfielder, saved three runs with a leaping catch that robbed Johnny Lindell of a home run.

Unfortunately, it's a nine-inning game. In the bottom of the fourth, I walked the leadoff man, a terrible idea. With Henrich taking a lead at first, Billy Johnson singled and now the Yanks had men at the corners. I took a deep breath and faced Hank Bauer, a guy who could hit me with the lights out. I hit him with a pitch. It had to hurt, but he was happy to take it for the team. He laughed all the way to first base, and Johnson moved up to second.

Maybe I would've struck out the next 18 batters. (Sure, and maybe the U.S. Cavalry would've galloped onto the field to my rescue.) But with the bases full and a season at stake, McCarthy was taking no chances with a 20-year-old. Out I went, and in came Jack Kramer. A good move. Not for me, for the team. The final, with Kinder holding the Yanks scoreless the last two innings: Red Sox 7, Enemy 6. When the game ended, we were a game ahead of the Yanks.

The fact that I'd pitched a no-hitter for three innings did not impress the local sportswriters. Next day, Tommy Byrne and I starred in a sports page cartoon caricature that showed us in a batting cage, five feet apart, throwing baseballs at one another. There were balls all over the cage. The caption read: "And nobody got hurt."

One game ahead, three to play against Washington, and the final two at Yankee Stadium. Perfect. We'd already beaten the Senators 16 times, lost only 3. With a little luck, the Yankee Stadium games wouldn't mean a thing. But a little luck was all we had. We won two out of three. Facing the A's, so did the Yankees. It was on to the Bronx to play the Bombers.

We had a lot to be confident about. Kinder and Parnell were in the middle of streaks in which they couldn't seem to lose a game, and the last two games were theirs to win. But almost every time we played the Yankees, something out of the ordinary, something almost spooky, would happen. You had to wonder.

So here we were playing the next-to-last game of the regular season. With Allie Reynolds and reliever Joe Page both wild for the Yanks, we jumped out to a 4–0 lead, and Parnell cruised through the first three innings. But Mel had been carrying the team on his left shoulder for too many weeks. In the fourth, the Yanks scored two, then another off Parnell in the fifth, 4–3. With two men on and one out, McCarthy called on Joe Dobson to relieve. When Joe couldn't handle a savage DiMaggio line drive through the middle, which with a little luck could have been an inning-ending double play, the bases were loaded. On the next pitch, Joe got the double play, but in waltzed the tying run.

Johnny Lindell homered in the eighth, putting the Yanks ahead 5–4, but then it was our turn. With men on first and third, *our* DiMaggio—also known as the Little Professor—came to the plate. The Little Professor? Well, his eyeglasses, unusual in baseball, contributed. Still, it's not your usual baseball nickname.

Dom earned the name with his nonviolent but eloquent response to an umpire's preposterous third-strike call. Williams would have shouted, "You stupid c-sucker!" Dominic came to a boil on the long walk back to the dugout and then boiled over. Standing on the steps, he railed at the ump, "I have never witnessed such incompetence in my entire career!" We all broke up. McCarthy, always the gentleman, just covered his face with his hands and walked toward the tunnel laughing all the way.

Now, with the Professor up, came the witching moment. With Pesky dancing off third, Dom lashed a rope to right field. As Pesky tensed to run for the plate, it happened. Clouds had been darkening. Now, as if on cue, a gusty wind whipped through the Yankee bullpen in right field and spewed a thick tornado of dust on the field between third base and the right-field wall. Dom's line drive vanished into it.

Pesky was caught between the devil and a deep gray dust cloud. Was it a hit, or had Mapes caught the ball? Blinded by this unexpected whim of nature, Johnny couldn't tell. He shot a glance at the third-base coach. No clue there either. If he ran and the ball was caught, he'd be doubled up by a quick throw to third. The only thing to do was tag up and wait for the dust storm to clear. When it did, Pesky saw the ball bounce into Mapes' glove.

Johnny gave it everything he had to get that tying run home, but he was thrown out at home plate. That, followed by a third out, stifled what could have been the game-winning rally. Stuff like that made us wonder if God was a Yankees fan.

So we're all tied up. One game left to decide the pennant race, and McCarthy went with Yankee-killer Kinder who had already beaten them four times in '49. Kinder was prepared to prepare the way he always did—drinking everyone else under the table in his favorite saloon. McCarthy wasn't having it. This was New York City. Who knew what could happen to a loose howitzer like Kinder? He could get mugged, rolled, lost, or bumped off by gamblers who had their money on the Yankees. Or he could fall so far into the bottle that, heaven forfend, he'd repeat the catastrophe that had given me my first major league win, against Chicago.

To flat-out tell Kinder this would be to lose the argument. To threaten him with a fine would guarantee his staying out 'til the sun rose over the Empire State Building. Not even McCarthy could tell this tough Tennesseean what to do. But though McCarthy never led his horses to water, he sure knew how to get them to drink.

Once when slugging Junior Stephens was down on himself for hitting into double plays something like 10 days in a row, McCarthy uncharacteristically tore into him for doing it. It was the old psychologist at work—get Junior riled up and, by building a fire under his butt, get him out of his rut. It worked. Junior started attacking the ball again. And a couple of days later, McCarthy invited him for a sit-down with a bottle between them. It was a maudlin scene with McCarthy apologizing, "I'm sorry, Junior. I shouldn't have said that to you." And Junior, "That's OK, Joe. Let's have another drink." Real men don't cry, but there were tears in both their eyes. Ah well, maybe it was the whiskey fumes.

So the night before the big game, master strategist and psychologist McCarthy did not lecture Kinder on the dangers of drink and the perils of New York City streets after dark. Instead he showed up at Kinder's room early in the evening "to discuss strategy."

Kinder was flattered. You went to McCarthy. He didn't come to you. And here was the man who'd managed Babe Ruth and Lou Gehrig asking him, a country boy, what he thought would work best in the next day's game. And encouraging him with, "Ellis, you beat the bastards four times already this year, and you can do it again." Came a knock on the door: "Room service." In on a tray came some chilled glasses and a couple of bottles of the best, ordered in timely fashion by previous arrangement with traveling secretary Tom Dowd.

The smile on Kinder's face must have been wide enough to drive the team bus through. Now this was really special. McCarthy rarely drank with a team member. So they talked about baseball, about past campaigns, about Kinder's determination to chew up the Yanks and spit them out like a chaw of Red Dog. Somewhere around 3:00 A.M., McCarthy looked at his watch, "Well, well. Good night, son. About time to go to bed. Get yourself a good night's sleep." Whatever works. And this did.

The following morning, a mere half gallon of black coffee later, Kinder was ready for prime time. In a great at-bat in the Yankees half of the first, Phil Rizzuto reached out and punched an excellent pitch down the line at third base past Johnny Pesky. In the left-field corner, Williams waited for the ball to rebound into his glove. Instead, it bounced along the wall past his outstretched arm, and the fleet Rizzuto had himself a triple. A soft well-placed Henrich grounder brought him home.

After that, Kinder gave them nothing but aggravation, but with one out in our half of the eighth, McCarthy, whose crystal ball was foggy that fateful day, made a move he would never forget and always regret. He yanked a pitcher hurling a one-hitter.

Kinder, a good-hitting pitcher, had his bat in hand. McCarthy waved him back to the bench—you could've sailed a yacht on the collective sigh of relief from the Yankees bench—and called on Tom Wright, a kid (well, he was five years older than I was) just up from the minors, to pinch-hit. The kid had a good at-bat. He walked. OK, I thought, watching from the bullpen, maybe it wasn't such a bad move.

But then misfortune's tape measure did us in. Two men on and Dom DiMaggio scorched a Joe Page fastball through the box, headed for the hole between Jerry Coleman and Phil Rizzuto. Page couldn't react fast enough to stop it, but Lady Luck was the Yankees' 10th player. The ball hit the rubber and caromed right into Rizzuto's glove—an inning-ending double play instead of two RBIs. Baseball: a game of inches.

In the last of the eighth, McCarthy called on yesterday's starter, gallant but weary Mel Parnell. Henrich, who hit Parnell as well as Hank Bauer hit me, did it again, and the ball he drove deep into the stands for a home run gave the Yanks a 2–0 lead. Berra singled, and McCarthy called for Tex Hughson. As Mel walked off, head down, umpire Cal Hubbard, a former all-time all-pro football player, said kindly, "That was a real good pitch you made, son. You keep doing that and you'll win a lot of ballgames."

"Thanks," Parnell said, "but I didn't fare too well with it today."

Hughson fared worse. He got DiMaggio to hit into a double play, but two singles and an intentional walk loaded the bases. Jerry Coleman popped up, but his location was perfect, between Bobby Doerr at second base and Al Zarilla in right field just inside the line for a two-base hit. He was out trying to stretch it, but three men had crossed the plate and it was 5–0 Yanks.

In the top of the ninth, we rallied for what should have been Kinder's three winning runs, but it was too little too late. The grim and silent locker room afterward was the first and only time I ever saw Ted Williams with tears in his eyes. Our inspired August to September run for World Series rings had been wasted and a pennant that coulda, shoulda, woulda been ours was theirs.

But, hey, that's baseball. And in baseball, as in life, there's always next year.

CHAPTER 7

Having a Wonderful Life

Maurice-About-Town

I paid a special visit to Grossinger's in New York's Catskill Mountains the winter of '49 to return a mezuzah to Rabbi Harry Stone. Short of stature but never of sense of humor, Rabbi Stone was the hotel padre. Every now and then, his little black yarmulke perched on his head, scouting for a 10th man for daily prayer services, he'd invite me to complete the evening minyan.

"Rabbi, I'm a Catholic!" I'd protest. "It's OK," he'd reply with a twinkle in his eye. "Before the service, we'll have a *bris*." (Do I have to explain that? I guess so. It's the circumcision ceremony when a baby boy is eight days old. I was not about to volunteer.)

The previous year when I worked (hmm, maybe that's not the right word) as Lou Goldstein's assistant winter sports director, my buddy the rabbi had presented me with a mezuzah—a religious object with a prayer in it that's nailed to the doorposts of Jewish homes—before I left for spring training.

"Here, Moishe," said the rabbi. "Wear it on a chain around your neck. You'll win 30 games."

"Thanks, rabbi," I said, "I've already got a crucifix on my chain."

He smiled and pressed it on me. "Moishe," he repeated. "Wear it. Don't be half safe."

Now I brought it back to Rabbi Stone. "Here," I said, "take your mezuzah. Please. Not only did I not win 30 games, but the last time I wore it Tommy Henrich hit a grand salami off me."

"Oy, Moishe," he said. "I'm sorry. Maybe it only works for Jewish pitchers."

He could have sent it to Joe Ginsberg. My old pal Joe came up in 1950 to catch for Detroit. He's "my pal Joe" now that our baseball wars are over, but friendly is not the word he'd have used to describe our relationship when his team (Williamsport) and my team (Scranton) collided repeatedly in the Eastern League. Here's how Joe tells the tale when we're on the baseball banquet circuit:

> I'm catching every day for Williamsport and hitting pretty good, too. We get to Scranton and my manager says, "There's a hard thrower out there. A left-hander." I tell him, "No problem." But when I get up at the plate, he's throwing BBs at me. He strikes me out twice. The third time I go up there angry. I think, "I'll get that SOB this time." He pops me up. And he keeps embarrassing me all season long.
>
> I get promoted to Toledo. Again I'm catching every day. We take a trip to Louisville, and who do you think is pitching? I tell myself I'm a better hitter than I was then. Turns out he's a better pitcher, too. He strikes me out again. And again. And again. I wind up hitting .285 for the season. I figure if it wasn't for McDermott, it would have been .300.
>
> I make it to Detroit the following year. I'm playing every day and I love it. Then we go to Boston. Red Rolfe, my manager, says, "Joe, how do you hit left-handers?" I say, "Pretty

good." He says, "Well, they've got the toughest lefty in the league pitching today." I look out at the skinny kid warming up on the mound. I say, "Oh no, not him again!" To make matters worse, now he's developed a great curveball to go with the heater. I feel like I'm swinging a toothbrush. My manager is watching. He makes up his mind. After that game, when there's a lefty pitching, my name's not on the lineup card.

So Mickey McDermott made a platoon player out of me. I hated him for that then, but a fella named Eddie Robinson of the Star Furniture Company used to throw parties for visiting baseball clubs. When the Red Sox came to town—well, thanks to Rolfe's decision I didn't have to hit against Mickey anymore. We got to be good friends.

I wonder if Willard Nixon and Minnie Minoso ever got to be friends. Willard came up to the Red Sox with me from Louisville. When his pitching career ended, he made his mark as chief of police of Rome, Georgia. Nixon, an under-.500 lifetime pitcher, had already made his mark regularly on Minoso, a Havana-born .298 lifetime hitter who played in the majors on and off for almost 30 years.

Willard made it a habit to hit Minoso every time he faced him. Minnie knew why he was being hit, and he must have thought about it a lot. Finally one day, after the seventh or eighth pop, Minnie bent down in the batter's box and rubbed white chalk from the first-base line on his face. "OK, Willard," he said loud and clear. "Enough of that stuff. Now I'm a white guy."

Boston was now a team that had finished second five times in the last 10 years. Writers were arguing that, yeah, Ted Williams helped the team, but a guy like Joe DiMaggio would have helped them win the pennant. Talk began about a three-way trade. DiMaggio to the Sox for Williams. Williams then traded to Detroit for half their team.

Passing McCarthy's train compartment one day (and, OK, I admit it, pausing to eavesdrop), I heard him arguing with Joe Cronin. "There'll be no trading Ted Williams," I heard McCarthy say. "Not as long as I'm on this club." But Cronin's logic was interesting.

"It'll be good for us and good for DiMaggio," he said. "In Yankee Stadium, where he pulls balls and hits 390-foot flies, there's so much room out there in left field that they get caught. At Fenway, with only 290 feet to the wall, they'd splash into the Charles. In Detroit, the right-field fence is only 300 feet, and here Ted hits them 450 feet right over the roof. So it's good for him, too. Hell, they'd both make Babe Ruth look like a Little Leaguer." Eventually, the story hit the papers, created a lot of excitement, and then died. If you took DiMaggio out of New York, they'd kill you. If you took Williams out of Boston, there'd be a riot.

Nineteen fifty was the year, a little more than one-third of the way through the season, that McCarthy called it quits. The two last-game-of-the-season rolls of the dice that came up snake eyes wounded this wonderful gentleman's pride. I'm sure he felt that, like Kinder, the team no longer trusted his judgment. Maybe he'd stopped trusting it, too.

Marse Joe had a long history of managing pennant winners and near winners for Yankees teams since 1931. But what had he done for them lately? Dumped in midseason in '46 in favor of his catcher, Bill Dickey, he came to the Red Sox determined to beat the bejabbers out of his old team. Edging them out in '48 was sweet, but losing that playoff game to the Indians soured the season. In '49, his disastrous decision to yank Kinder hurt even more. On the long, gloomy train ride back to Boston, Ellis had caught up with McCarthy and called him a drunk and a stupid SOB who had made the worst managerial decision in the history of baseball: "A one-hitter. You yanked a pitcher who was pitching a one-hitter!" The worst part was that McCarthy agreed with him.

McCarthy had done his share of drinking in '48 and '49. He seemed to be drinking more in '50. The Red Sox were a mediocre and dispirited 31 wins and 28 losses the night I approached the front desk of our Chicago hotel a couple of hours after a game with the White Sox. (We probably

I'm "Lefty" on the far left, as a 10-year-old on a local keep-them-off-the-streets basketball team. In high school I was an all-state forward, but it was easy to turn down a college scholarship when the Red Sox offered my old man $5,000 on signing. The beer trucks rolled up and filled our cellar.

From the personal collection of Mickey McDermott.

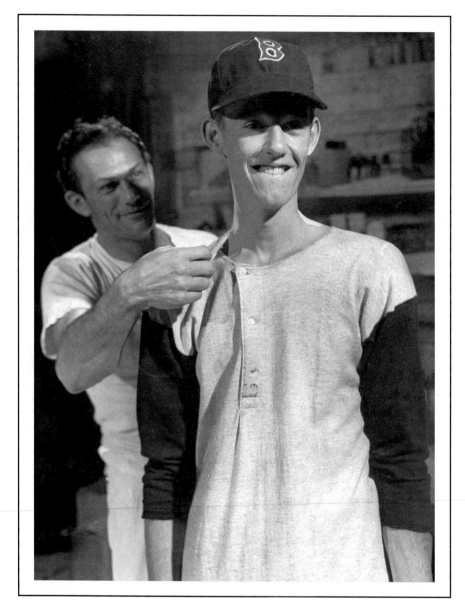

"The Rookie," said *Life* magazine, "his face reflecting the eternal glow of optimism, is a more certain harbinger of spring in the U.S. than the first robin. Above is Morris McDermott . . . who might have walked out of the pages of Ring Lardner into the training camp of the pennant-seeking Boston Red Sox. . . . His gawky neck, broiled by a relentless sun, had to be especially treated . . . and he became the butt of all manner of training camp gags. But through it all he grinned as only a rookie can."

Photo courtesy of Frank Scherschel/TimePix.

Warming up for real in Boston. The first time he saw me pitch batting practice, in spring training a couple of years earlier with 100-mph fastballs sailing all over the place, Ted Williams declined to participate. He loved hitting, but he loved living more.

From the personal collection of Mickey McDermott.

Spring training
with the Red Sox
in Sarasota with,
left to right,
Chuck Stobbs,
me (those jug ears
tell me I was
about 19 at the
time), the incredi-
ble Ellis Kinder,
and my roomie
Mel Parnell. If
there's one pitch
out of thousands
I'd love to take
back, it's the one
that broke Mel's
left wrist when I
pitched for the
Senators.

*From the personal
collection of Mickey
McDermott.*

Barbara's mother wanted her to marry a socialite, not "a baseball bum," and if I remember correctly, she boycotted the wedding. One thing's
for sure: she would have loved to chase me out
of town with one of the bats that Cleveland
catcher Jim Hegan (left) and Red Sox first baseman Walt Dropo (right) crossed over us.

Photo courtesy of the Boston Record-American.

Mugging backstage at a signing with Walt Dropo. Years later he got me out of his pad when I'd overstayed by a couple of months by taking out an ad on the scoreboard at Fenway Park that read, "Mickey, go home."

From the personal collection of Mickey McDermott.

With lessons from the master, my pal Richard Hyman of the Harmonicats, I picked up the harmonica fast. Listen: doesn't it just tear your heart out to hear me play "Peg of My Heart"?

Photo courtesy of AP/Wide World photos.

Singing an Al Jolson–style "Mamie" at Steuben's in Boston always brought me to my knees. When the Red Sox traded me to Washington, I said, through the hurt, "Tell Bucky Harris he's getting a triple threat player: I can pitch. I can hit. And, if I have to, I can sing." (A half-dozen years later when I loaded the bases pitching against the Tigers, Detroit manager Freddie Hutchinson shouted, "OK, Mac, let's see you sing your way out of this one!")

Photo courtesy of AP/Wide World Photos.

So I had this ball that represented the 18th win of my 1953 Red Sox season, and suddenly I learned I'd been traded to Siberia—the Washington Senators. There, I slid from 18–10 to 7–15. President Eisenhower wanted to know what happened. I explained: "Washington is what happened."

Photo courtesy of AP/Wide World Photos.

Birdie Tebbetts (right) did it all — as catcher, coach, manager, scout, and teller of tall baseball tales. Here we are on the "Rubber Chicken Circuit" (those $150 banquet speaking fees kept our families in groceries) playing "Can You Top This?" Birdie won.

From the personal collection of Mickey McDermott.

Here we see, left to right, Bob Turley, Whitey Ford, Tommy Byrne, and the next Lefty Grove (maybe in my next life). Don't ask me who I signed the photo to. Billy Martin, maybe?

From the personal collection of Mickey McDermott.

lost, but who remembers?) There was McCarthy. I was about to open my mouth to greet him when he threw his room key on the counter and, as though rehearsing a conversation with Boston's GM, said, "I quit." He strode angrily away. Instead of, "Evening, Mr. McCarthy," I said, "Uh-oh." It didn't seem the right time to wish him pleasant dreams.

Next day, it was press conference time, and it turned out that he meant what he'd said at the desk. We were a great ballclub, he told assembled sportswriters, with a great tradition, and if he couldn't do better than play .500 ball with a team batting better than .300, it was time to quit managing.

So it was curtains for McCarthy, and the curtain rose on Steve O'Neill. Our new manager jollied a 63–32 record out of us, but it was too late to do anything better than finish a game behind his old team, the Tigers, who finished on the heels of the Yankees. McCarthy lived to be 90, and I regret to this day that I didn't visit him in his old age. He would have enjoyed it. I would have enjoyed it even more. He was a great man, but Buffalo seemed like such a long way away. And a few years later, I had a drinking problem myself.

O'Neill was a great guy and a darned good manager. His Detroit teams had finished second a couple of times in the forties and first in '45 when Hank Greenberg came back from the war in time to hit a pennant-winning grand slam homer. O'Neill, observing how fast I could warm up and feeling I'd been pushed too fast, put me in the bullpen. I acquired five saves before he made me a starter again. But they weren't counted at the time—and neither were nine more I picked up later on other teams—because that stat didn't become official until 1969. Too bad. Nowadays they compile stats on everything. They count it if you take a leak.

There's one stat they missed completely: HBO—hit by osprey. It had to happen to either me or Kinder (it couldn't happen to serious guys like Parnell or Williams), and Ellis was the one who got lucky. You can't make this stuff up. An afternoon crowd of thirty thousand or so was enjoying the game when an osprey, looking for a nice quiet place to eat lunch away from noisy Boston Harbor tourists, swooped over Fenway Park with a plump fish in its beak. The roar of the crowd as Kinder struck out yet another ballplayer must have shocked the big bird. Startled (or maybe wanting to squawk, "Hooray for the Red Sox!"), the osprey made the mistake of opening its beak. Suddenly it was "Bombs away!"

That darned bird must have stolen the Norden bombsight. The fish plummeted down with pinpoint accuracy, landing on Kinder's head as he went into his windup, and drove the rugged ex–farm boy and pipe fitter to his knees, giving Kinder the distinction of being the first pitcher ever to be knocked out of the box by a herring. A sports cartoon in the *Boston Globe* followed next day. (Did the other team win as a result of the bombing? Don't recall. If it did there was something fishy about it.)

A churchgoing man might have thought, "Somebody up there is trying to tell me something." But not Ellis. A herring from the blue didn't change him one bit. Toward the end of the season, when the farmhands came up during roster expansion, a young pitcher new to the clubhouse asked to be introduced to Kinder.

"Mr. Kinder," he asked, "what does it take to stay in the big leagues?" Kinder pondered that for a moment.

"Do you drink?" he asked.

"No, sir."

"Do you get laid regularly?"

"No, sir. I'm a churchgoer."

"Do you smoke or chew tobacco?"

"No, sir."

"You don't drink. You don't smoke. You don't get laid."

Kinder turned away. "Kid," he said over his shoulder, "you'll be up here for about an hour." It took a little longer than that, but, in fact, about this Mr. Clean anyway, Kinder was correct.

I had never been quite as clean as Mr. Clean, and now as I put miles on my odometer and got out from under my old man's heavy hand, away from motivational put-downs like, "You couldn't pitch in a girls Sunday School league," I moved into a new phase: Maurice-About-Town. I'd been a rebel since I was a kid. I think I was born a Pancho Villa without sombrero. Part of it was because my father was so much into discipline. I hated being told what to do, and if we'd had a woodshed, I'd have spent a helluva lot more time in there than I did doing my homework.

Now as a grown Red Sock, I enlivened bus rides with harmonica playing, did comedy routines I'd picked up at Grossinger's, or, in a spring training game, slipped to my knees to pitch to pint-sized Yankees shortstop Phil Rizzuto. Ted would say, "Bush, you'll never change. You're a free spirit." But I was just doin' what comes naturally. I was like a genie in a bottle. Once the cork came off, the tornado came out. And now, free, wiseass, and 21, earning the salary of guys twice my age, traveling from city to city, pursuing and being pursued by women who thought baseball players were the cat's pajamas and had no objection to my taking mine off, the cork was definitely out of the bottle.

It was the Yankees' superreliever Joe Page who turned me into a social drinker, which, you betcha, was the first step toward Kinder and McCarthy–type serious drinking. Of course, in those days (Kinder was only half joking when he dismissed Mr. Clean) if you didn't drink, you weren't one of the boys. And that, of course, was what every rookie wanted to be. Today few players pal around together after games. They retreat to their luxury condos, slip into something comfortable, turn on their surround sound and home theaters or step up to their in-home bowling alleys, and they're in a world of their own. Hell, we even palled around with the enemy.

So one night after a game against the Yankees, I decided to see more of the bright lights and the big city. I'd heard that Joe DiMaggio and some of the other Yankees hung out at the Edison Hotel on Broadway, so I paid it a visit. The bar was quite a place. Kind of a Sistine chapel tribute to the Bronx Bomber with bigger-than-life Michelangelo-type ceiling frescoes of DiMaggio batting, DiMaggio running, DiMaggio fielding, DiMaggio sliding. All this and Carmen Cavallero playing the piano, too. No wonder he liked it here.

And, wait a minute, there he was, big as life, standing at the bar with pitcher Joe Page, a wacko like me but 10 years older. DiMaggio was famously a private person. So when the Yankees' superreliever waved me over, this was Acceptance (with a capital A), and I went gladly. "Pour the kid a Scotch," Handsome Joe said to the bartender. Then a bevy of great-looking women, probably emerging from his stash in the drawers of his hotel room, joined us. This is it, I thought. This is the big leagues. The Scotch tasted like crabgrass, but drinking it seemed like the grown-up thing to do. Down my hatch it went.

I smiled. A new phase in my life had begun. You could say I had turned the Page. Or even begun a new chapter.

CHAPTER 8

The Singing Fool

Great Days (and Nights) with the Red Sox

Everybody drank, or almost everybody, so what could be bad? Well, for one thing, it started me dissimulating. Well, fibbing. OK. Lying. One day I got the word that Joe Cronin wanted to see me in his office.

"You've got to stop running around with Ellis Kinder," he told me. "The closest that bastard has been to water in his life is to take a shower. He won't drink it. He's afraid it'll rust his pipes. But that old man can still get men out, and I'm not so sure about you. I hear you were with him at Ken's Steak House last night drinking grasshoppers."

I put on my innocent face. "Me? No way. I don't drink grasshoppers."

"Oh, yeah? Well, take a look in that mirror and stick out your tongue. You look like a goddamn leprechaun." I looked. I gulped. He had me dead to rights. Absinthe makes the tongue grow greener. Mine looked like a shamrock.

I told myself (we all have conversations like this) that a little social drinking couldn't affect my pitching. I nodded in agreement. "In fact, for a relatively new guy on the mound, you're not doing half bad." (I agreed with that, too.) "Look at those two games you pitched that were almost no-hitters!" (I looked. Why, even a guy who'd never had a drink in his life would have been proud of them.)

I had "it" big time both those days. Against Cleveland, I was two outs away from a no-hitter when Larry Doby hit a ground ball down the middle that hit the rubber, snaked past my glove, and went through for a single. Well, it never pays to celebrate too soon. The next two batters stranded Doby, and I had the consolation prize.

The other game was even more exasperating. One last out to go in the ninth and Washington's Mel Hoderlein came up. Good deal. It wasn't Mickey Vernon, who was batting in the .330s. Or Jim Busby, who was not far behind. Hoderlein was a utility infielder who probably wouldn't get 50 at-bats all season, and at the moment he was hitting under .200.

I threw a tough pitch to hit—a 99-miler inside at the fists. He barely got his bat around. The ball plunked off the wood toward Walt Dropo at first. I thought easy out. But it kept traveling. I stood and stared and talked to myself as it drifted over Walter's head. Dropo was running, running, extending those long arms of his. I was watching and praying, "Let him catch it, or let it be foul!"

My prayer was either unheard because the crowd was making so much noise, or it was misunderstood. The ball kicked up white dust smack in the center of the foul line. Where was Rip Collins (remember the good-hearted player/manager who saved my first minor league no-hitter six chapters ago?) when I needed him? Later, Tom Yawkey told a reporter to thank Hoderlein for him. "He saved me a lot of money," he said. "McDermott would have demanded $100,000 next season." Oh, well. It wasn't much of a dinger, but, "Good-bye, no-hitter."

And hello, musical career. I was at a party one night and a guy named Danny Biancino, a talent agent also known as Danny White (a reasonable translation of his name from the original Italian) was there. He booked his wife into cocktail lounges around town playing piano, and that night she sat down and started to play pop standards. I like to sing. I fooled around singing duets with Eddie Fisher at Grossinger's when he sang with Eddie Ashman's Band in the Terrace Room there. I got up and sang with Mrs. W. When we finished, Danny said, "You can carry a tune, Mac. And you've got a good voice. A little coaching and I can get you booked here in Boston in the wintertime. You won't have to shovel driveways."

That sounded good to me. I loved singing almost as much as pitching. Tino Barzie, who had played clarinet for Glenn Miller (and luckily wasn't with him during a World War II USO tour when Miller's plane disappeared over the mid-Atlantic), had been one of my biggest fans and best buddies for years. He managed Tommy Dorsey's orchestra and whenever Tommy played a band date in the Scranton area, Tino would come to watch me pitch. Tommy was big-league Irish, loved baseball, and when he heard there was a shamrock pitching, sent Tino to scout me on a night when I struck out 17. "Gee, the kid really pitches," Dorsey said proudly. He was in my fan club from that time on. I was already in his.

Every few months, Tino would send me the band's itinerary. When Tommy played the Meadowbrook in Jersey and the Red Sox were in New York, he'd call and say, "Bring the whole club. I'll have my bus pick you up." We'd all have dinner as his guests in the ballroom.

Brother Jimmy Dorsey's band was just as welcoming. A few years later, when Jimmy regularly packed the ballroom of the old Pennsylvania Hotel, I was with the Yankees. We had just won the '56 World Series, and Jimmy called a half-dozen of us onstage to be introduced to the cheering crowd. (Well, there were a few raspberries from Brooklyn Dodger fans, still in pain after their valiant loss to us in seven games after taking the first two.)

Back at our table, Tommy Byrne looked wistful. "I'd love to sing with that band," he confided. "If you could fix it, I'd give you my World Series ring."

"Already got one," I said. (Not that Tommy couldn't spare one. He already had two and was headed for another.) "Decide what you wanna sing. I'll go ask Jimmy." I don't remember what Tommy sang. I do remember that he stayed in tune and that Jimmy didn't fire his singer, Bob Eberle.

But afterward, Tommy, who'd beaten Brooklyn with a complete game five-hitter in the '55 World Series, sighed and said, "Mickey, that was the biggest thrill of my life!" I think he exaggerated. Just a little.

But singing onstage was great fun, and being a big frog in a small pond (no, that is not a description of my singing voice) was fine with me. So I was raring to go when Danny White hired local disc jockey Sherm Feller's wife to write an act for me with some special songs and booked me into Steuben's, a nightclub owned by brothers Max and Joe Schneider.

I still remember one of the songs. To the tune of Eddie Cantor's "Whoopee," I warbled:

> I used to sleep in days gone by
> And dream of shutouts and RBIs
> Then I met Barbara and began dreaming
> Of making whoopee.
> We started dating and pitching woo.
> She had ideas. I had some, too.
> Then to the courthouse to get a license
> For making whoopee.
>
> We honeymooned all winter
> Blissful as we could be;
> Spring training soon was over;
> Suddenly we were three.
> And now at night instead of dream
> The baby hollers 'til I could scream.
> So don't forget folks. That's what you get folks.
> For making whoopee.

I can see now I should have talked my publisher into including a CD with this book. (How deprived you must feel, Gentle Reader—I hope there's at least one of you—able to read the lyrics but missing the glorious experience of me caroling them.) But let's just put that behind us and go on—which is what I had to do after my one and only experience singing the national anthem at Fenway Park.

The Ink Spots, a very mellow singing group, were headlining at Blinstrub's in town, and their PR guy asked if I'd join them for the anthem. I was game. I always was. But singing out there in front of tens of thousands of music fans was tougher on the nerves than listening to baseball fans boo. I cruised through "Oh, say can you see by the dawn's early light?" Then my light failed. With my mind as blank as a first-grader's new composition book, the best I could do was mouth the rest. Thank heavens for the Ink Spots. They carried me.

At Steuben's, I not only had the time of my life singing and clowning around (hey, by now you know I'm not shy), but got paid $500 a week besides. With my $7,500 salary (by that time, I'd gotten a couple of raises) spread out over seven or eight months, I didn't need an adding machine to figure I was getting paid as much for a week of singing as I got for two weeks of pitching. And the best part: every night was New Year's Eve.

I sang at Steuben's a couple of winters, packed them in, and wanted to do more. So (peeking ahead just a little) when I came back to town in the winter of '54 after being traded to the Senators after my best year with the Red Sox, I called on Joe Schneider. "Season's over," I said. "Want to book me for a few weeks?" Joe's answer came straight from the pocketbook. "Moishe," he said, "18 and 10 in Boston? Oh, what a beautiful voice! Seven and fifteen in Washington? You don't sing so good no more." Joe never let me pay for a drink at Steuben's, but I couldn't sing there. Ah, how fleeting is fame.

Actually, I had already learned that lesson. Johnny Pesky was one of Boston's (and the game's) all-time great shortstops. In 1946 under Joe Cronin, the Red Sox won their first pennant in 28 years and faced St. Louis in the World Series. It went seven games, and in the grand finale, Boston tied the game in the top of the eighth at 3–3. In the bottom of the inning, Enos Slaughter singled for the Cards and Harry Walker followed with a double to center field. Leon Culberson had replaced Dom DiMaggio in center when Dom pulled a muscle running out a double. Culberson threw to Pesky, the cutoff man.

The St. Louis fans, tasting victory, cheered like Romans rooting for the lions—so loud that Johnny, with his back to the runner, couldn't hear Bobby Doerr or Pinky Higgins shouting, "Home, Johnny! Throw it home!" He wheeled and hesitated momentarily, trying to pick up the runner. That was the moment Slaughter needed. Off at the bang of the bat, he had already rounded third and was halfway home. Johnny whipped the ball to the plate. Too late. Slaughter's dramatic slide brought in the fourth and World Series–winning run.

Pesky, just out of the army, only 26 years old, had hit .335 that year, only 7 points behind Ted Williams. He had 43 doubles. He had fielded brilliantly. (In his rookie year, 1942, before three years of military service, he'd hit .331.) But Boston fans were bitter and unforgiving. Johnny couldn't go out for dinner. ("Here comes that stupid sonovabitch, Pesky!") And so many rocks crashed through the windows of his house in Lynn that Johnny and Ruth had to get out of town—back to his hometown in Oregon for the winter. (Well, they say Bostonians are just as hard to please at the theater. New York producers used to open shows in Boston. If one ticket holder in the audience applauded, they knew they had a hit, and it was on to Broadway.)

Before he left town, Pesky attended an Oregon State–Boston College football game. It was a cold, wet day, and the Oregon quarterback fumbled in the mud on the one-foot line. Suddenly an iron-lunged beery voice was heard in the crowd: "Give the ball to Pesky. He knows how to hold it." Johnny felt like three tons of stampeding football players had trampled him into the mud. But that didn't keep him from giving the Red Sox 1,000 percent for another five years before he was traded away and then returning to bulldog through one final career-closing year.

Meanwhile, back at Fenway Park (before my trade to Washington) my batting skills had spawned some lively differences of opinion. Over the years I had hit home runs off some of the best pitchers in the league: Bob Feller, Bob Lemon, and Early Wynn among them. Our new catcher, Gus Niarhos, was not a little upset when Lou Boudreau, now our manager, wrote my name in as number six or seven in the lineup (something he did with superb-hitting pitcher Mel Parnell, too) and moved Gus down to number nine: "the pitcher's spot."

"You SOB," Gus told me, "you're humiliating me. My kids read the box scores, and when I come home they raise hell. They're saying, 'Daddy, can't you hit? They put the pitcher up ahead of you.'"

I was truly sympathetic. I offered to give Gus hitting lessons.

Meanwhile Williams, who gave hitting advice even to guys on other teams, was telling me how to go from being a good hitter to a great one. "The trick," he'd say, "is to hit the ball out in front of you." That worked fine if you had 10–20 vision like his.

One day we were playing Detroit and Virgil Trucks was on the mound. Trucks was someone Ted could hit with handcuffs on at midnight. He always knew exactly what Trucks was going to throw. So when Boudreau looked at me and said, "Grab a bat. You're pinch-hitting," Ted urged, "Watch for the sliders." I struck out—bang, bang, bang—waiting patiently for the slider that never came.

"Bush, what happened?" Ted asked when I returned dejectedly to the bench. "You know damn well what happened," I said. My f'g name is not Ted Williams. He threw you sliders. Me, he threw all fastballs." Williams grinned and hit me with his favorite line: "Now you're getting smart, Bush."

Still, there was no one I'd rather take batting tips from. As a rookie with Boston's Minneapolis Millers farm team, Ted was already launching balls over walls. One memorable clout they're still talking about broke a plate-glass window in the bank across the street. It was a night game, so thanks to bankers' hours, nobody was hurt. But the police came in a hurry, all set to recapture John Dillinger when the alarm went off, and some cop got a real great souvenir. Or did the ball end up locked up forever in the evidence room? Or, better still, will we, one of these days, see it for sale on eBay?

Williams campaigned with Yawkey to do what had been done many years earlier with Red Sox pitcher Babe Ruth—convert me into an outfielder. "The kid's got a natural swing," Ted argued, "and he's got too much talent to be out there only one day in four. He's got power, and I can teach him how to pull the ball. If he stays a pitcher, he's gonna throw one day and be in some bar crooning on his three days off." Yawkey didn't buy it. Ignoring the fact that I'd hit the longest home run ever by a pitcher at Fenway (oops, I forgot Babe Ruth)—over the center-field wall and 10 rows into the bleachers—he insisted, "McDermott sells tickets. We need him out there throwing those high hard ones."

Years later, Joe DiMaggio echoed Ted. "I never told you this, Mac, but I'm gonna tell you now. They made a mistake with you. They should have put you at first base or in the outfield. You could run. You could hit. You had all the tools. The only problem is you'd have had to go to bed. And they'd have had to lock the door and throw away the key."

Today, brother Dominic still believes the mound was the wrong position for me. He remembers me fooling around at first base during infield practice and soft hands scooping up short and wild throws left, right, and overhead. (Well, sure. That was the first position I played at St. Pat's, 10 years earlier.) "You were the ideal fielding first baseman," Dominic says. "And on top of that, you could hit for distance and run like a gazelle. Matter of fact, you could do anything with a baseball but get it over the plate. There you were wild as a March hare. For years I tried to talk them into making a first baseman out of you. Nobody listened."

I sure didn't. Pitchers made the wheels go round. Oh, in later years at Kansas City when my fastball wasn't what it used to be, I filled in at first a couple of games, and stretching halfway to the pitcher's mound for the throw from third base felt great. But center stage, out on the mound—that's where I really wanted to be.

The Little Professor was right about the gazelle part. I was pitching against Detroit, and just before my at-bat I ducked into the tunnel for a quick smoke. I squashed the butt, jammed it in my back pocket, grabbed a Louisville Slugger from the rack, and headed for the on-deck circle. I took charge of a hanging curveball and drove it high off the left-center-field wall.

I started flying around the bases, thinking Secretariat, the Triple Crown winner, taking the Belmont by 31 lengths. The Tiger crowd was roaring. (I guess seeing a pitcher dent the wall is exciting even if it's the other team's pitcher.) I didn't break stride. The coach frantically waved me on to third. I left my feet and slid the last dozen feet in a cloud of dust and a trail of smoke. Of smoke?

What was it? A smoldering cigarette butt? Friction from that long slide? A combination of both? All I know is something had ignited an open book of matches in my rear pocket, and it was burning the hell out of my butt. I screamed, jumped to my feet, and with the third baseman, the coach, and the umpire laughing hysterically—not to mention the crowd—I started slapping my backside to put out the fire. They didn't have to call the Boston Fire Department, but it burned through my underwear and I wound up with a fat blister. I thought of suggesting that when I came up to bat they should have started keeping a fire extinguisher on the third-base line. But Professor DiMaggio, this baseball player runs faster than a gazelle. He runs like a wildfire.

I was hot that day, but I was even hotter in a matchup against Early Wynn of Cleveland. I singled my first time up, stole second (there's that gazelle again), and later scored. The Indians tied the game, and it was a pitchers' battle at 1–1 until I came up in the last of the ninth with two men out. It was do it then or go into extra innings, and that would spoil my plans for the evening. So I homered and won the game.

Talk about spoiling. Mel Parnell blames Bill Veeck for spoiling a perfectly good W one afternoon in Cleveland. Veeck was the P. T. Barnum of baseball—sportswriter Ed Linn wrote three books with or about him—and one of the funniest, most creative guys I ever met. I guess he learned to laugh at life when, as a marine pilot, he got a leg shot off. Veeck didn't let that interfere with his love of life, ladies, and liquor. He smoked a foot-long cigar and extinguished it on his wooden leg. Women would see that and say, "Ooh, isn't this man something? It didn't even hurt him." One night he unscrewed the leg and lobbed it onstage where Abby Lane was singing with Xavier Cugat. Cugat dropped his baton. The band stopped. The Cuban bombshell fainted dead away.

Veeck constantly came up with new ways to fill Municipal Stadium. To bring in women, he flew in orchids from Hawaii, gave away nylons, and installed a nursery for baby-sitting. He had horses, real Native

Americans, war whoops, and pageantry that matched Ringling Brothers. At Municipal, you never knew what would happen next. And Mel Parnell, cruising along in the bottom of the fifth inning on a beautiful sunny day, had the Indians beat when, suddenly, a huge black cloud swept in from Lake Erie, blotted out the sun, and dumped tons of water on the field. Mel ran into the dugout cussing. "That damn Veeck," he said, "now the sonovabitch is making it rain!" Game called on account of Veeck.

Pitching against Cleveland always seemed to bring out the best in me, so I was furious as I sat in the visitors' clubhouse when catcher Gus Niarhos asked, "Didja read the paper this morning? Holbrook said the reason you're not pitching this series is you're afraid to face the Indians." The Indians? Hell, that was the team I could beat the easiest. Bob Holbrook of the *Christian Science Monitor* wrote it as he saw it, but he couldn't see the athlete's foot all the way up to my groin that the trainer hadn't been able to do anything about.

I was hot, irritable, scratching, and, now, itching for a fight. When Holbrook came into the locker room, I demanded an apology.

He refused. I lost it and popped him. It was just a glancing blow, but Williams applauded. "Way to go," he said. "You're the first player to pop a writer in 20 years." Kinder joined in. "Don't knock him out," he said. "I want to hit him, too." But manager Boudreau was not amused. "You're gonna have to apologize to the writers," he said in his office later that day. Tact was not one of my more visible traits. Still hot under my wool collar, I suggested a warm destination for the writers. But eventually I cooled down and apologized, and Holbrook and I became good friends.

I generally got along pretty well with writers, but you could do a guy a favor and next day he'd stab you in the pitching arm. That was especially true of Dave Egan, a heavy drinker known as the Colonel, who wrote a vitriolic sports column for the *Record*. Ted was his favorite target, but he took sadistic potshots at everyone else on the home team as well. Boston fans couldn't wait to read his column to see who his victim of the day was.

Egan called me one day and asked, "Morris, will you do a benefit for me?" I agreed, went to the show, and sang my songs. Next day I read in his column: "McDermott can't pitch, he can't hit, and he can't sing. What's more, he's got nightclub pallor." I called him up and asked, "What was that all about? I do you a favor and you cut me up?" He said, "Sorry, buddy, I can't write you're a nice boy. It doesn't sell newspapers."

Niarhos, a tough Greek from Alabama we'd picked up from the White Sox, did more than get me in trouble with Bob Holbrook. He got me in a winning groove, too. In my first several years with the Red Sox, I had not exactly lived up to my early promise and press clippings. Lefty Grove? Lefty Gomez? Cy Young? Not really. Not yet. In '48, my 0–0 record and 6.17 ERA were based on 23⅓ innings pitched. In '49, I appeared in a dozen games, had a 5–4 record, and had a 4.05 ERA. In '50, I won 7, lost 3, appeared in 38 games, and had an undistinguished 5.19 ERA. The following year, I went 8–8 in 34 games, actually had 35 more Ks than bases on balls (wow!), and slashed my ERA to 3.35. So why, you're beginning to wonder, am I writing a book? Well, it's not all about pitching.

Come to think of it, maybe what it's about is the days when baseball was played more for love than for money. Oh sure, we longed for more and absolutely wouldn't have turned it down. But we didn't have a choice. The owners held all the aces and—except for Yawkey, who other owners felt "spoiled" his players—they didn't believe in sharing the wealth. They glued their billfolds into their pockets.

Even an extra thousand was a big deal, so when the season was over, I enlisted—along with Al Rosen, Johnny Groth, Joe Ginsberg, and Art Houtteman—in Birdie Tebbetts' All-Stars to play 30 games in 30 days against New England semipro and high school teams for $1,000. Birdie was more generous with World Series stars like Phil Rizzuto and Eddie Lopat of the Yankees. They held out for five times what the peons got.

Steady Eddie was a great pitcher who had won 21 games that year with superb control and a fastball that he threw in three speeds: slow, slower, and slowest. In the majors, Lopat could set you up with pitches like that.

Guys would fall all over themselves swinging at oxygen molecules. But one day in Fall River, we played a high school team that didn't know from finesse pitching. They just hit what they saw, and what they saw was a pitch that took a nap on the way to the plate. After the game, I told Eddie I'd seen three birds poop on one of his pitches before it reached home. But Eddie didn't hang around long after that game. The kids slammed his pitches all over the field and beat us 12–1. "The hell with this," Eddie said, "I'm ruining my reputation here. I'm going home." And he did.

The reputation he had with me was being the Yanks' foremost bench jockey. Players don't holler today. They sit on the bench and think about their sneaker endorsements, or they duck back into the clubhouse for a snack and watch the game on TV, just so they know when to get their asses back out there. But back then, everybody on the bench was a cheerleader, and Lopat excelled: "We're gonna get you!" "Get a Seeing Eye dog!" "Grab a towel. You're going to the showers!" He got me so mad one day, I waited 'til there was a man on first and then, pretending to throw my pickoff wild, fired the ball straight at Lopat in the adjacent Yankees dugout. He and the other guys scattered like leaves in a hurricane. And I'm sure the announcer had a lot of fun with that one: "Sonovagun! Wild Man McDermott is at it again."

In '52, with Ted Williams off to fly with the marines in Korea (but batting .400 before he left), we sank to sixth place. I struck out 25 more than I walked and managed a 10–9 record with a 3.72 ERA, only two wins behind club leader Parnell, enough to lift me to that magnificent $7,500 salary. And then came 1953.

That was the year that Red Sox patience with me paid off at last, and Gus Niarhos was a big reason. By then, I was a pretty good pitcher. I'd lost a bit off my fastball. I could no longer just plain overpower the opposition for nine innings. But I was at my peak. I could throw strikes. I'd developed one of the best change-ups in the game, but I rarely used it. I preferred to throw the ball high and tight, knock the batter on his ass, and then follow up with a curve that, with him backing off from the plate and extending my strike zone, he wouldn't be set to hit.

Gus was a skinny little Caesar. He'd come running out to the mound and say, "Mac, your curve is great today. So's your fastball. But let's have some fun with your change-up and watch them fall on their faces." He'd go back, squat behind the plate, call for the change . . . and I'd shake him off. He'd call for it again. I'd shake him off again. But Gus wasn't about to let me win that argument. He called for the change-up over and over again until I got tired of standing out there. And it won games for me. I went 18 and 10—second best on the staff behind 21-game-winning Marvelous Mel—and closed with a very respectable 3.01 ERA. (Damn, one or two runs less and I'd have broken into the 2.00s.)

That last number reminds me of a bet I made with outfielder Bob Nieman of the Tigers. Bob had reason to love me—my pitching arm anyway. When he broke in with the St. Louis Browns in 1951, I put him in the record books. His first two at-bats in the major leagues, guess what? He hit back-to-back home runs against me.

By '53, Bob is hitting homers for Detroit, and he still has my number, but we're good friends. The Tigers come to town and I invite him to dinner at the country club where Charlie Spivak's Orchestra is entertaining. We're eating and talking baseball, and he says, "$200 says I go two for four against you tomorrow." I take the bet, but I raise him $100. Sure he hit me well, but he wouldn't this time.

He steps up to the plate for his first at-bat, and I hit him in the kneecap with my first pitch. Not 98 miles an hour. Just enough to throw him off stride for the rest of the game when he swings. But he goes down hard and they have to carry him off the field. Later, between innings, I do the 60-yard dash to the visitors' clubhouse. Nieman is in the whirlpool moaning and groaning.

"Quick," I says to the clubhouse kid, "open the trunk." The players' money and watches were kept there in numbered boxes.

"Mr. McDermott!" the kid exclaims. "I can't do that."

"Look," I says. "I work here. He doesn't."

He knew about end-of-season tips. He opens the trunk. Nieman is struggling to get to his feet and out of the whirlpool. I grab his wallet, pull out three bills, and run like hell. We win 2–1. He's out 10 days, but he still manages to play 142 games, pop 15 homers, and bat .281. Next time we had dinner I said, "I told you you wouldn't get a hit."

So I was having a great season, living every sandlot kid's dream, and I was sure it was only going to get better. And then I made two more monumental mistakes. (Popping the writer had been strike one.) Cockily popping off to the press about money after the season ended became strike three. ("After all those years of paying me peanuts," I ranted, "if they want me for '54, they're going to have to pay through the nose. I'm ready to hold out 'til Little Bo Peep's sheep come home.")

Strike two had come earlier. It had been one of those days when suddenly Cleveland not only was *not* the easiest team for me to beat but beat me to a pulp in the first inning. I jogged toward the showers in a cloud of rage and ignominy.

I slammed into the locker room throwing towels and pop bottles in every direction, showered, dressed, and headed, head down and still foaming at the mouth, to the fenced-in players' parking lot.

As I approached the gate, a woman approaching it from inside the lot spoke: "Morris," she said, "there's always tomorrow."

I didn't wonder, how does she know my name? I didn't look up to see who she was. I just kept going, slammed through the gate, which almost bowled her over, exclaimed, "Eff you, lady" (only I didn't abbreviate it), got in my car, revved it, and drove away.

The next day I learned that the woman was Mrs. Yawkey, the owner's wife. On her way to Fenway, she had been listening to the game on the radio. Her comment had been kind. My conduct, toward an owner's wife or not, had been unforgivably rude. My pal Ted chortled in the clubhouse, "Mac, you're going to love it in Washington."

CHAPTER 9

Washington

In Siberia with the Senators

I didn't love it in Washington.

     I learned about the trade on TV, and for me the news was on a personal Richter scale somewhere between the San Francisco Earthquake and Pearl Harbor. It was during the winter of '53, and I was snoozing late after a night of singing at Steuben's. I may have been chuckling in my sleep because my good buddy, Walt Dropo, had bopped in that night with a lovely lady on each arm. There was a big, happy smile on his face as I introduced him with, "Ladies and gentlemen, let's have a round of applause for the fabulous Boston Red Sox first baseman, formerly Rookie of the Year, Walt Dropo." The smile vanished as I continued, "Walter is so famous they named a town in Massachusetts after him . . . Marblehead." Dropo jumped up and tried to brain me with the microphone, but hey, you can't please everybody.

     Barbara had been up early feeding our practically brand-new daughter, Bobbie, and performing assorted motherly tasks we macho men of yesteryear preferred to remain ignorant of—like changing nappies and preparing them for the diaper service pickup. While doing her thing, she'd tuned in to a TV sports news show, which, for a baseball wife, is more important than the soaps. The news was not good. She broke into the bedroom hurriedly, bursting the placid bubble of my sleep. "You better look at this," she said. "You've been traded to the Washington Senators for Jackie Jensen."

That got me out of bed fast. By the time I flopped in front of the RCA Victor, ex-jock pundits were already busily speculating about which team got the better deal. They quoted Washington manager Bucky Harris, who sounded like a nice guy, as saying, "I like those 18 games he won for the Red Sox last season in that little Boston park. McDermott won every game he pitched at night—10 straight. We play a lot of night ball in Washington."

All I could do was sit and absorb the shock. It wasn't April 1, but I wanted to believe this was some kind of joke. My heart and my left arm belonged to Boston. I was 23 years old. I'd started in the Red Sox farm system before I turned 16. That was a third of my life, all my adult life so far, and I had naïvely believed I'd spend the rest of my baseball life playing for Boston. I felt I'd proved myself, that I'd finally matured into the winning pitcher I always knew I could be. And I was sure I could do even better. How could they do this? And with no warning. Not even a polite phone call.

And yet it made sense. I'd popped a writer, shot off my mouth to the press about holding out for a fat raise, and almost knocked the owner's wife on her fanny. Jensen, a power hitter, would be a perfect fit in the batting order behind Williams, reducing the chances that in RBI situations they'd walk Ted. If they didn't, there was a good chance that with his swing—and particularly with that short porch in Fenway—swat, just like that the other team would be two runs behind. (But they preferred facing Jensen. Ted drew a league-leading 136 walks in '54 anyway.)

Baseball was a business—a business with no place for loyalty. And time marches on. I'd learned both those lessons when the Red Sox traded Johnny Pesky to Detroit in '52 and took center field away from the Little Professor in '53. After a great career that included a lifetime batting average just four points under .300, Dom, 36, came to work one day to find his name missing from the lineup card, replaced by Tommy Umphlett, 23.

"What's going on here?" he asked manager Boudreau.

"Management wants a younger team."

"Really? OK. Well then you don't need me anymore. See you around." Dom wasn't interested in being somebody's backup. He didn't have financial problems. He cleaned out his locker, shook hands all around, and took a cab. A couple of dozen years later, with Tom Yawkey gone, he formed a syndicate and tried to buy the club. Mrs. Yawkey refused to sell. (I hoped it wasn't because he was a friend of mine.) But, hey, wouldn't it have been great if Dom had put his old uniform back on for a couple of games and made baseball history as the first player/owner?

Well, if I had to play for Washington, they'd have to pay through the proboscis. My last Boston contract read $12,500. Washington offered $19,500. "No thanks," I said, "I'm not signing," and I held out all winter. I had no agent, no lawyer, and I didn't realize that I held aces. I could have gone to the bank, taken out a loan based on the contract, and held out forever. The trade for Jensen couldn't come off until I signed on that old dotted line.

But what do you know when you're 23? To me baseball was still fun. I didn't know that owners would cut your throat for a $10 bill. But buying my own food, paying for my own hotel room, I was rapidly going broke. And they had the infamous reserve clause in reserve. Sure, I could refuse to go to Washington. But if I'd said, "Hell, no, I won't go!" they could have barred me from baseball forever. Today, owners and players are more evenly matched. But back then, we were slaves who were sold up or down the river at the whim of our masters.

Two weeks before the start of spring training, I sat on a park bench in Florida with Mickey Vernon. As a Senator in '53, Mickey had led the American League in hitting with a .337 batting average, nosing out Al Rosen of Cleveland for the championship.

"Did you know," I asked Mickey, "that I won that title for you?" He admitted that he hadn't been grateful enough, but then, very reasonably, asked why I deserved credit for his 205 hits. "You beat out Rosen by one point, right? Well, Rosen came up to bat against me 43 times last season, and I gave him only two hits. That's 2 for 43. Who else won that batting championship for you?"

Like me, Mickey had held out all winter. Now he said apologetically, "I got a family, Mac. I gotta sign." He wanted $50,000. Clark Griffith, in a generous mood, gave him $21,500.

That made me the last holdout. With my support group gone, I caved, too. But I got in one last lick. I checked into the Senators' hotel, demanded a suite, called a half dozen buddies with hearty appetites, got room service to send up steaks, baked potatoes, and drinks for 20, and signed the tab on the Washington Senators. I pictured Clark Griffith having a heart attack when the hotel bill hit his desk, and that felt really good.

The hardest thing to get over when the '54 season started was the feeling that I wasn't where I belonged. In Boston in '53, I'd felt as though Hal Newhouser's prediction had come true, and I finally owned the mound. But apparently I'd been wrong. Tom Yawkey owned it. I—any of us—was just a piece of movable meat, one of the herd in the corral, and if the owner thought we were worth more as steak, it was, "Going once, going twice, sold!" Dom DiMaggio's replacement, Tommy Umphlett, who, after that one short season in beautiful Boston went with me to Washington, must have felt as discouraged as I was. He dropped 64 points on his batting average.

So in the beginning, I felt lost. But hit the mound and you're back again, maybe not pitching for a pennant—fat chance of that with the Senators—but at least for pride. I cared if I won or lost, but that little extra oomph that made a difference between winning and losing was missing in action. With a so-so club—and the '54 Senators were 22 games under .500 by the end of the season—you don't have the Ted Ws and the Dom Ds hitting homers for you on days when you can't find your curveball. Or old reliable Ellis Kinder charging in to relieve like the Fighting 69th. I pitched pretty good ball, and my 3.44 ERA could have won 17 or 18 games for me in Boston, but—hey, that's baseball—I got beat in a lot of 2–1 and 3–2 games. And there were days when I just plain got knocked around.

The embarrassing truth is that while Jackie Jensen was flourishing in Boston, upping his batting average a dozen points and his home-run production from 10 to 25, and four years later winning the MVP, I was winning 7 and losing 15. And apparently that didn't disappoint only the head of the house back home in Poughkeepsie, New York, it disappointed the head of our country, too.

President Dwight D. Eisenhower, a baseball fan who had expected an 18-game winner from Boston to give the local team a lift, was quoted on the sports pages as asking, "What's wrong with McDermott?" I was flattered that he took time from affairs of state to notice me, but didn't he have enough to worry about without putting me in the Oval Office mix? My reply was simple: "What's wrong, Mr. President? Washington! That's what's wrong."

For example, I was in the bullpen with catcher Joe Tipton one night when the call came in: "Get McDermott up." Joe was a happy-go-lucky McCaysville, Georgia, boy who enjoyed distilling bootleg White Lightning back home in the off-season. He enjoyed drinking it, too. I turned to Joe and said, "Skipper wants me. Give me a ball. I gotta get loose."

Tipton shrugged. "Ain't got no ball."

"Joe, stop horsin' around. Where's the ball?"

"Ain't got none."

Just then an eager young voice from just outside the bullpen was heard: "Here, Mr. Tipton. Here's your beer." While I was dozing in the sun, every time Joe had gotten thirsty he'd given a kid an autographed baseball to fetch him a beer. It must have been a lot of beers.

Tipton played a starring role in a dumb prank (this story brought to you courtesy of Rudy Riska, ex-pitcher in the Yankees organization and now of the Downtown Athletic Club, who reminded me of it) that could only have happened in pre-air-conditioned Washington, where clubhouse toilets were constantly stopping up and you did anything you could to get your mind off the heat and humidity. What Tipton did was daub feces in pitching coach and ex–Washington pitcher Joe Haynes' glove, an event Haynes didn't notice 'til he stuck his hand in the glove on the way to batting practice. He went nuts, and when the guffawing was over, got even.

He daubed Capsolin in, of all places, Tipton's jockstrap. Now Capsolin, also know as the Atomic Balm, is a liniment so hot it had to be diluted with oil before being rubbed on racehorses' legs. It burned so many pitchers' arms and shoulders, including Riska's, that trainers finally stopped using it. Haynes couldn't have chosen a more sensitive location or a more powerful weapon of mass destruction. There was only one place Tipton could go after letting out a howl of anguish and yanking off his jock, and that was the hospital. And there were only two things they could do—rinse and ice until the swelling went down. Talk about white lightning.

And one more morsel of Tipton memorabilia. Years later, Mickey Mantle, who could empty a shot glass pretty well himself, spotted me at a party in Miami and burst out laughing. "What's the joke, Mick?" I asked. "Is my fly open?"

"Goddang, McDermott," he said, "I gotta tell you this. Remember when you were pitching for Washington how I got to hitting you pretty good?" I remembered all right. No matter what I threw, he seemed able to anticipate every pitch and hit it out.

"Well," Mantle continued, "your catcher, Joe Tipton, was betting me $10 bills on how far I could hit it. He fed me the signals. Watch out! Gang way! There she goes: 450 feet. Ten dollars, please." No wonder we finished sixth. And, yes, no wonder that was Joe's last year in the majors.

Joe wasn't throwing the game. Nope. It, like the season, was already a lost cause. With all the empty seats, Griffith Stadium looked as though a smallpox epidemic had swept through it. One fan held up a sign that read, "Be Kind to the Animals." Local nightclub comics did routines about us, like: First Fan: How are you enjoying the game? Second Fan: Game? What game? I'm here to get a suntan. Or: Game? What game? I'm a hermit. I came here for the peace and quiet.

I need to add that Joe Tipton was a helluva ballplayer. He was a fair hitter and was both strong and intelligent. He might even have been a Hall of Famer if he put his mind to it. But he was another McDermott—having too much fun to think about the road to Cooperstown. (Well, I guess the day Haynes got even with him wasn't very much fun.)

The man they named the stadium for, Clark Griffith, had to be the cheapest owner in baseball. Bob Porterfield wore the same cap for two seasons, and it absorbed so much salt sweat that when it fell off his head one day, it cracked. At least, that's what he said. When he asked for a new one, he was told, "That'll cost you $7.50," and the clubhouse boy put it on his tab.

If we wanted sanitaries—the necessary white socks under our team athletic socks—Griffith made us buy our own. We were allotted $5.50 a day for meal money on the road (couldn't they have made it an even six?), so we made it through the day by ordering buckets of White Castle hamburgers. We wore the same uniform for the whole season. We used to say the fans—the few there were—could smell us coming out on the field before they could see us.

And fielding? When we pulled off a double play, we threw a party. Fielding one surefire double-play ball, our shortstop, Jerry Snyder, somehow managed to get hit on the head with the ball. (OK, it took a bad hop.) He was knocked out. A run scored. That kind of play behind us did not inspire confidence in Washington pitchers. The base running wasn't all that hot either. One day when we had two men on and were actually threatening to score, I got beat by the Yanks on the first triple play in Yankee Stadium in its 31-year history.

Ed Fitz Gerald and Joe Tipton caught me. Cliff Courtney, my beer-drinking buddy who joined the team in 1955, said I had a 10-cent head with a million-dollar arm. He had problems of his own. He could throw out a runner, but, like infielder Chuck Knoblauch of the Yankees years later, who had trouble making the throw to first, Cliff had a psychological block when it came to throwing the ball back to the pitcher. Sometimes he'd have to walk or bounce it back. And sometimes he'd stop in the middle of a signal and start all over again. I told him he had a nickel head on a 10-dollar arm.

But all things considered, I loved our manager, Bucky Harris. While Washington burned and sank ever lower in the standings, he sat on the bench eating peanuts, smoking, shaking like a leaf (he had Parkinson's before anybody knew what it was), and remembering better teams and better days—maybe as a player, but never, in a dozen years with Washington teams, as a manager. The Senators (formerly known as the Nationals) had won the pennant in 1933 under shortstop player/manager Joe Cronin but averaged sixth place forever after. So good-natured but unfortunate Bucky was accustomed to losing.

One day late in a game, when it was third baseman Eddie Yost's turn to be hit on the head and knocked out of action, Bucky, playing managerial chess, called out, "Where in the goddamn hell is that football player?"

"Who?"

"Killywill, or whatever his name is."

Harmon Killebrew, our recently acquired 18-year-old bonus baby second baseman, stepped forward: "Yes, Mr. Harris." Harmon was there because of a bizarre league rule that forced teams to keep bonus babies on their major league rosters rather than send them to the minors for seasoning—the idea being to discourage anarchist owners from spending too generously on promising young talent. Gosh, it might set a dangerous precedent.

"Grab a mitt. You're playing third base."

"Third base?"

"That's right. Grab a mitt and get out there."

In the next 20 years, Harmon would slug his way into the Hall of Fame. That day he was just a hanging-around rookie with four hits in a very limited season. But Harmon had more desire than any young guy I ever saw. He was at the ballpark early every day taking extra fielding and hitting practice. And one night the next season against the Yankees, he clouted the ball 480 feet to dead center field and over the speakers in Griffith Stadium. People who witnessed that mighty blow didn't know that 572 more home runs would follow, but they were mightily impressed. I know I was.

I was less impressed with our new manager Chuck Dressen, who replaced Bucky Harris in '55 and skillfully guided us from sixth place to last. Dressen would rather fine you for coming in late than win a ballgame. A few years later during spring training in Florida, managing the

Milwaukee Braves, he got himself a ladder and climbed a young palm tree one night during spring training to ambush Warren Spahn and Lew Burdette, guys he suspected of breaking curfew. They spotted him and paid a bellhop to remove his ladder. Dressen shinnied down and hit the ground in a timely fashion—just at the moment that a timer turned on the hotel lawn sprinklers. Spahn and Burdette escaped. Dressen sloshed to his room looking like the lifeguards had just pulled him out of the swimming pool.

Dressen strolled through the clubhouse dispensing his unique brand of evenhanded justice, fines that depended on how late you'd been out: "Shea, you didn't get in 'til 2:00 A.M. That'll cost you $200. McDermott, you were out 'til 3:00. That'll be $300." How did he know, we wondered. Then we got it. Whenever we came in, the hotel night clerk would ask us for an autograph—for a brother, a cousin, an uncle. We'd oblige. He— a spy on a $25 nightly retainer—would write down the time we'd signed in and slip it to Dressen in the morning.

My relationship with Dressen began poorly and got worse. He called a meeting the first day of spring training to announce the Dressen Proclamation: "We have five guys on this club whose reputations precede them: Mickey McDermott, Bob Porterfield, Frank Shea, Johnny Schmitz, and Dick Wakefield. If any of you takes so much as one beer, I'm fining you $500." That was a lot of money for a Budweiser, but I was ready to risk it after I asked to go home for the night—my house was just a mile from the ballpark—and he turned me down.

I went out for a drink that became a lot of drinks with an old friend, County Commissioner Jimmy Spanos, and arrived at 4:00 in the morning at the room I shared with Spec Shea at the old Sarasota Terrace Hotel. I could have used a compass to locate the doorknob and a map to find the keyhole. Unaccustomed to major drinking, I flopped on the bed without undressing, but I felt so sick that I stumbled, head spinning, to the toilet bowl and knelt to do what comes naturally. Afterward, I reached for the towel rod above me to get to my feet. It snapped, and a couple of hand cloths fell into the bowl. Too plastered to notice, I cleverly flushed the toilet and staggered back to bed.

A couple of hours later, I heard Spec's voice, "McDermott, you SOB, what have you done now?" The water looked to be six inches high, and socks, shoes, and souvenirs of my upchucking were floating past my bleary eyes. The water flowed under the door out into the corridor and cascaded down the stairs and into the lobby. Some of the water took a shortcut. I heard screams from the room below us. Plaster was raining down on a man and his wife in bed. Naturally, Shea wanted to kill me. The way I felt it would have been a mercy killing. But when he got over the initial shock, laughter replaced anger. "Only McDermott could do this," Spec said. (That made me kind of proud.) But what Dressen said was, "You're fined $500." I thought about arguing that it was the plumber's fault.

When we played the A's in their last year in Philadelphia, I led a bunch of fellow protesters against Dressen's Law on an exploration of local saloons. At about 3:00 A.M., we returned to the old Ben Franklin Hotel. "Not through the lobby," I said. "He's probably got somebody staked out there. I got a better way." Earlier, I had scouted the alley beside the hotel. A fire escape led straight to my window on the third floor, and I'd conveniently left that open. Single file and silently, we made our way to the fire escape. I leaped and yanked it down. So far, so good. But as it reached the ground, the old lead counterweight sash broke, the ladder instantly changed direction, and I rocketed skyward screaming for help. As I dangled helplessly in midair, windows opened and faces appeared—Dressen's unfortunately among them. The fire department came. The police department came. And nobody ever wanted to sneak in with me again.

I was not fond of Charlie Dressen. He bragged so often about his managerial moves with endless variations of, "Well, I sure won that one for you!" that we started to call him the "I" man. But I resisted a faint but growing desire to punch him out until the day my sister called me at the clubhouse to try to get tickets to a game and somehow the call came in on Charlie's phone in the dugout. Pitcher Camilo Pascual, who happened to be there, hurried to where I was out on the field waiting to take batting practice. "Meekey, Meekey," he asked, "you haff a seester?" I said I did.

"Well, she call you on Dressen's phone. He refuse to take call. He say, 'It's jus' some pussy—one of McDermott's whores.'"

I dropped my bat and sprinted to the dugout where Dressen was talking to a group of sportswriters. "So my sister's a whore, is she?" I shouted. I dove on Dressen from the top step of the dugout and began to politely strangle him. Carlos Paula, a burly 6'3" outfielder from Havana, pulled me off Dressen. "Meekey," he said, "don't keel heem. Let me keel him for you one meellion times." Somehow management quashed the story.

I took my anger out on the baseball when I got up to bat. I was proud of being a hitting pitcher. With Boston in 1953 I'd batted .301, with eight doubles and one homer, and I ached for more of the same—especially home runs.

In my first Senators spring training, I'd overheard Bucky Harris say that he needed a left-handed-hitting outfielder. "I know just the kid for you," I said, "Tommy Wright. I played with him in Boston. He'd be perfect." I knew Tommy was out of a job, and when I phoned and told him to hurry on down, he got one. But what is it they say about no good deed going unpunished? Tommy was on first base one day in Baltimore when I came up to bat. I stepped into Jim Wilson's pitch and hit it right at the right-field flagpole. Tommy started running. Suddenly he stopped. I was about to catch up to him. "Keep running, you dumb bastard," I shouted. "What are you stopping for?" But he just stood there. Now the first-base ump, who wasn't sure whether to call it fair or foul, had the clue he needed. If my own teammate thought it was foul, it damn sure must have been foul. That's what he called it, and there went my next home run. (I did swat one in my second season with the Senators and seven more before I put my bat in the rack for the last time in 1961.)

Not a lot of good things happened in Washington, but the worst came in a game I pitched my first season there against the Red Sox and my old roomie, Mel Parnell. I threw a fastball that sailed high and inside. Mel reflexively threw up his left arm in self-defense. The ball plowed into his wrist, and clutching it, he went down. I rushed to home plate and knelt beside him. "Mel," I asked, "are you alright?"

"Am I alright?" he asked, repeating my idiotic question. Then he answered by throwing up his breakfast.

I visited his hospital room after the game, and when he told me the wrist was broken, tears came to my eyes. "Forget it," Mel said. "It was just one of those things. It was my fault, not yours. I just didn't get out of the way fast enough."

It was an accident, but that didn't make me feel any better. Mel had a great southpaw arm and the pitching smarts to go with it. He was coming off a great 21–8 season in '53. But says Mel, "Lou Boudreau enticed me into coming back too soon toward the end of the '54 season. Management always wants to know where you're at before they fill in the numbers on your next year's contract. Anyway, my arm was never the same. Basically, that was the downfall of my career."

Mel's record slumped to 3–7 in '54 and 2–3 in '55. But he went out with a bang in '56, his last year, pitching a no-hitter against the White Sox before becoming an announcer for Boston. *If* is an uncertain word, but if it hadn't been for me breaking his wrist, Parnell could have added another 100 or so Ws to his lifetime 123–75, and be in the Hall of Fame today. One thing's for sure. He's got my vote. But it still hurts when I think about it.

Now I was having trouble with my own arm. When my shoulder popped a couple of years earlier in Chicago, I'd started favoring it. Like Koufax, I snapped the ball with my elbow, and every time I pitched the following year, the elbow inflated like a small balloon. At first it hadn't been severe, but in Washington it caught up to me. Cleveland's Al Lopez had been right. He knew that if I went up to the bigs too soon, before my body filled out and when all I had was 160 pounds to support a 100-mile-an-hour fastball, sooner or later I'd get hurt. (It is, I'm afraid—and I hope I'm wrong—what's going to happen to Boston ace Pedro Martinez. He's strong, but only about 165 pounds. To me, that spells arm trouble.)

Dr. George Resta from Georgetown University was our club physician. Midway into the '54 season, my elbow was swollen and clearly in trouble, but Bucky Harris needed a starter.

"Can you pitch?" Bucky asked.

"I don't know."

What I did know was that I had an elbow full of bone chips. One in the shape of a needle had sneaked into my bursa sac and emerged unexpectedly one night when I picked up a bottle of beer at a bar. The woman on my left suddenly screamed. I turned toward her. What in the. . . ? With blood all over her face and her dress, she looked like she'd been mugged. I looked back at my arm. Bending my elbow had launched a needle-nosed bone chip through the skin, closely followed by a small geyser of blood. The guys I was with fell off the bar stools laughing. The lady on the adjoining stool didn't think it was funny.

"Doc Resta has something new that could help your arm," Bucky said. "Are you game to try it?"

Resta had been involved in the development of cortisone at Georgetown, and I may have been his first baseball guinea pig. He came at me with a needle so long I thought he was going to knit a sweater. "Here," he said, handing me what looked like a rubber doggy bone, "bite down on this and don't look at me. Mr. Shea will squeeze your hand to distract you while I do the injection."

Spec Shea, my roommate at Washington, got a firm grip on my left hand and squeezed. But nobody had told him not to look. The doctor inserted the needle into my bursa sac. The pressure on my hand suddenly ceased. I looked at where Spec had been standing. He had vanished. I looked down. There he was curled up in the fetal position on the floor. He had fainted dead away. The doctor revived a very embarrassed baseball player. "Geez, don't ever ask me to do any crap like that again," Shea said.

The elbow ached all night, but in the morning the swelling was down and it felt fine. Cortisone, I thought. Why, it's the greatest thing since Crown Royal. I pitched a shutout against Detroit, but after that, though I continued to take cortisone shots, every time I threw hard my arm strength felt diminished. I was not happy. It was, I started to worry, only a matter of time before I wouldn't be fit to pitch in Scranton—unless someone came up with some miracle surgery.

Someone did, but too late for me. Today, bone chips in the elbow are no worse than blisters on a pitching finger. Calcium deposits aren't either. They just laser them away. And even better, they have the Tommy John procedure, moving tendons from elsewhere, putting them in the elbow, and bringing a dead and painful arm back to a brand-new life.

In *The Summer of '49*, his classic book about the epic seesaw Boston–New York race for the pennant, David Halberstam wrote an elegant epilogue in which he panned forward 40 years to relate what became of key players after their diamond lives ended. Researching his book in the late eighties, he sat me down for a two-hour interview, and I told him my favorite stories. Who knew I'd write a book and need a few myself? I am now about to repossess an anecdote. It won't be the only one.

The Senators were playing the Tigers and I was on the mound, not having one of my better days. A couple of seasons earlier, Tigers manager Fred Hutchinson had been one of many baseball people who, happening to be in Boston off-season, taxied to Steuben's to hear the seventh wonder of the singing world perform. Then, Hutch had applauded. Now, with the bases loaded and a 3–0 count, I heard his voice ring out from the Tigers bench: "OK, McDermott, let's see you sing your way out of this one."

At age 19 and 20 with the Red Sox, I drank malted milks. When I was 21, Joe Page introduced me to malt Scotch, but for the most part, with occasional exceptions like the grasshopper episode, I had remained largely a social and beer drinker. Until the trade to the Senators. There I progressed. At first, even in Washington, despite the occasional toilet-hugging binge, the words *heavy drinker* didn't apply. The elbow trouble changed that. I felt the end was coming, and I didn't want to think about it. The Crown Royal helped.

At the end of the '55 season, I went home to Sarasota still not wanting to think about it. I drove there in a new green Buick Dynaflow, the biggest one in the Washington, D.C., showroom of the Cleveland pitcher Early Wynn's father-in-law.

Sarasota in those days was all dirt roads, hound dogs, and Southern crackers, with a population still under five digits. I bought a home on the 12th tee of the Sarasota Bay Country Club for $11,000. (Today it's probably worth a couple of million, but, alas, I am no longer the proud owner.) Hall of Famers Heinie Manush, a .330 lifetime slugger for six clubs, and Paul Waner, known as "Big Poison," who hit .333 lifetime for four (as distinguished from brother Lloyd, known as "Little Poison," who hit only .316), were fellow club members. Under the mistaken impression that I was one of the rich new breed of players with money to light my cigarettes with, they urged, "Buy the golf course. You can get it for $40,000. And only $2,000 down." I explained that after buying the Buick, I couldn't afford the golf club.

Drinking was becoming a serious business for me now, and every other weekend I found myself in a ditch getting towed out. Fortunately, the local lockup only had room for two, or I'd have been a steady boarder. Meanwhile, Braves pitcher Lew Burdette (who the next year would beat the Yankees almost single-armed, shutting them out twice and winning three World Series games) had moved into town. He was about my weight and height—a fact that may seem unimportant now but will shortly become relevant.

One morning, Lew was being a good father and driving his kids to school. He pulled his green Buick into the school parking lot and was just about to unload his children when a police car that had been tailing him pulled up alongside.

"Get out of that car, McDermott," one of the cops commanded. Burdette was taken aback.

"McDermott? My name's not McDermott. It's Burdette."

"None of your lip, McDermott. There's too damn many tickets you haven't paid. We're taking you in." They ignored his protests, yanked him out of the car, and cuffed him. His kids were temporarily paralyzed, but with great presence of mind, one of them trotted into the school and came back with her teacher in tow.

"No, no," the teacher declared. "This is a case of mistaken identity. I know this gentleman, and he is Mr. Burdette, not Mr. McDermott." Burdette was then allowed to introduce his driver's license into evidence, and the cops were finally convinced. They apologized and cruised away. Burdette dropped off his children, drove home, and telephoned me.

"You sonovabitch," he said. "Today the police arrested me instead of you. And in my kids' schoolyard no less. How do you think my poor children felt watching them put handcuffs on their father? I love that green Buick Dynaflow of mine, but I'm putting an ad in the paper to sell it. Today. I'll never drive that car again. Everything you do, I'll get blamed for."

"Lew," I said, trying to calm him down. "Look at it this way. You might've gone to San Quentin for me. Think how lucky you are."

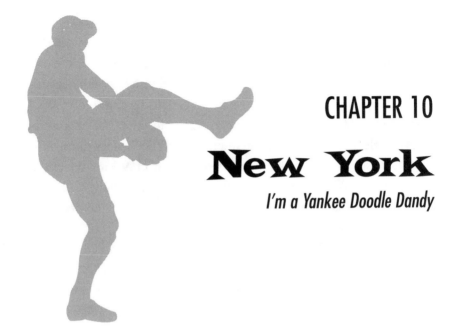

CHAPTER 10

New York

I'm a Yankee Doodle Dandy

My own luck was about to change. For the better.

I was out on the golf course about to tee off when I was called to the phone. I was about to say, "Don't bother me. I'm trying to break 200," when a sportswriter for the local paper interrupted me.

"This just came in over the wire," he said excitedly. "You've been traded to the New York Yankees. What's your reaction?"

"My reaction? As soon as I hang up, I'm gonna sing 'Hallelujah!,' get on my knees, and give thanks. I'm never going back to Washington. Well, maybe. If they elect me the senator from Florida."

You think that's far-fetched? The good citizens of Kentucky elected Jim Bunning their senator, and he won only three times as many games as I did. We pitched together at Detroit in '58, and several years ago when we did a baseball card show together, I asked, "Do I still call you Jim? Or is it Mr. Senator now?" Bunning's baseball cap still fit him. "Call me anything," he said, "except what players called me when I struck them out."

He struck out a lot of them—2,855 to be exact. And walked only 1,000. Oh well, control freaks.

When I finished my round and returned to the clubhouse, golfers who'd seen a report of my trade on TV put down their drinks and stood to applaud me. Heinie Manush and Paul Waner begged to differ. "It's the end of a dynasty," they agreed. "With you in pinstripes, the Yanks will finish last."

My trade to the Yanks incurred the wrath of Whitey Herzog, also known as the "White Rat," who still denounces me whenever I run into him. He and four other players, mostly minor league prospects, and a rumored $100,000 went to Washington for me. (See what a hot item I was? Now you understand why I'm writing a book.) "You SOB," Whitey said pugnaciously, "I'm in a Yankee uniform for an hour and a half and I find out I've been traded to Washington." I told him, "Sure, but look what I did for you. I made you a star." (Fact is, I didn't have a thing to do with his going on to star as one of the shrewdest managers the St. Louis Cards ever had, but while he's trying to figure out what I'm talking about, I escape.)

I could understand Whitey's being upset. For me, to pitch for Boston had been a major thrill. But for anyone, to play in Yankee Stadium for the Yankees was to be in baseball heaven. It was the House That Ruth Built, the house he played in and filled to capacity and beyond. Babe Ruth—first 94–46 as a pitcher with a 2.28 ERA and then hitting .342 lifetime with 714 home runs as the Sultan of Swat. (Gee, those press guys made up silly names.) Ruth was the hitting pitcher I'd always wanted to be and deep inside still hoped and prayed, even at this late stage, I'd somehow miraculously become.

Two years in Washington had drowned a lot of my dreams, and at this point, putting aside the Mutt and Jeff differences in our physiques, I was not looking like a Babe Ruth clone. But that rare hitting-pitcher combination I represented seemed to be why the Yanks were willing to pay dearly for me. That season I'd led the pitching staff of the last-place Senators' with a 10–10 record and a 3.75 ERA. (Well, Johnny Schmitz had a 3.71, but he won three fewer games.) I'd had one save, and I'd been a handy pinch-hitter. My .263 batting average included a homer and four doubles and, hey, I outhit future Hall of Famer Harmon Killebrew by 63 points. (Of course, he was only 19 at the time.) I was a lefty, which would make me a useful supplement to Whitey Ford and Tommy Byrne. And I was only 26. There was always the hope that this would be a major turnaround year—that cagey Casey Stengel would motivate my left arm to its first 20-game season. Which would be just fine with me. Except . . .

Except how would my arm behave when called upon to operate from a mound instead of a golf tee? The Yankees wanted the answer to that question, too. They sent me to Johns Hopkins in Baltimore for a battery of tests. Somehow the elbow chips escaped detection—they must have had a nurse's aide read the X-ray films—and along with the bills the Hopkins docs sent to George Weiss they included a clean bill of health for me. I hoped they were right. A World Series ring would look great on my pitching hand. I might even be able to scuff the ball with it.

I reported to spring training camp at St. Pete and got my roommate assignment: Hank Bauer. Better and better. Here was a dividend I hadn't thought about: the one batter I couldn't get out if my afterlife depended on it, and I wouldn't have to face him anymore. Except a time or two in spring training. In one intrasquad game, I pitched the ball at him with the glove still on it. He hit them both. In the past all I could throw at him as he circled the bases was the glove. The ball was already gone. Over the fence.

I knocked on the door. Bauer opened it.

"McDermott? What do you want?" Apparently he hadn't been reading the sports pages.

"Good news, Henry! I'm your new roomie."

"Oh, no. You're with us?" He slammed the door in my face. I knocked again. Harder this time.

"Henry, what are you doing? Let me in. I can't sleep in the hall. There's no place to put my toothbrush." He opened it again.

"Henry, what kind of welcome is this for an old pal who fed you all those home-run balls?"

"McDermott, you bastard. There goes 50 points off my average."

Actually, he only lost 37 points—from .278 to .241. But his home-run production went up from 20 to 26. He must have studied my batting swing.

The following morning I said, "Hank, I hate to do this, but I forgot to buy toothpaste. Can I use some of yours?"

"Sure, take your choice."

I almost got bombed. He had Scotch toothpaste, rye toothpaste, and bourbon toothpaste. He got drunk in the morning cleaning his teeth. I don't think they make that stuff anymore. If they do, I don't want any part of it. Anymore.

I had reported in good shape, and I looked better than good pitching a complete-game six-hitter against the Cardinals as spring training came to a close. In the *New York Daily News*, Jimmy Powers' column asked, "Did the Yanks grab themselves another pennant when they stole Mickey McDermott?" (I wish.)

Lefty Tommy Byrne immediately challenged me. "I hear you can hit pretty good," he said. "Let's see who hits the most home runs in batting practice by the end of the season." You're allowed 10 swings in BP, and we made the most of them. By the end of the season, Tommy had hit 76. He beat me by one, but Hank Bauer—yep, him again—made a helluva leaping catch at the wall, and I was robbed. I made up for it by becoming one of only a handful of pitchers ever to hit an inside-the-park home run.

We were playing Baltimore at Yankee Stadium. Knuckleballer Harold "Skinny" Brown, a pal from my Scranton Miners days, was on the mound. I pointed toward him, challenging. "Go ahead, Skinny," I called out, "I dare you to throw me a fastball." Later in the dugout, guys told me they thought I was doing a Babe Ruth—pointing at where I planned to hit a home run.

Skinny threw me the fastball I wanted, and I drove it 420 feet to deep center field. They're gone now, but then there were three memorial "tombstones" out there with plaques on them honoring Babe Ruth, Lou Gehrig, and Miller Huggins. The ball flew beyond them, and I knew the fielder would have to slow down or take extra steps to make his way between or around them. My wife, Barbara, was in the stands that night.

She screamed so hard that—there is no way to say this delicately—she wet herself.

I rounded second with my eye on third-base coach Frankie Crosetti. He kept waving, and I kept running. I crossed home plate standing up, ahead of the relay throw to a standing ovation that a rock star would envy.

I did not get an ovation from Casey Stengel, our esteemed manager, and neither did Mickey Mantle, Billy Martin, Whitey Ford, Hank Bauer, or Billy Hunter, when we missed the Yankees troop train headed home after a series at Fenway. It was my town, and after the game some of the guys wanted to pay a short, relaxing visit to an after-hours club, one of many run by the local mob, before we caught "the next train."

Time flies when you're having drinks. The short visit became a long one, long enough so we missed the last train. It was enough time for Billy Martin, who never felt an evening was well spent unless it included at least one fight, to tangle with the owner of the club. This was not very smart because this gent had no shortage of muscle on his side. Still, out-manned or not, we couldn't let Billy fight it out alone, so we all joined in. But some pretty big bouncers had us out on the sidewalk in no time. We emerged to find Whitey Ford waiting for us.

"Where in the hell were you?" Billy asked Whitey through a split lip.

"Well, while you were fighting, somebody had to line up a couple of cabs for a quick getaway to Logan Airport. I volunteered. By the way, how'd you guys do in there?" No wonder the Yankees called him the Chairman of the Board. (My old man sure was impressed with him. Once, after umpiring a game at Hyde Park, New York, that Whitey pitched as a member of an army team, he phoned to tell me, "Hey, Big Shot, I just saw the best left-hander I've ever seen. Now you're only number two." Whitey was equally impressed with my father. "I left my wallet in the locker room," he told me. "Your dad found it and drove 50 miles to return it to me.")

We got to Logan after 3:00 A.M. and managed to get an early plane to D.C. a couple of hours later. But before we did—and I can't remember why or how—we managed to turn the airport lounge upside down. At the hotel by 6:00, we agreed to separate, go to our rooms to change, come down 10 minutes apart, and carefully avoid sitting at the same table for breakfast. No use attracting attention. It was a brilliant plan, but it didn't take into consideration the freedom of the press.

On my way to the table, I passed Casey Stengel sitting in the corner reading a newspaper sports section. He took note of my passage and moved the paper aside just enough so I could see a big fat "gotcha" grin on his face. He waved the paper and I got a quick glance at the damning head-line: something like "Yankee Players Start Riot in Boston." I retreated to a table and became the condemned man eating a hearty breakfast. Later that day in the locker room, Casey, the Associated Press story under his arm, fined everybody else $100. "But you, McDermott," he said, "I'm fining you $200. That's because you're not a Yankee yet." Meaning, I sup-posed, I hadn't yet earned my pinstripes.

Maybe not, but the Boston massacre sure solidified my reputation as a guy who deserved to wear them. The Yankees were a club that had always enjoyed themselves off the field as well as on. Off-season, too, because in those days we were a brotherhood of ballplayers. We enjoyed playing hearts on the long train rides, the steaks and beers after the games, and the impractical jokes we played on one another. When the long season ended, we hated to go our separate ways. And sometimes we didn't.

A few years earlier, Spec Shea, Joe Page, Tommy Henrich, and Snuffy Stirnweiss didn't. Hunters all, they chipped in and bought a no-frills lodge in Maine instead. And then the "fun" began. Joe shot a black bear early in the day, and neither he nor the others said a word about it to Snuffy. Of indoor plumbing, there was none, but the real estate included a very useful outhouse about 20 yards back of the cabin. That, of course, when you play cards and drink a lot of beer, is a place a man needs to visit now and then.

That night, the conspirators all went easy on the beer, waiting for Snuffy to make the first move. Finally Stirnweiss stood up, stretched, and headed for the outhouse. The guys waited until he was halfway there. Then, in the pitch blackness of the forest clearing, fighting off laughter, they followed. Snuffy, unbuttoning his fly, opened the wooden door. The dim outhouse bulb went on automatically, suddenly revealing a huge six-foot bear—neatly suspended on the inside of the door, lifeless but extraordinarily lifelike, its arms spread, its jaws open wide, apparently eager to enjoy a midnight Snuffy snack.

Snuffy was only human. He let out a piercing scream that must have alarmed every creature in the woods and set off burglar alarms as far away as Portland. He backed off slowly and then, bouncing off trees and tripping over bushes, ran for his life. When he burst into the cabin shouting, "Grab your rifles. There's a bear in the outhouse," the others just looked up and grinned. "Really?" asked Joe, "did you check to see if it's alive?"

Snuffy, whose heart was still pounding 200 miles an hour, suddenly realized what was going down. He sat down. "Deal me in," he said slowly. After a while he added, "Just wait. I'll get you guys." If he did, nobody's told me that story yet.

That spring, it looked like I'd earn my pinstripes fast. I got everybody out. Well, not everybody. Solly Hemus, for example. One impressive fastball in an exhibition game against the Cardinals sliced the button right off the top of Solly's cap. I wonder. Is there a stat on that?

I had reported in fairly good shape, but the more time I spent on bar stools instead of in bed, the worse it got. When the Yanks signed me, Casey said the fourth spot in the rotation was mine to earn. I didn't. My elbow didn't let me. You know you're in trouble when you start asking your catcher, "How's my stuff?" and he doesn't answer. As the season progressed, I'd come in as a reliever, throw my warm-ups, and see Yogi Berra look at Stengel on the bench and shake his head. It didn't take long to break that code: "McDermott ain't got nuthin' today." And I wouldn't be in there long.

It didn't bother just me. It bothered old friends of mine as well. After a game with the Senators at Griffith Stadium, the writers were getting their usual shot at postgame questioning when an old sportswriter friend of mine asked Casey, "How come you're not pitching my boy, McDermott?" His answer was pure Stengel, "Eleven other managers tried that, and they ain't managing."

Sure, that was a bit of an exaggeration, but there was enough truth in it to hurt like hell. I think I hid it pretty well, but deep down I felt that my

Good-Time-Mickey approach to baseball had done me in every bit as much as my arm trouble had. Paul Anka hadn't even written "My Way" for Sinatra yet, but I could sing the lyrics already: "And now, the end is near. I see the final curtain." Not that I couldn't get guys out. I could. And once in a while my arm would pleasantly surprise me. But after four or five starts I couldn't finish, I spent most of my time in the bullpen. Stengel called on me to get a couple of hitters out or to mop up in games that had already gotten away. And I did a lot of pinch-hitting.

None of that kept me from having a wonderful time. Too wonderful, my manager thought. I knew the back entrances of service elevator locations of every team hotel in every city, and one 4:00 A.M. I got the hungers and snuck downstairs to get a bag of White Castle hamburgers at an all-night joint. I thought I was home free until the room service elevator stopped and Casey Stengel himself climbed aboard.

"Drunk again!" Stengel accused.

"Really? Me, too," I replied, burping innocently. Stengel started to laugh, then muffled it with his hand. He waved me away. "Get away from me," he said. "Go to bed." (Good news for the bank clerk in charge of McDermott overdrafts. No fine.)

Occasionally, I even got paid for having fun. Mickey Mantle and I got booked for a guest spot on the Arthur Murray TV show. Mickey jitter-bugged with a partner. I did the same, letting it all hang out and throwing my partner around like a sack of feathers. When it was time for the audience to judge, Mickey scored well on the applause meter, but it went over the top for me and my gal. Afterward the booking agent said, "What did you think you were doing? Mantle was supposed to win." I had no idea the fix was in. If I did, I'd have tripped.

Stage-struck ham that I was, I did not indiscriminately accept any and all TV guest shot invitations. For instance, once Barbara and I, driving home from a friend's place late one night, suddenly felt overwhelmingly passionate. (OK, there was a trigger. We'd been watching a very sexy movie.) Delayed gratification never having been my strong suit, I spied a secluded beachside lane near the Fontainbleu Hotel, pulled over, and parked on a dark strip of sand. Wasting no time, Babs and I went at it, oblivious to all around us.

It was one of those wonderfully unforgettable moments until a harsh voice, shattering our romantic mood, made it even more unforgettable: "All right buster, out of the car—you and that hooker." Pulling myself together as best I could, I got out. But when the party pooper refused to listen to reason ("Officer, this lady is no hooker. She's my wife."), I punched him out. To his insult, I added injury. I was cuffed and hauled forthwith to the station house.

The next day the McDermotts' amour interruptus story was all over the papers in lurid detail. And within hours, I got a call from *I've Got a Secret*, a popular TV show, inviting me to share my secret with 20 million voyeurs. "No thanks," I said. "I'm going fishing." And I did. With Barbara. On a boat with a cabin, a guy can have some privacy. And oh yes, the cop. When Barbara's father, an attorney with friends in very high places, heard what the cop had called his daughter, he steamed like Mt. Vesuvius. Next day, the cop was looking for a new job.

My pals tried to help me regain control of the pitching mound. But once more Maurice "Pighead" McDermott didn't listen. When you lose velocity on your fastball, of course you have to come up with command of another major pitch. Throw the sinker. Throw the change. Or, as Whitey suggested, for base-runners-at-the-corners situations, learn to load 'em up. Not the bases, the balls.

Half the guys in the Hall of Fame wouldn't be there if they hadn't learned the tricks of the trade. Guys who aren't there used them, too. Butterfingers helped. The infielders would whip the ball around the infield after an out, ending with the third baseman. He was supposed to walk the ball to the pitcher (a Hall of Famer who, sorry, must be nameless here) and hand it to him. Instead, after surreptitiously spitting a Boston oyster on it, the infielder would lob it underhand to the pitcher, who, looking the other way, would drop the ball, then grind it into the dirt as he picked it up. The joke used to be that when Pitcher X pitched, the umpires had to wear raincoats.

Ground crews sometimes played helpful games too. Put 6'10" Randy Johnson on top of a 23" mound and he's as menacing as Goliath on stilts. But Bob Porterfield was only 6', so the crew would quietly raise the mound for him. And when a sidearm pitcher was scheduled, a few inches were surreptitiously sliced off it. Hey, every little bit helps.

Catchers could be helpful. He never stabbed anyone with it, but the rumor was that our backstop, Elston Howard, sharpened his belt buckle so he could crease a new ball before tossing it to the pitcher. Nobody thought of it as criminal activity. Like hollowed-out and corked bats, it was a way to get an edge, to outsmart the opposition, to experience the ultimate thrill—committing a misdemeanor with fifty thousand eyewitnesses looking on. So when a Braves Hall of Famer was accused of using a foreign substance on the ball, it was the challenge to his patriotism that bothered him. "Shoot, no," he declared righteously, "The stuff I use is made right here in the U.S. of A."

Lew Burdette had the best spitball ever. He was a walking oil well. Oil on his belt, his sleeve, the bill of his cap. When he pitched, the bottom would fall out, and the batter would find himself swinging at air. Of course, every pitcher rejoiced when the ball was kept in play after somebody hit it hard. If you wanted it to dance, there was nothing better than a ball with a dent in it. Nowadays they're casually tossed to the fans. I never did that. Better to pitch with it. Anyway, if you sent a ball into the bleachers during the fifties, management would fine your fanny. Especially in Washington, the capital of cheap. Waste not, want not.

Joe DiMaggio had limped off the Yankee stage in 1951 batting .263 and hitting only 12 home runs. Dom had followed two years later. They had played passionately for passionately rival teams. Dom went on to a successful business career. Joe made a career of being Joe DiMaggio. There was a line a mile long waiting to sign him up for endorsements or to buy something—anything—with his autograph on it.

But behind that poker face lurked a sense of humor. At a benefit many years later for B.A.T. (the Baseball Assistance Team), a group that offers financial aid and health benefits to old timers who never had the chance to sign eight-digit contracts, I had been shooting the breeze with Stan Musial and Ralph Kiner. Later I walked past the table where Joe was sitting with a young girl and doing signings. Smiling, he called me. "Morris," he said, "come here and meet my granddaughter. I want to sign a ball for you." Afterward I strolled back to Kiner and Musial. "What is this?" Kiner asked. "How come he signs baseballs for you and he won't even talk to us?"

"Here's how come," I said. I handed him the ball. The inscription read, "Dear Mickey, thanks for all those good pitches at Fenway Park."

I've already told you about my childhood. I can't tell you about Joe's. I don't know how it made him such a private person, a man who inhabited a private space, pretty much aloof even from his teammates. When anyone messed with what little privacy was left to a guy with a face as well known as the president on the penny, he really got upset. Like the time Yankees GM George Weiss called Joe into his office to say that he'd gotten reports Joe was staying out late with a woman. Nobody could talk that way to Joe. Not even the boss.

"Oh, so you're hiring detectives to watch me," he fumed. "Well, I'll give you their next assignment. Have 'em try to find me. I'm outta here." Weiss called off the PIs. At contract time, Joe demanded and got the first $100,000 contract in baseball.

But I guess if I'd had songs written about me, had Marilyn Monroe sleeping with me, owned the longest hitting streak in baseball history, and had a reputation as "America's Guest" because I never picked up a tab in a restaurant and they never gave me one, I'd have had at least as inflated an ego as Joe's. But he was given to grand gestures, too—like the ball he signed for me and the three rare signed bats in a rack in the office of his buddy Rudy Riska, of the Downtown Athletic Club. It may have been the only time he ever signed three bats to one man, and in today's eBay world, they are worth a fortune. My ball probably is, too.

The Yankees boasted a lineup of legends, and Yogi Berra, briefly my roommate, is among, as he might say, the legendariest. Yogi was a legend to me before I joined the club. I was pitching for the Red Sox. It was the top of the ninth. The Yanks trailed 2–1, and there was a man on first with no one out. Berra came in to pinch hit. It was an obvious bunt situation, but this was Berra, one of baseball's all-time great power-hitting catchers, so how could you be certain? (That's one of the great things about the game of baseball. You can never be certain.)

Birdie Tebbetts called time and came to the mound. "OK, Bush," said the old pro, "here's how we find out for sure what this guy is up to. Take the ball and throw it right at his f'g head. If he squares around, we know what he's gonna do."

I wound up, aimed between the eyes, and fired. If he didn't duck, he would get creamed. But he didn't duck. Neither did he square to bunt. He just hit it a mile to dead center for a home run. I was furious. I retired the next two batters and then I trotted in, ranting and raving. In Fenway the dugouts were adjacent. I spotted Yogi on the Yankees bench and detoured.

"What the hell were you doing?" I yelled. "That was a bunt situation."

There was the bottom of the ninth still to come, but he had just basically won the ballgame. Still he apologized. "Gee, Mick, I'm sorry," he said. "I missed the bunt sign."

Rooming with Yogi was more fun than pitching against him. One night the phone rang. Yogi picked it up, greeted his wife, listened a while, talked a while. There was a pause. His wife had finally gotten around to the point of this phone call. Yogi's voice changed. "Whaddya mean you're pregnant again?" he bellowed. "You can't be! I bought you a diagram!" Laughter was not the appropriate response at a moment like that, but I couldn't help myself.

Yogi was as creative with the English language as he was in calling signals behind the plate. One night I tiptoed into our room about 2:00 A.M. and was about to slip under the covers when I heard a plaintive voice. It was Yogi: "Hey, Mick, would you have a cigarette with me? I'm insomniated." Once in Kansas City, I came back in the middle of the night after partying and drinking gin with a bunch of cowboys I met in the lobby, spent the next hour embracing the toilet bowl, and then slept the deep sleep of the guilty. When I woke up, the sun was high enough in the sky to make me wince, the room was empty, and a look at my watch told me I had missed the team plane. Luckily, the next day was an off-day and I caught them without being fined. When I asked Yogi why he'd left without me, he said, "Mick, I tried. Heaven knows I tried. But a siren couldn't wake you. A bomb could go off and it wouldn't wake you. Maybe I should've tried a bomb. I finally gave up and left."

I shouldn't tell stories you've probably heard before, but then again, I'd feel terrible if you hadn't heard them. So . . .

No discussion of Yogi could possibly be complete without his classic comment about Stan Musial's restaurant in St. Louis: "No wonder nobody goes there. It's always crowded." Or his polite request of Bobby Brown, the third baseman/med student, who was reading a medical text, "When you're finished, tell me how it ends." And then there was his immortal remark after watching Steve McQueen as "Bullitt" in a movie of the week, "That sonovabitch became a great actor since he died."

Speaking of Yankees legends, let us not forget the notorious "Jerry the Crasher." Jerry appears dead center in full uniform in a Yankees team photograph that, when it appeared in the official Yankees yearbook, led to the inevitable question by devoted fans (and players, including me), "Hey, who's that?" Which in turn led to a second question from an embarrassed management, "How the hell did Jerry the Crasher manage to pull that one off?"

Yogi managed the club in 1964, rewarded for years of sterling catching (14 of them) and home runs (358 of them). It's easier to relax as a player than as a manager. With his team in third place in mid-August after three straight pennants under Ralph Houk, Yogi was not in the mood for a harmonica concert on the bus after another loss. Phil Linz, the 24-year-old supersub who played short, third, and the outfield, didn't know that.

Linz was in the back of the bus, sitting near Mickey Mantle. Yogi jumped up and roared from the front, "Stop that f'g playing," but the roar of the bus motor and the sounds of busy New York traffic drowned his words. Chuckling, Mantle translated for Linz: "Skip says keep playing. He likes it." Linz played on, only louder. Yogi jumped up again and repeated his command. Once more, Mantle interpreted: "He says that's his favorite song, play it again."

This time Yogi jumped up and down fit to go through the floorboards, and Linz didn't need an interpreter. What he shouted was, "You're fined $1,000. And throw that f'g harmonica out the window!" Mantle, the world's greatest instigator, didn't pay Linz's fine, but maybe he should have. On the other hand, the incident may have been just what the Yankees needed to show them who was in charge. Bolstered by Mantle's return from a leg injury, the team woke up, lost only six games in September, and clinched the pennant a day before the season ended.

I certainly didn't win it alone, and I will not claim the Yanks couldn't have done it without me. That's because the record shows that I did not exactly set the stadium on fire when the ding-ding-ding to the bullpen came in. I wended my way to the mound in 23 games, pitched an average of three and a half innings, gave up almost a hit an inning, and finished the season with a not-very-dazzling 4.24 ERA. Not a team worst—the ERAs of Gerry Staley, Jim Konstanty, Jim Coates, Ralph Terry, and Bob Turley were higher. But Bob had an 8–4 record, and mine was a regrettable 2–6. Poor Gerry got credit—maybe that should read debit—for one-third of an inning with an unforgettable ERA of 108.00.

Is that a record? I don't know, but it's not very kind of me to remind him, so I've got to add that it was an aberration. Traded to the White Sox, Gerry had a 5–1 record in relief the following year with a team-low 2.06 ERA. See how a stat can fool you? In all, he pitched for six teams, won 134 games, and had a lifetime ERA of 3.70. Which I say, hanging my head in embarrassment (by now you know I have no shame), was a better overall record than mine.

My first World Series. (OK, and my last.) Things did not start well for us. The Brooklyn Dodgers had beaten out the Yanks in '55 and took the first two games in '56. But Whitey Ford and Tom Sturdivant evened the score, with significant help from Mickey Mantle and Hank Bauer. And then it was Don Larsen's turn.

The night before, when we went out to have some good old Big Apple fun, Don didn't know that. Personally, I was having too much fun to be a reliable witness, so I'm forced to take Yankees exec Art Richman's word for what happened that night. Art, who was then handling press for the team, tells me that before things got out of hand he rescued young Donald—who, being a year younger than I, needed his beauty sleep—and made sure that he was in bed by midnight.

Whatever. All I know is that out in the bullpen the next day with Larsen on the mound, I marveled at Mantle's flying catch of Gil Hodges' long bid for extra bases. He hurt his leg, aggravating his osteomyelitis, but you wouldn't have known it at the time. I had no idea Larsen was pitching a perfect game until a sudden hush fell over the stadium in the top of the ninth. It was so quiet you could hear a name drop. I thought someone had died until I looked up at the scoreboard and saw all those goose eggs.

Larsen almost lost el perfecto, but a bunt that would have been a hit went foul at the last possible moment. Babe Pinelli was the umpire, and as time went on the game got tougher and tougher to call. A lot rode on whether a strike he called a fourth ball put a man on base or a bad pitch he called a strike cost the Dodgers a runner.

When he pumped his right arm in the air for strike three on the final batter in the first World Series perfect game, Pinelli tossed his balls-and-strikes indicator up in the air, too. Then he tossed his mask on the ground. "I've seen it all now," he said. "I quit." But he did hang around for the final two games.

I got in my innings, too, but not quite as spectacularly. The score was 11–7 in the sixth inning of the second game with the Dodgers on top when I got the call. I did nobly in the sixth and seventh, and adequately in the eighth. I did distinguish myself with the bat though. I got to hit for myself in the top of the eighth; I singled up the middle against Don Bessent. My 1956 World Series batting average: a perfect 1.000. Babe Ruth, whaddya think of that?

Everyone I knew wanted World Series tickets, of course. Comedian Larry Storch had been backstage when Mantle and I jitterbugged on the Arthur Murray TV show. "Moishe," he said, "I've gotta have two for the game." I left them at the gate in his name. Later he said, "Moishe, what did you do to me? They put me in the third deck. The game was a rumor. I asked the guy next to me if he was enjoying the game. He said, 'What game? I'm flying the mail to Pittsburgh.'" Never do a favor for a comic.

My old man was more appreciative. When I gave him his ticket at the hotel, he said, "Great! I'll grab a cab to Ebbets Field."

"You're not taking a cab all the way to Brooklyn," I said. "You're coming on the bus with us."

"Can I take him?" I asked the traveling secretary. "He played at Hartford in the Yankees system. Gehrig took his job at first base." The answer made him the happiest father in New York, and when we went to Toots Shor's after the game he headed straight for the piano to spread his happiness around. A crowd gathered immediately, and—shades of the old Poughkeepsie firehouse—his first song was "Mamie Riley." But he didn't stop 'til he'd sung every Irish song he knew, and then he started over at the beginning. He was having such a good time, I don't think he got around to eating his steak.

Phil Rizzuto had played 13 years for the Yankees when 1956 ended. He'd have played three more if, in 1943, Uncle Sam hadn't invited him to play a bigger game. That last season, he'd played short in only 30 games, spending most of his time in my territory as bullpen coach. GM George Weiss called him into his office one day, slapped a list on the table, and said, "Phil, I want you to go over this with me and see who we should let go next season."

Phil wondered what this is all about. Kind of, "Why me?" He smelled a mouse. They went over the list and got to the last two guys: McDermott and Rizzuto. Phil said, "Oh, yeah. McDermott?" Weiss said, "No." Phil said, "You mean me?" And Weiss said, "Sorry, Phil, I do."

It sounds like some kind of upper-echelon sadism, but, in fact, it was the best thing that could have happened to the Scooter. They offered him a job in the broadcast booth, and he made more money talking baseball in the next couple of years than he had in his 13 years playing it—and kept on making it for almost 40 more years.

My name stayed on Weiss' hit list though. With that ballclub, if you don't do great, you're gone. And he added another nine players to the list when he had the chance to obtain lefty Bobby Shantz and righty Art Ditmar from Lou Boudreau's Kansas City A's. I had a feeling that maybe Boudreau wanted me back on his team because he felt guilty about trading me from Boston to Washington after my 18-win season. But who knows? Maybe he was a cockeyed optimist and thought he could get me to push it up to 20 this time around.

Anyway, along with Billy Hunter, Rip Coleman, Tom Morgan, Irv Noren, and some minor leaguers, now I was off to K.C. It could have been worse. I had a bunch of good buddies with me. And this time I was wearing a World Series ring.

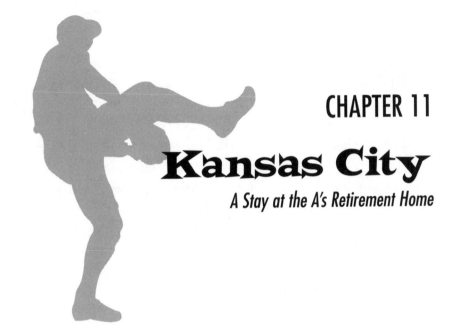

CHAPTER 11

Kansas City

A Stay at the A's Retirement Home

Like a soldier of fortune, I wore a lot of different uniforms. Now I wish I'd saved them, but who knew my dried sweat would be worth a small fortune someday? I sure didn't until an old pal called a while back to say, "Quick, Mickey, tune in eBay. Somebody's selling your Washington Senators shirt for $3,700." Gee, I hope they washed it first.

No longer proud in pinstripes, I gypsied to my fourth team in five years. From New York to Kansas City. From the penthouse to a cellar club. And the sad truth is that I was starting not to care. Another last-place team? So what?

Another truth: I wasn't feeling very good about myself. Barely 10 years ago, I had been a phenom. One of the chosen. Destined for stardom. All those things. I had been convinced more and more with every rocket I launched, every strikeout I racked up, that my arm and I were headed in the general direction of Cooperstown. Of course, when that audacious thought slipped into my head, I shooed it out. No use jinxing yourself. But the thought was like a pink elephant. Someone says, "Don't think about a pink elephant," and your head is suddenly so full of tusks and trunks that you can't shake them out.

People kept saying and headline writers kept writing: "They're Calling Maury the Greatest Lefty Today." "McDermott Ranked with Grove, Gomez." "A Sure Thing for the Hall of Fame." And now the mighty had fallen. "Casey at the Bat" and "McDermott on the Mound" were blood brothers.

I didn't realize until recently, resurrecting memories for this book, how down on myself I was when I left the Yankees. I loved wearing that World Series ring. I still do. But deep down, I felt it was on my finger not because I earned it but just because my name happened to be on the 1956 roster.

Sure, everybody on the team deserved a ring, no matter what the size of his contribution. Everybody couldn't be Mickey Mantle or Whitey Ford. They needed help. I'd gotten some key outs and some key hits, but in my teenage World Series dreams of glory, I hadn't been the spot reliever or pinch-hitter but the hero—the hero pitching on two days' rest who won three games and the honor and glory that went along with it.

So in thinking about my years in baseball, I was amazed to recall a note I wrote to Ted Williams in the winter of '56 that I hadn't thought about for 46 years. I had a standing invitation to go fishing with Ted, so, back home in Miami after my season with the Yankees ended, I paid a promised visit to Ted's home in Isla Mirada in the Florida Keys. The door was open, but there was no Ted inside. He was, I figured, already out fishing.

Wrong. Next day, when I asked Ted where he'd been, he said, "Playing tennis. Returning a serve or a smash is great. It keeps my hand-and-eye coordination in shape over the winter. But if you ever tell, I'll kill you." Tennis might have been good for Ted's hitting eye and batting average, but it was embarrassingly unmacho. Women played it, for heaven's sake.

Ted's home was magnificent. I had a pretty nice one myself, but this was one I couldn't help but admire. A few years earlier, a passing hurricane had carried most of Ted's house to parts unknown, leaving the fireplace and little more. Gone were the mementos of a magnificent career—silver Louisville Slugger bats earned for batting championships, MVP plaques, and trophies and awards galore. Apparently his underwear survived. Or he replaced it at an army-navy store. When I stayed overnight, he was still wearing his old reliable button-down white skivvies imprinted with "United States Marine Corps." (Or maybe it said U.S. Marines. I didn't look that closely.)

But Ted had friends in high places. Boston Braves owner Lou Perrini, who'd made his fortune in construction, decided to build Ted a palace. Red Sox owner Yawkey made some phone calls and pretty soon there were new silver bats, new plaques, and new trophies to replace what had been lost. We should all have friends like that. But the note I left for Ted the day he was out playing tennis identified me as a friend of a different color. It read: "The Failure was here. See you later."

"The Failure." I didn't write it. My subconscious did. But the next day when we went fishing, Ted never said a word about it. He practiced baseball, not psychotherapy. I know now that two-word self-portrait was a cry of pain from—I've gotta say it—a broken heart. What I was admitting to Ted was simply the verdict that Judge Maurice McDermott—severe, unforgiving, black-robed, and seated deep in the confines of my brain—had, with an authoritative rap of his gavel, passed as my life sentence. And, with the velocity of my once-high-powered fastball gone, gone, good-bye, there didn't seem to be any possibility of appeal.

Oh, there might have been if we'd had surgeons performing Tommy John elbow procedures in the fifties. If we did, Sandy Koufax and I would have pitched competitively for another five years. And possibly, with increased smarts, better than ever. I know what I should have done. I know because, several years later, I did it in the Mexican League. But now, instead of a "fight team, fight" attitude, instead of thinking, I'll show them—over the winter I'm gonna develop a couple of new pitches—I just headed for the nearest cocktail lounge to cry in my beer. To brood and to rationalize: "OK, the average player lasts only three years in the majors. What's to complain about? I've had six pretty good ones already. From now on, whatever happens happens."

The main "whatever" that happened was thinking about how long my arm would last before I became a men's room attendant, watching well-dressed men use the urinals and handing out towels for quarter tips. Well, it wouldn't be that bad. But drinking was a great way to avoid thinking, and I knew my days in baseball were numbered. From now on, I'd have to fake my way through.

I know I appeared in 29 games, pitched 69 innings of relief, had a pitiful 1–4 record and a 5.48 ERA, and that my main redeeming feature was hitting four home runs with a slugging average of .510. I know only because the stats tell me so, but I don't remember too many games in Kansas City. I call those my blurry years.

It's like Mickey Mantle said in a surprised tone of voice when liver cancer forced him to stop drinking: "I actually don't remember 10 years of my life." And he was breaking records at the time. Mickey talked about getting a liver implant, and somebody suggested Billy Martin. "Hell, no," he said, "if they put Billy's liver in me, I'd be dead in 10 minutes." Mine would have given him at least 15.

When it comes to remembering what happened in Kansas City, my five scrapbooks are no help at all. After my season with the Yankees, the pages are blank. That's partly because my dad, who was addicted to collecting the clippings, got sick. And my wife, who pasted them in, had become a pretty heavy drinker herself and was ready to divorce me.

Instead of clips, I'd started to collect DWIs—which, for those of you who drink nothing stronger than Diet Coke, translates into "driving while intoxicated." And that's even stupider, I freely admit, than going through a revolving door while intoxicated.

I did that one night at the old New Yorker Hotel when K.C. was playing the Yankees. After the game, Johnny Groth and I did a little eating and a lot of drinking at Toots Shor's. Johnny's anatomy was unusual. He had two hollow legs and a hollow arm. How else could he slurp Scotch Royals as though they were glasses of orange juice—Scotch Royals, a drink so potent that after you down two or three you're ready to take on a regiment of Highlanders?

Well, we got out of the cab and Johnny cruised through the revolving door like it was, well, a revolving door. I entered and I couldn't find my way out. Every time I got to the exit, I missed it. I circled around again and missed it again. This happened four or five times, and now I was even dizzier than when I got in. Groth and the people standing in the lobby were convulsed with laughter. Why not? This was a very entertaining show. A heroic bellhop risked life and limb to save me from turning into a puddle of butter. Finally, with a little help from my new friend—I tipped him royally—I made it inside. My audience stood and applauded.

I wasn't K.C.'s only eccentric. We had a great kid named Lou Skizas, nicknamed in *The Sports Encyclopedia: Baseball 2002*, as the "Nervous Greek." Why Lou was nervous I'm not prepared to say, but I can say that he always wore two wash-and-wear suits. Not separately. One on top of the other. He'd come into the locker room, remove the inside one, wash it, and hang it up to dry during the game. When he dressed afterward, the inside one became the outside one. I don't know. Maybe his apartment didn't have a closet.

Baseball players, never having outgrown their adolescence, are inveterate pranksters, and Skizas came back after the game one day to find that the suit he'd washed now had short pants. What could he do? He bought another pair of matching long pants. Actually, the guy with the scissors was doing Lou a favor. If he'd taken the hint, he wouldn't have been picked up for vagrancy in Palm Beach. That was a pretty ritzy town in those days. "Look at that guy. He's wearing two suits. He must be homeless. Lock the bastard up." And they did.

Lou came from a solid family. His father owned a restaurant in Chicago, but when Lou took me there, I'm afraid his dad overdid the big fat Greek hospitality just a little. Anyway, he shouldn't have left that bottle of ouzo on the table. Ouzo? It hit me like an Uzi. I never got so bombed in my life. (Well, at least not that month.) Lou was one smart fella—the only baseball player I know who went on to become a professor at a university. Kansas State, I think. If he wore two suits there, I'm sure nobody noticed. Professors are supposed to be absentminded.

Another one of our team characters was an outfielder (you will soon understand why he must remain nameless) who refused to shower at the ballpark. One day, a ball was hit between him and center, and the only way he was going to get to it was to make a running catch. He ran, hobbling like a dog with bad legs, and didn't get anywhere near the ball. Nothing was said, but he was pulled from the lineup and sent to see a specialist. Turned out our teammate had what was indelicately termed "the clap." That explained why he showered only in the privacy of his own apartment. He'd been afraid to tell the trainer or the team doc, and he'd let it go too long. So the reason he couldn't run was impure and simple: swollen testicles. A series of penicillin shots solved the problem.

Playing for K.C. was a downer for a lot of us. We had nothing against Kansas City, the city, but after playing in New York, it was like being in another world. Hell, even if we won the pennant, who would notice? We had some great over-the-hill players on the team, but the A's were more like a retirement home than a ballclub. We played to win, but we didn't expect to. In the winter, you'd run into an old friend who'd ask where you were playing.

"Kansas City."

"Kansas City? Where's that?"

The people and the steaks were great in Kansas City—the steaks equal to Chicago's and the people even friendlier. (Chicago's got the best hot dogs though. I oughtta know. On my gradually decreasing salary—players who didn't deliver got cuts, not raises, in those days—I ate a lot of them.) K.C. nightlife was great, too. Big time jazz. Mississippi riverboats and gambling. But I didn't go near the boats. (I didn't even know they had a river.) I never had a problem with gambling. You've gotta have money to bet, and besides, I never got that far. I stopped at the nearest bar hoping to forget where I was. Sometimes it worked too well and I wouldn't remember how to get home.

Home was with my roomie, Virgil Trucks, one hard-nosed baseball player, who pitched two no-hitters in one season when he was with the Tigers. We called him "Fire" Trucks because he came on like a house afire. You didn't mess with anyone on our team when Virgil was on the mound. In a preseason exhibition game played in a Kansas City snowstorm, a

Dodger pitcher had the temerity to knock down Vic Power, a good guy and a helluva first baseman. Next inning came the payback. Virgil floored Don Zimmer with a fastball right between the eyes. Then, before anybody could charge the mound, he charged the Dodger dugout and challenged the whole bench to a fight. His preemptive strike was so unexpected that nobody moved a muscle. Virgil was a 205-pound animal, but he was our animal.

Trucks was from Birmingham, Alabama, where people and water fountains were still segregated. Vic Power was the opposite of white, but Virgil didn't care about his skin color. He was on the team. That made him family. And maybe an earlier episode in a small cracker town in Florida during spring training had something to do with raising Virgil's consciousness.

Our bus had pulled up to a roadside diner and we all piled out. The sign in the window said "Whites Only," but we didn't think that applied to baseball players. We were wrong. The owner refused to serve Vic Power, and Vic was not happy with that. Neither were we. With Harry Craft leading the way, we all walked out together. Our bus hadn't gone two miles down the road when we heard the sirens. Two sheriff's department patrol cars pulled us over and four deputies boarded the bus with shotguns at the ready and yanked Vic out of his seat.

"We know what this boy did," the sheriff drawled. "We have a complaint and we're gonna take him in." There was a long pause and then he continued. "Tell y'all what we're gonna do, boys. Whip out your wallets or we take this nigger with us. But if you can come up with $500, we'll let y'all go on your way."

We all looked around. All most of us had was the $5 meal money we'd been about to spend. (Nowadays, players' appetites must be a lot bigger. Meal money is $150.) Well, maybe they'd settle for less. Baseball caps started to move from the front and back of the bus with players dropping in fives and tens, but not enough of them. Little Jack Urban, a pitcher who gambled on horses, dogs, and anything else that ran, called a halt to the collection. The day before he'd won $600 on a horse. "Don't worry about it, guys," he said. "I got it." He peeled off a batch of $50s and handed them over. The sheriff shoved the $500 in a pocket and then gave us his version of Southern hospitality: "Better get his black ass outta here, or we'll string him up."

Virgil and I were left behind to take whirlpool treatments when the team headed north. He had a hamstring pull. My elbow was tender. We checked into a little $5-a-night frame motel, the kind of place that when you see it by the side of the road, you speed up to pass it by. We had a booking to speak at an Elks banquet, and a friend who owned a car agency offered to lend me a Rolls Royce touring car so we could suitably impress our audience.

With its thick glass partition and built-in speaking tube to command the chauffeur from the rear seats, it would have impressed Liberace. To me, it looked like Hitler's car, the one we used to see in the newsreels, and seemed solid enough to flatten a tank. It turned out I was not cut out to be a tank driver. When I returned to the motel to pick up Virgil, my turn as I approached the parking space in front of our corner room was too wide and I had to back up.

Unaccustomed to the Rolls Royce's five-speed shift, I miscalculated. Instead of shifting into reverse, I put it into drive. The Rolls Royce shot forward into a wood post holding up the second-floor porch on which the motel owner sat all day long drinking beer. The Rolls demolished the post and kept right on going into the wall of our room. With one of its supports removed, the whole building tilted crazily, and when I hit the brakes, I found myself partially parked in our living room. Fortunately, Virgil was in the bathroom at the time. He emerged coughing dust.

"How in the hell did you get in the living room?"

"I took a left through the kitchen."

We were no longer alone. The stairs leading to the second level had collapsed, and the owner, beer in hand, slid involuntarily down the rubble, never spilling a drop. He looked bewildered by this sudden change in the condition of his property, but he was too drunk to get upset. The insurance, he assured me, would cover everything.

The Rolls Royce needed to be washed. Other than that it was in great shape, and we made it to the banquet only a few minutes behind schedule.

Virgil brought down the house, you might say, when he told the story of why we were late: "I'm waiting for McDermott in my room, and he doesn't walk in. He drives in."

Frank Lane, Kansas City's GM, who bought and sold players as swiftly and ruthlessly as a slave owner, was commonly referred to as Trader Vic. A busload of us slaves, returning from a road trip, were boarding the team bus at the airport when an adjacent bus began to fill with players from a team we'd be playing that night. "Geez," somebody said, "good thing Frank Lane isn't here. He'd step into the nearest phone booth, make a call, and trade this busload for that busload."

He couldn't wait to trade me. The season had hardly ended before I got a letter in the mail that basically said, "The Kansas City A's are no longer the proud owners of one Maurice 'Mickey' McDermott. Go directly to Detroit. Do not pass Go. Do not expect an increase in salary. In fact, expect a pay cut."

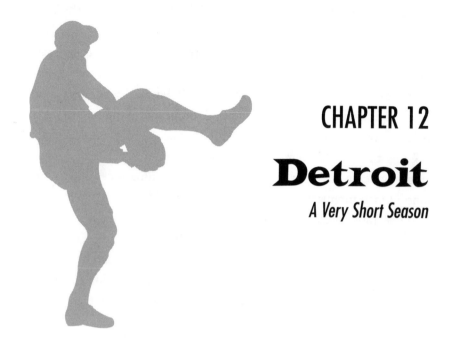

CHAPTER 12

Detroit

A Very Short Season

OK. That wasn't so bad. I had a lot of friends in Detroit. And not just bartenders. One of the best was Dick Wakefield, once the Tigers' prize bonus baby out of the University of Michigan. His signature earned him $50,000—at that point the biggest bonus ever. But Dick wanted a bonus on his bonus. He told Detroit owner Walter Briggs, "I won't sign unless you add a clause: a box of Havana cigars every week."

Briggs, who practically adopted Dick—he was welcome at Briggs' palatial lakefront estate anytime he felt like dropping in—grinned and signed on the dotted line. He got his money's worth. Dick, whose dad had been a catcher with Washington and Cleveland, hit .316 and .355 for the Tigers in '43 and '44 but then—maybe baseball seemed like kid stuff after World War II—never topped .300 again.

Wakefield had all the tools to be a superstar but, like me, after the first half-dozen years, though for reasons of his own, Dick didn't take baseball very seriously. It wasn't his life. It was just something he did—to the best of his ability—from February to September.

I'd met Wakefield earlier in spring training, but we became pals at Grossinger's resort in the Catskills when I worked there in the off-season. So when Detroit dumped Dick after the '49 season, I was happy to learn that the Yankees had offered him a walk-on in spring training to see what he could do. When we played an exhibition against New York, I told him the night before, "Richard, my first pitch is gonna be a nice and easy batting practice pitch right down the pike. Hit it nine miles and make the club." Good intentions, bad result. Dick popped it up.

The Yanks put him on their roster briefly anyway, but they traded him to the White Sox after only two official at-bats and a walk. Dick rejected Chicago's contract terms. Not enough cigars. Even though he was only 1 for 2, I suspect he told the White Sox that any player hitting .500 with the Yanks deserved more money. The argument, if, indeed, he made it, didn't wash. Chicago sat tight, and Richard sat out the season.

He spent that winter with me as a guest at my father-in-law's motel in Miami Beach. The only trouble with that was that every Sunday morning he yanked me out of the sack and dragged me to church. I warned him that sooner or later the church would fall down, but he took the risk.

As personable, intelligent, and articulate a charmer as you'd find anywhere in the world, Dick later ran for mayor of Detroit and narrowly missed winning the election. His opponent, a woman, got most of the women's vote. If she had been a he, handsome Richard would have been the people's choice, with women lining up all over Detroit to pull the lever for him.

I don't think he minded losing. Dick was so calm and serene that when he was standing up he looked like he was lying down. "Rats win rat races," he explained. "People need to lie back now and then and listen to the grass grow." Once he suggested to his pal Milton Blackstone, singer Eddie Fisher's manager, that when Eddie went on the road, he'd make a good road manager. Milton's deadpan reply: "Richard, are you kidding? I'd never see Eddie again." I guess he feared Dick would take Eddie to a scenic mountain lake instead of where he had to be—at a microphone in front of the Vegas crowd that was waiting for him to sing.

It's a metropolis now, but when the census taker did the numbers in Lakeland, Florida, in 1958, it was a spring-training town about as exciting as sleeping through a sermon, and he counted more iguanas than people. The biggest crop was sand, and by the time you got through a day of spring training, when you took off your shoes at night you had your own private beach beside your bed.

OK. I won't say it was a cemetery with lights. But the best place to eat in town was the Elks Club. I don't know if it was the only place to gamble, but you could always find a crap game underway, and Richard usually did. I guess he liked listening to the dice roll, too.

During the previous season, Detroit had been short-armed. In Jim Bunning they'd had a 20-game winner, but except for a 14–11 from Paul Foytack, all the other starters had losing records. Hell, I'd had losing records for the past three years, so what did they need me for? Walt Dropo's opinion's as good as any: "All Mickey had to do was work out with a club and they'd take a shot. They kept hoping their pitching coach could find the key to unlock his talent and find a 20-game winner inside." To which Walt added, "But he couldn't focus on baseball. He never grew up."

It's all true. GMs remembered my early press clippings, the predictions that I was gonna be the best there was, the nickname my fastball earned me as "the Fenway Rifle." They remembered my 18–10 season (which kept me in the big leagues for another six years), wishfully dismissed my recent inglorious history, and thought, well, maybe this time. But the truth is that by the time I got to Detroit I'd lost my stuff, and it didn't take them long to wise up to that.

I got along fine with manager Jack Tighe. But quickly realizing that my arm was as shot as a vintage 1776 musket, he didn't give me many opportunities to get myself in trouble. Two to be precise. In a grand total of two innings, I gave up six hits and two walks and racked up a sorry 9.00 ERA.

Actually I prefer to judge my short season—because it was short—by my boxing record. There the official tabulation was 1–0. Oh, there were other fights. When I'd passed stage one (friendly drunk) and stage two (garrulous drunk) and moved into stage three (belligerent drunk), I was the jerk who challenged you to a fight if you made a remark I took the wrong way. But my big fight was with Billy the "Intimidator" Martin.

Don't get me wrong. Billy was my barroom buddy. He had been Mickey Mantle's until the Yankees traded Billy (and probably me, too) to try to put the brakes on Mickey's drinking. But Billy got to stage three even faster than I did. And even cold sober on the ball field, he was always at stage three—as spoiling for a fight as an F-16 over Baghdad. It was part of his game: Intimidate. Intimidate. Intimidate and conquer.

That's what was going on back in 1952 (or maybe '53), in a game between the Yanks and the Red Sox when Jimmy Piersall slid into Billy, upending him at second base in the last out of the inning. Piersall, whose quick tongue often got him in trouble, came up taunting: "If I had a nose like yours, I'd put nickels in it and retire." Or words to that effect. To Billy, that was a challenge, and man, did he love to be challenged. He sprang to his feet and gave chase. Piersall ran like hell for the safety of the Boston dugout. Billy caught him at the steps and fists started to fly.

That startled Yankees coach Bill Dickey, who may have been dozing just a bit in the adjacent Yankees dugout. Dickey leaped to his feet to separate the combatants. Or, maybe, pile on. The top of Dickey's skull smacked the dugout's low ceiling. The ceiling was cement, and the brawny ex-catcher collapsed in a heap, the brawl's only casualty. Meanwhile Ellis Kinder, 6'3" and 220 pounds, stepped between Piersall and Martin, grabbed them by their collars, and banged their heads together in what sounded like a collision of two bowling balls. Fight called on account of Kinder's knocking some sense into their heads.

Now back to Baltimore where Billy and I were in a bar with ex-welterweight contender Rocky Castellani. Billy started to needle me with very long needles. I should have been laughing, but too many beers had drowned my sense of humor, and the last jab, attacking Barbara, demanded a response. "Ah, you ain't got any balls," he said. "I could screw your wife and you'd just leave the room."

That did it. "You c-sucker," I said. "Get your ass outside. We're gonna settle this right now." I slid off the bar stool, but Rocky's manager locked his arms around my chest to hold me back and calm me down. That's as far as it would have gone, but Billy took advantage of my immobilization to slap me hard in the face. I broke loose. "OK, Billy," I said, "that's it. Outside. And you go first. You're not gonna sucker punch me when my back is turned."

Billy was a tough little hombre, but I outweighed him by 40 pounds and outreached him by a hand span. We drew a crowd of 200 people in the parking lot—come to think of it, we should have charged admission—but the fight didn't last long enough for *Eyewitness News* to get there. They didn't come any gamer than Billy, and he belted me a couple of times like a 16-wheel truck, but I was too big for him. When it was over, I wasn't happy about it. There's never a winner when two friends fight.

Next morning, a phone call woke me up. "McDermott, this is Tighe. I hear you ruined my shortstop."

Uh-oh. My manager. "OK," I said, "I know you're gonna fine my ass. How much?"

He should have hit me for at least $500, but he only laughed. "No, no, Mac. We're playing an exhibition game in San Fran next week. I wanted to know if I could book you at the Cow Palace for a four-rounder." Now it was my turn to laugh. No fine? How did I get away with that one?

That night, pitcher Jim Bunning (soon, you may remember, to be Senator Bunning of Kentucky) came to the dugout after shagging flies in the outfield, looked at the lineup card, and, puzzled, asked, "Where's my shortstop? Where's Billy?"

"Mac and Billy were drinking," backup shortstop Reno Bertoia explained. "They got into it. Mac cleaned his clock, and Billy doesn't look too good today." In fact, Billy sat out the next couple of games on the bench—on the semidisabled list.

A couple of days later, we were in Washington, a city with very bad vibes for me. I woke up in D.C. with a hangover, stumbled into the bathroom, caught a glimpse of myself in the mirror, 29 years old and looking like the far side of 50, and asked myself, "What am I doing here?" I sat on the toilet, chin sunk in hands, waiting for an answer, but none came.

"The hell with it," I said aloud. "I'm going home to Miami to Barbara and play golf."

It was not a logical thing to do. I had maybe $1,000 in the bank. About the only thing I could afford to do on a golf course was caddy. What's more, I was under contract. Jumping the club was not a good idea. It could have finished me in baseball. But I felt like I was finished anyway, and alcoholism knows no logic. You're just gonna have one drink. But that first drink numbs the brain's judgment center and puts it out of commission. Suddenly, one drink turns into a half-dozen. And if you have as much to regret and forget as I did, even that's not enough.

Forget about textbooks. I can tell you firsthand that when people say of a drinker, "The guy's crazy," they're not far from the truth. It's a form of insanity. You don't know or care what you're doing, or who, besides yourself, you're hurting. Everything is immediate gratification. Impulsive. I want a car. I pick it out now. I'm lost. I'm disgusted. I want to go home. Why not now? Right now!

I went to the ballpark. Billy was taking a shower. We were still pals. There was no way the fight could break up our friendship. We both knew it was the devil's fault—the devil in the bottle.

"Billy," I said, "I need $100." His voice cut through the steam, "Take it out of my wallet." I did, and I caught a plane home. My wife was surprised to see me. She wasn't happy that I was broke. But hey, what else was new? On fifties baseball salaries, we were always broke.

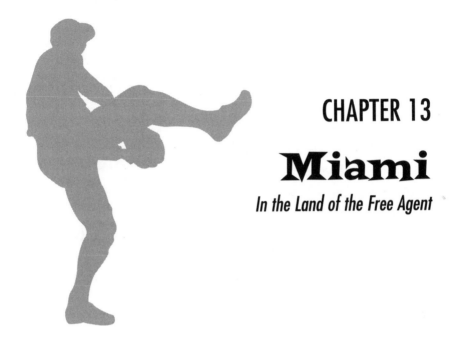

CHAPTER 13

Miami

In the Land of the Free Agent

Well, I didn't want to caddy, and after a few weeks at home fighting with Barbara—who'd started drinking to keep me company and had gotten to be almost as good a drinker as I was—I was surprised to get a telegram from Dallas. When I opened it, I blew a row of gaskets. Without saying a word to me, Detroit GM John McHale had sold me to Dallas–Ft. Worth in the Texas League.

"You're going back to the minors?" Barbara asked in alarm.

"Hell, no," I told her. "First of all, playing in that climate would be like playing in hell with tumbleweed. Second of all, McHale can't do that. I've got 10 years in the majors. I'm pretty sure that makes me a free agent. And that means the $75,000 he sold me to Dallas for belongs to me."

Welcome to the slave market. The day after I communicated that sentiment to Detroit, I got a telegram from the league commissioner, Ford Frick, that Albert Einstein and two Supreme Court justices would have had trouble understanding. But while I was puzzling over it, I got a phone call from New York from two labor lawyers who'd gotten wind of what was going on.

"You're a free agent, aren't you?" they asked.

"I think I am. I've got 10 years in the majors."

"Well then, let us take your case to court. That $75,000 is rightfully yours." (Well, of course, they'd get some of it, too.)

They interpreted the telegram: (a) because of the reserve clause, the money belongs to Detroit, and (b) if you don't sign with Dallas, you'll be blackballed and never play baseball again.

Furious, I phoned Frick, finally reached him at a banquet, and told him he was spelling his name wrong, that it should start with a consonant much further up the alphabet. (Well, actually, I spelled it out for him.) After I hung up, I phoned Ted Williams to ask for advice. It was clear and to the point: "Mac, you're not gonna beat them. They'll run you out of the game. They're so powerful they won't even let you in a ballpark to watch. You're just going to have to go along with it."

Ted was right. My lawyers did their thing, but the majors did their thing better. They moved to dismiss my case because of the reserve clause in my (and everyone else's) baseball contract that bound a player forever and a day to the team that signed him—in effect permanently reserving the owner's right to do whatever he wanted. Their motion was granted.

About 10 years later, a .293 lifetime outfielder and all-around great guy named Curt Flood, who had more brains and endurance than I did, refused to "go along" when the Cards traded him to the Phillies. And he refused to let a lower court dismissal stop him. He took his case against the reserve clause all the way to the U.S. Supreme Court. Except for a final 35 at-bats in '71 with the Senators, that pretty much ended his 13-year baseball career, but his battle helped to eventually erase the reserve clause and changed baseball salaries and the economics of the game forever. Curt, who had studied in Spain and was a successful artist, had other sources of income anyway—a nightclub in St. Louis, where he remained a very popular guy, and the sale of his paintings for as much as $25,000. Or so I heard. He didn't quite make it to 60. I don't know what he died of, and I'm sure not a doctor, but whatever it was, I wouldn't be surprised if major stress from his reserve clause legal battles, weakening his immune system, had something to do with his early death of throat cancer.

There was no way I was going on Dallas' terms. I told management that I'd changed my mind and I'd be happy to go. There were just a few little things I wanted—a hotel suite in every city they played in, a $100 bonus for every game I won, and my major league salary. That cooked that goose.

The dispute hit the newspapers, and not long after, I got a phone call from Joe Ryan, GM of the Miami Marlins of the Triple A International League. Miami? Well, I lived there. Why not play there? I agreed to terms somewhat less demanding than my Dallas ultimatum and headed for Ryan's office to sign a contract for $1,500 a month.

Ryan was a great guy but a character and a half, known to the team as Mr. Magoo. I found out why when I signed the contract. When it was his turn, he missed the paper and signed his desk. He would sit in the owner's box wearing eyeglasses with lenses that looked like 20 pounds of ice, listening to the game on the radio because he couldn't see the ballplayers. I told him he should have been an umpire. One day at Miami International Airport, Joe excused himself to find a phone booth. Instead he slid into a photo booth. He fumbled around until he found a slot, and then he started to put in a coin. "Joe," I interrupted, "what in the hell are you doing? Taking a picture for your wife?"

Maybe that's why, when scouting for players, Ryan preferred to sign the tried and true rather than the new. So in '59, my second season with the Marlins, Ryan added 177-game winner Virgil Trucks, most recently of the Yankees, and ageless Satchel Paige, who, mostly in relief, had won 28 games and saved 32 with Cleveland, the St. Louis Browns, and Kansas City, but before that had won uncounted hundreds as a starter in the Negro leagues.

Satch moved with the speed of iced molasses when summoned from the bullpen. I asked him how come it took him so long to get to the pitching mound. "Bo," he said mournfully (he called everybody but the manager Bo because learning names was too much trouble), "Bo, it's somepin' I learned a long time ago. You never rushes into trouble."

A Funny Thing Happened on the Way to Cooperstown

Satch behaved the same in front of forty thousand people as he did in the privacy of his hotel room. That's how many were watching him one afternoon when he pitched for Cleveland against the Red Sox back in '49. Came time to throw the ball, he just stood on the mound holding his belly with an odd look on his face. Stepping off, Satch waved his buddy, pitcher Bob Lemon, in from the Cleveland dugout.

Lemon suspected what the problem was—the bourbon from the night before (or from that morning) working its way up from Satch's toes to his gut. With manager Lou Boudreau's blessing, he trotted out to ask what was wrong. Satch shook his head, "You know what's wrong, Bo. I jes' got to get this burp out." He frowned and concentrated. Lemon went behind Satch, wrapped his arms around him, and yanked in a modified Heimlich–Jack Daniels Maneuver. Immediately, a howitzer-like explosion rent the air, probably audible all the way to Bunker Hill. Satch beamed. "Oh, that's good, Bo," he said. "I'm ready to pitch now." And he proceeded to beat us.

Satch sure wasn't ready the afternoon he was scheduled to start against the Yankees. Game time was 1:05, and he and catcher Jim Hegan were supposed to meet in the manager's office 45 minutes beforehand to go over the hitters' strengths and weaknesses. "Where the hell is Satch?" Boudreau asked Hegan. "Don't know. Haven't seen him in the clubhouse." Boudreau, who was accustomed to expect the unexpected from Satch, started to panic.

Had Satch been killed in a cab accident? Kidnapped for ransom? Or, heaven forbid, had this stud, who claimed to have sired 90 children with assorted lady friends and to have paid $100,000 in maternity bills, forgotten that he was pitching? Was he even now shacked up in his hotel room in the arms of yet another mother-to-be?

The last theory seemed to Boudreau the most plausible. He phoned the club's hotel and asked for Paige's room. His pitcher answered. "Satch, get your ass down here to the ballpark," Boudreau demanded. "Sixty thousand people in Yankee Stadium are waiting to see you pitch, and the game is about to begin."

"Mr. Lou," said Paige, "I can tell from the way my rheumatiz is rheumitatin' that we ain't gonna play no ballgame. My arm hurts. My back hurts. I hurts all over. Look out the window. The biggest blackest clouds you ever seen in your life got to be headed your way. There is gonna be a hellacious rain."

Boudreau looked. The sky had suddenly darkened. Thunder boomed in the distance. Lightning rent the sky. And, exactly as Satch had predicted, the game was postponed on account of rain. Torrents of rain.

Satchel Paige didn't pay a lot of attention to club rules. He knew that a box-office draw of his caliber could make his own. When he played for the Browns, they put a rocking chair in the bullpen under a big umbrella to keep the sun off him. Early in the season, the Marlins flew to Canada for a series in Montreal—long before their roofed Olympic Stadium was built. As our descending plane broke through the cloud cover, Satch peered out the window. "What is that white shit?" he asked aloud. Thoroughly alarmed, he answered his own question. "That's snow!" He swiveled in his seat toward manager Pepper Martin. "Mr. Pepper," he said firmly, "Ol' Satch ain't playin' in no blizzard. My ass is goin' right back to Miami." Ignoring Martin's remonstrations, cajoling, and threats, the minute we disembarked from our charter, Satch headed for the nearest Air Canada desk and booked himself a return flight to sunny Florida.

First time I saw Satch, the lively legend, was when Cleveland played us in Boston. As he trudged to the bullpen in deep center before the game carrying a bucket covered by a towel, all eyes were on him, wondering what in the world was in that bucket. When he reached the bullpen, the suspense was over. Satch pulled back the towel, revealed a half-dozen cans buried in ice, and popped a beer.

"Geez, Satch, put that sonovabitch away," George Susce, who was our bullpen coach and had been Paige's in Cleveland, exclaimed. "Satch, you know you can't drink beer on the field. They'll fine your ass."

Satch was unperturbed. When he made black baseball history with the Kansas City Monarchs where a lot of people think he may have been the greatest pitcher of all time (yes, even including me), the only regulation was that for this man there were no regulations. With the Monarchs, if he wanted to sip from a fifth in the dugout for a refresher between innings, that was just fine. Especially if he happened to be pitching another no-hitter at the time. In the majors, when he got bored in the pen, he used the bullpen coach's phone to call old flames all over the country. He'd just tell the switchboard lady: "This is ol' Satch. Give me Los Angeles information," and go from there. He ran up three-figure phone bills in every ballpark, but nobody ever held the legend accountable. Well, I guess there was an occasional reprimand when the manager called for a relief pitcher and the line was busy.

At Cleveland, GM Bill Veeck was busy on the phone himself. He claimed he was fielding phone calls from all over the country from women who wanted Satch to sire a son for them. He was a thoroughbred like Secretariat, and they wanted to take in some of his solid gold pitching genes. There were calls from women who'd already had one by him, too, and Veeck would send them toys for their kids, Christmas trees, and money.

Humility was not a problem for Satch. At one time he drove a pink Cadillac with "S.P., The World's Greatest Pitcher" emblazoned on the door. He never bothered to get a license. Once he was picked up for driving without one. When the judge informed him that driving without government certification was against the law, Satch said, "Oh, I didn't know that. How much I owes you?" (I considered doing "M.M., The World's Second-Greatest Pitcher" on my Buick, but thought better of it.)

After a game, he'd hit the nightclubs, and it didn't take much to get him to saunter onstage to play his banjo—which he rarely failed to bring along—and then throw in a Bill Robinson tap dance for good measure. He was good. He could've made a living at it.

When I knew him, Satch was already a legend. Now, 20 years after his death, he's still a giant. He could have stood even taller, could have been the first of his race to break the major league color barrier. He was on the short list, but Branch Rickey nixed him. "He drinks," said Rickey. "He screws anything with legs. And he won't listen. I'm going with Jackie Robinson. He's clean-cut, a college graduate, and he was an army officer so he knows discipline. He's a better choice."

As anybody over 40 knows, Rickey told Robinson, "It isn't going to be easy. You're going to be biting your tongue a lot. You'll either ruin it or make it for your people." Look at any major league roster and you know Jackie sure didn't ruin it. But, sadly, a great many young African-American players (and Hispanic players, because he bulldozed a path for them, too) not only don't know how much they owe him, they've never even heard of him.

I had a ball with the Marlins. I had learned how to pitch a little. Not just throw smoke. Pitch. Toss the change-up. Toss the slider. Close them out with the curve now and then instead of the fastball they were expecting. Keep them off balance.

Having the lowest ERA in the league excused a multitude of my sins. Like the time Larry King, then a Florida DJ, was interviewing me on his show. We were both having such a good time that I forgot what time it was. Finally, Larry asked, "Aren't you supposed to be at the ballpark?" I looked at the studio clock. "Oops!" I said. "Oh, well, if they've got the radio on, they know where to find me." P.S.: I missed the game. But that wasn't as bad as the time I missed two games. I lost track of time for an entirely different reason in a bar across the street and blew a doubleheader.

That may have been the time a guy followed me into the men's room. No. No, that was a nightclub in Toronto. I recognized the nightclub manager in the mirror behind me as I was soaping my hands. When I'd dried them, he handed me a thick envelope. There was no stamp or address on it.

"What's this?"

"Open it."

I tore open the envelope. It was very green. Stuffed with $100 bills.

"This is a lot of money. What did I do to deserve it?"

"There's $10,000 in there. And it's not for what you did. It's for what you're gonna do. Simple things. Like phone me now and then. You know. Kinda keep me on the inside about what's what on the club. Who's injured. Who's hittin'. Things like that. Stuff that'll give us a little edge."

"No way," I said, "that's a felony." And I walked out. Fast.

A Funny Thing Happened on the Way to Cooperstown

It wasn't only a felony, but if it got out that I was involved with gamblers betting on games, I'd have lost not only whatever tattered reputation I had left but my pension, too. Of course, the pension was only $350 a month at the time. (Later it grew to $1,300—which is even less than it sounds because they take out $600 a month for health insurance, plus withholding. It took a dozen years and a lot more pleas for even that to happen.) Administrators of the Major League Baseball Players Pension Plan seemed oblivious to the difference between the $150,000-a-year pensions the new retirees were getting and the $4,200 a year for us older vets. Scrooge was writing our checks. King Midas was writing theirs.

Miami was fun. I could be myself. When I wasn't pitching, I often played first base. One day manager Pepper Martin did the mound walk to yank a pitcher who was in trouble. As he was walking him to the dugout, he heard footsteps behind him. He turned. It was me.

"Where are you going? Get back to first base."

"Oh, sorry, Skip. I'm so used to being yanked, I thought I was supposed to go, too." I was a very clean pitcher. I took a lot of showers.

Not everything in Miami was fun and games. In fact, the game was about up between me and Barbara. By this time—seems like playing for a Florida team I was home more often than she could tolerate—our marriage was, like the liquids we both indulged in too much, pretty much on the rocks. But we kept trying. A good offer came along from Havana in the Cuban League—$4,000 a month for three games a week of winter ball—and I grabbed it.

"Hey, Babs," I said. "How'd you like to spend the winter in Havana?"

CHAPTER 14

Havana and Caracas

Comes the Revolution

Havana. The league we played in wasn't much to wire home about. Only four teams: Havana, Marianao, Cienfuegos, and Almendares. (Did I get that right? I hope so, Señor Castro.) But they had hustle and muscle, and you could have moved any one of them to the majors and they wouldn't have finished last. It was the first league I ever played in where a baseball game was called on account of a revolution. About which more ("patience, patience!") shortly.

Each team was allowed four Americans. One of ours was a dynamite little 5'5" outfielder (I think he exaggerated an inch or so), Albie Pearson, who played for Baltimore, the Cal Angels, and a couple of other teams. I'm not sure how they classified two pitcher pals of mine from the Senators—Camilo Pascual and Pedro Ramos, who were born in Cuba but played in the States. In '55, my last year in Washington, none of us had impressive records. (I was 10–10, Camilo 2–12, and Pedro 5–11. But everyone has a bad year now and then. And a few years later, Camilo went 20–11 and 21–9 in consecutive years for Minnesota.) But what the heck? We were beeg-time players from Estados Unidos. We ran into Tommy Lasorda every now and then. He pitched—not very well—for Almendares. Of course, I was pitching—not very well—for Havana. And Lasorda, after going 0–4 for life in his cup of coffee with Brooklyn and Kansas City, put that behind him and made a name for himself managing the Dodgers for 21 years.

Pedro was a Cuban cowboy movie star when he wasn't pitching. And when he wasn't staring batters down, pitcher Jose "Mike" Fornieles, who played for five teams in the majors from '52 to '63, dealt in gold and imported U.S. cars. He had a dresser drawer full of gold watches, chains, and rings. If I had the brains a flea is born with, I could have bought enough gold Rolex watches from Mike at $75 apiece to open a jewelry store in Miami. When he was in the States, he would buy American cars four or five at a time and hire drivers to smuggle them into Cuba. Eventually the authorities caught on, but he was a big baseball idol so they looked the other way.

I had bought a new Ford station wagon. (Not from Mike. In the States on a drive-now-pay-later plan.) Babs and I had decided that wintering in Cuba with little Barbara and littler Michelle would be a great family togetherness experience, maybe even good for our marriage. We loaded the kids in back, took the ferry from Key West to Havana, and moved into a gorgeous marble villa on Marianao Beach with two maids—one to take care of the kids and the other to cook and polish the floors.

It wasn't long before I had myself a reputation among the locals. After I'd pitched a couple of games, I walked through the turnstile at Marianao's private beach one morning, and the attendant recognized me enthusiastically.

"Oh, I know you. You Meekey McDermo. Sí, sí. You throw ball here. You throw ball there. You throw ball everywhere. Only you never throw ball over plate." Well, it was a bit of an exaggeration, but all I could say was, "Geez, they already know me in Havana."

The team's three-games-a-week schedule had me thinking I was on winter vacation all winter. Pitching only once every two weeks made fooling around at night too easy. So did invitations like the one I got at a game one day.

Our manager, Mike Guerra, approached me as I was warming up on the sidelines. "Meekey," he said, "a man in the box seats wants to talk to you."

"You're Mickey McDermott?"

"Yes, sir."

"Tell your ballplayers any time they want to come to the International Hotel, they're welcome. Dinner, drinks, everything comped."

"Well, thank you. That's very generous."

Afterward, Mike asked, "Meekey, you know who that was?" I admitted I didn't. "That was Meyer Lansky."

Now I knew who he was—the brains behind what used to be called the mob. Hollywood star George Raft, who got gunned down regularly as a slick-haired fast-talking mob chief in a score of films but apparently always wanted to be a real mobster, fronted a hotel for them in Havana.

It might have been the Copa, where I ran into Rocky Marciano. "Hey," I said, "are you down here to catch batting practice?" I'd first met him at Fenway Park in the early fifties, on a day when I was pitching BP to loosen up between starts. As the heavyweight champ of the world from Massachusetts, good-natured Rocky could do anything he desired, and he and his brother desired to catch batting practice. I did not pick a fight with him.

It might have been the Tropicana, where they made so much money separating tourists from the family farm at the roulette wheels and crap tables that a magnum of champagne cost only $1.50. Xavier Cugat played rumbas, the roof opened, and a next-to-nude chorus line of lithe Latin beauties and imported blondes made a spectacular entrance languidly descending the steps of circular stairways wrapped around 50-foot monkey trees. (How in the hell did they get up there without boosts from a half-dozen backstage Tarzans? Later they showed me. They had ramps backstage.)

It was easy to see why Cuban players were so good. Pint-sized and quart-sized kids all over Havana specialized in two things: begging for change and playing baseball. They played in empty lots and on the streets.

A Funny Thing Happened on the Way to Cooperstown

They played with broomstick bats and worn, fuzzless tennis balls, and in what Fidel aimed to turn into an atheistic society, baseball players were their gods. When we went into the ballpark, they were playing in the street outside. When we emerged, they were still playing by twilight. Kind of reminded me of me when I was a kid.

All day long, we heard, "Señor, señor, you got the nickel? I need the *dinero*." One of the more entrepreneurial *chicos* in the pack offered me a deal: "Señor Meekey, I be your chauffeur. I take care your car."

I thought about that. Driving was out of the question. He could barely see over the steering wheel. But he was a nice kid. "OK," I said. "You mind the car so nobody steals it."

"I take care, Meekey. I take care good."

One morning I came out and found my caretaker surrounded by his buddies, squatting over the motor with a wrench in his hand. The smoking gun. Only now the motor wasn't in the car. It was spread all over the street.

"What in the hell is going on here?"

He calmly continued taking it apart. "I feex for you, Señor Meekey."

"Feex?" I shouted. "You no have to feex. It works fine. This car is brand-new. You feex it so it don't go."

I think even a Cuban court would have sanctioned my killing him on the spot, which was, frankly, my first impulse. Instead I phoned for a mechanic to put it back together. There were some nuts and bolts missing, but when he got finished, the motor turned over and got me around just fine. I relented and gave my "chauffeur" his job back, this time with orders prohibiting further showboating for his amigos—or borrowing parts—which might have been what that scene was all about. He was to watch it, not feex it.

But Gene Bearden's Cadillac suffered greater indignities than my Ford. Gene was the heartbreaker who had pitched Cleveland to victory in the one-game American League pennant race tiebreaker with the Red Sox back in 1948. Since then, like me, he'd been around the block a time or two—with Washington, Detroit, the St. Louis Browns, and the White

Sox. With no stoplights at intersections, the blocks in Havana were more dangerous than a revolution. Gene reported that his Caddy had been squashed between two big buses, so badly that the door handles almost touched each other. He got out unhurt—how, I have no idea. It wasn't funny, but it reminded me of a joke I'd heard Myron Cohen tell in the Catskills. The punch line was, "Anybody wanna buy a tall thin Cadillac?"

I never let Pascual drive my car. Not after Washington. I had a clunker there, and one day Camilo had said, "Meekey, I learn how to drive. You lend me your car?" I said, "Sure, why not?" He brought it back without fenders. "Meekey," he apologized, "honest! I try my best not to miss the light pole." All he knew how to drive was the horn. In traffic-light-free Havana, you have to learn that real fast.

While I was struggling with the language barrier, I returned from a road trip to find my little three- and four-year-old speaking Spanish with their playmates. Who says grown-ups are smarter than kids? The first day of "spring training" for winter ball, Camilo Pascual (nicknamed "Little Potato," despite being taller than his older brother Carlos, or "Big Potato," who'd pitched briefly for the Senators in 1950) gave me my first Spanish lesson.

"Meekey, tell this to Guerra. He will like you for speak our language: 'El brazo madwayray. No pocheo conyo.'" (That's spelled phonetically the way he taught it to me. For heaven's sake, don't ask me to spell it right.)

I went to the manager with a big smile. He smiled back. Like a trained parrot, I repeated what Camilo taught me. Instantly Guerra's smile disappeared. It was replaced by a scowl. "You're full of it," he said. "You're pitching, sore arm or not." Pascual was watching. He fell off the bench laughing.

Came the revolution, he wasn't laughing. Nobody was. The game started peacefully enough. There were more than ten thousand people in the stands when Fidel Castro and company stormed down from the Sierra Maestra late in December 1958 to overthrow the Cuban dictator, Colonel Batista. The revolution had begun, and suddenly we were in the line of fire. Or what our presidents have lately begun to call "harm's way."

A Funny Thing Happened on the Way to Cooperstown

We were at bat trying to inflict harm on the other team when shots rang out in the streets outside the ball field. Fireworks. Some kind of Cuban holiday, I thought. Then, suddenly, our third-base coach fell to the ground. What the hell? These crazy Cubans celebrate with real bullets? Luckily for him, our coach was wearing a batting helmet. Why, I'll never know. Maybe he could read Spanish, read the papers, and knew something we didn't. Anyway, that helmet saved his life when the spent bullet that struck him knocked him cold instead of dead.

Another bullet hit Leo "Chico" Cardenas in the leg. (He healed just fine. In 1960 this great little shortstop joined Cincinnati and went on to a four-team, 16-year career in the majors.) Somebody very sensible shouted, "Run for the bus." It was almost a mile from the ballpark, but I had no trouble breaking Mickey Mantle's record. (Before the osteo-arthritis got to him, and even then, pain or no pain, Mickey always ran as though someone he owed money to was chasing him with a shotgun.)

We made it back to the team hotel and holed up there for the next three days while the streets echoed with shots and screams. We stayed under the beds eating crackers, periodically coming out from under to cautiously raid the hotel kitchen for more provisions. Meanwhile, Castro's squads rounded up Batista supporters (the colonel himself had instantly decided in favor of discretion and Swiss bank accounts instead of valor and fled on the first plane out) and carried out speedy trials and summary executions in a local coliseum.

On the third day, Castro showed up at the hotel and delivered a fiery speech containing the line we'd all been praying for: "Yanquis, go home." We didn't waste time arguing. We were outta there—which made us luckier than some of the Cuban ballplayers. Castro held onto them.

I don't know whether it's the climate or something in the water, but revolutions seemed to pop up wherever I played winter ball. The following year it was Caracas, where a military coup having something to do with U.S. oil companies—what do I know about geopolitics?—tried to overthrow President Betancourt. All I know is when I heard bursts of machine-gun bullets flying in the street, I threw myself under the bed. As usual.

That wasn't easy. The bases on Venezuelan diamonds are mounted a little higher than in the States, and I'd broken an ankle running to first base, which must have been stuffed with old baseballs. My ankle was in a cast. The club had insisted on holding my passport and return plane tickets when I signed my two-grand-a-month contract with Caracas, but Chicago (and Cleveland and K.C. and Baltimore) shortstop Chico Carrasquel, who owned the club, relented when I insisted longer and louder on holding onto them.

It was a good thing. When the sounds of firing moved off into the distance, I hobbled to the U.S. embassy and said to the marine guard at the gate, "Get me out of here." I guess in the excitement he'd forgotten about the halls of Montezuma and the shores of Tripoli. He grinned and said, "Here, you take the rifle and get me out of here!" I didn't take the rifle, but I got to the airport and outta there pretty damn quick. So quick that I left my first baseman's mitt behind.

I was in the airport. I felt a tap on the shoulder. My sunburn turned white. Uh-oh, they're gonna nail me now. This Yanqui isn't gonna be allowed to go home—they're gonna shoot me at the nearest pillar.

I turned around slowly. I didn't see any *polizia*. What was going on?

"I am journalist. I write sports. I hear you go home. I got job for you at Ponce in Puerto Rico." (Which, by the way, is where some of the best ballplayers are coming from now.)

I said, "You take it. I'm going home to Miami Beach."

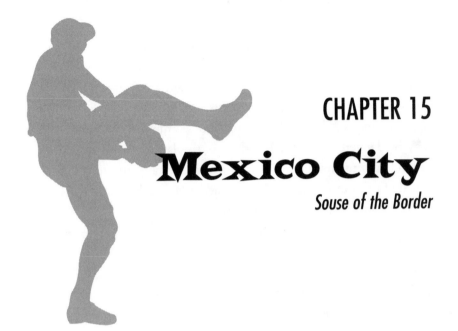

CHAPTER 15

Mexico City

Souse of the Border

I can't say I wasn't warned.

When I told an old baseball buddy that I'd be playing in Mexico that winter, he said, no doubt thinking of my reputation as Señor Nonchalance, "Mac, they take their baseball very seriously down there."

Al Schroll—he pitched briefly for the Red Sox and a couple of other teams—gave me an example: "We had men on first and second and one out. The batter missed the bunt sign, hit into a double play, and cost us the game. Our manager pulled out a pistol, chased him around the field, trapped him in the left-field corner, and, with a big grin on his face, plugged him in the leg."

Dimly, through a haze of last night's residual tequila fumes, that conversation came back to haunt me in the first inning of a game I pitched for the Reynosa Broncos. Was I at a bullfight or a baseball game? And was I the toreador or the bull? What I was was bombed—so bombed that I hit four consecutive batters in the kneecap.

A Funny Thing Happened on the Way to Cooperstown

A cloud of garlic hung over the stands and the crowd, and the menacing faces under a sea of sombreros sucking on bottles of tequila began to make threatening noises. Yes, they took their baseball seriously all right. *Soldados* crouched over machine guns mounted outside the foul lines at opposite ends of the outfield as a silent warning to the crowd: "Rioting may be dangerous to your health." As the last guy I hit writhed on the ground and my first victim limped toward home plate from third base, a squad of rifle-toting military police suddenly marched onto the field.

"Uh-oh," I thought, "it's the firing squad."

I didn't have time to worry if the bandana they were going to bind over my eyes would be clean. (Wouldn't you hate to be buried with an eye infection?) As they deployed on the first- and third-base lines, I sighed with relief. They were facing the crowd, not me. They were my amigos, standing fast to keep me from being tarred, feathered, and pinned to the town's tallest cactus. And I was luckier than the Dodgers' Don Newcombe the year he played winter ball in Mexico. All he did was drill two guys in the kneecaps and they marched him off to el jailo.

I felt like I had a lot more reasons than the fans in the stands to get bombed. Even more than usual. Sure, the pay was good for a hungry pitcher with no place to go—$1,000 a month and no taxes. And I didn't mind that they were allowed only three gringos to a club. I didn't know the word for jail yet, but my Spanish was good enough so I could say, "*una mas cerveza*" when I wanted another beer. And, yes, my arm hurt more every time I pitched, but I didn't notice it as much because I was drinking more, and I'd learned to turn the ball over a bit. Gripping it between the seams, I'd developed a pretty good sinker and change-up. Even a knuckleball.

No, it was the bus rides. And the food. Before one game in Mexico City, one of the ballplayers invited me to his mother's house for dinner. "Mama makes great *arroz con pollo*," he told me. (At least, that's what I thought I heard: *arroz con pollo*—chicken with rice.)

"You will love it," he said with conviction. I didn't take much convincing. Home cooking. That sounded good. It had to be better than the restaurants I'd been patronizing in Reynosa. We ate. It was delicious. I accepted seconds. My teammate said, "You like, Meekey?"

I said, "Great!" and asked him to transmit my compliments to the chef. "We got great woof-woofs here," he said proudly.

"Woof-woofs? You mean dogs? You mean that was *arroz con perro?*"

I excused myself and headed for the john. I remembered now what I'd noticed hanging in butcher shop windows. Dogs. Cats, too. I bent over the toilet bowl (Is this starting to sound familiar?) and bid my dinner farewell.

The food, yes. And the bus rides. Take the trip from Reynosa, just south of the border near McAllen, Texas, down to Mexico City. After two months, I couldn't. Twenty-four hours on bumpy, winding mountain roads without guardrails on the brink of precipices that would discourage a Tibetan guide, in springless buses so old they must have been driving this route when Pancho Villa was still worried about pimples. And then home the way we came.

I have two choices: pray or drink. I doubt Sister Teresa would approve, but I do them both at the same time. I have two bottles of tequila in my bag to help me sleep through the ride. In the middle of the night, I'm awakened by the screech of brakes and the acrid smell of burning rubber. Now what?

A bridge has washed out and the driver, to avoid drowning the whole team, had swerved off the road at the last moment, skidding and bouncing 50 or so yards into a rocky field. When my heart stops pounding, I figure I might as well empty my bladder, which I suddenly realize is about to burst. I stumble to the door and step outside. There are no stars. It is darker than the inside of a whale, and I am suddenly very sympathetic to Jonah.

I unzip and am in the process of obtaining dramatic relief when I hear thundering hooves behind me. What in the hell? I hear my name called, "Meekey, Meekey, run for your life." I don't ask questions. I am stiff and sore and unfinished, but I hastily interrupt what I am doing and scurry to safety. The door closes, the bus driver leans on his horn, and the disappointed herd of bulls—yes, we are in the middle of a *toro* ranch—

unable to execute its plan to butt me back to Boston, paws the turf unhappily. I find my way back to my seat, finish the remains of my tequila, and contemplate the fact that if you weren't an alcoholic, playing in this league you'd become one. As I doze off, I mutter to myself, "I've gotta get out of here."

At dawn, the sound of rushing waters awakened me. Our bus was in the middle of a river on a wooden raft that served as a rudimentary ferry. There was no engine. We were being hauled across by a sweating crew on the other side tugging on ropes. The maneuver was completed and we took a pit stop on the other side of the river at what looked like a gypsy camp. It was breakfast time and they were eating tacos and biting the heads off what looked like raw fish. I was suddenly not hungry.

I hoped for the best and went back to sleep. Some hours later, I smelled exhaust fumes instead of coffee, and, even with my eyes closed, I knew I was inhaling good old Mexico City. We checked in at our hotel, and I learned that Eddie Fisher was in town singing at the Hilton. My prayers worked. I said, "Thank you, Lord." I phoned Eddie.

"Lefty," he asked, "what are you doing here?"

"I'm with the Reynosa Broncos. No, no. I'm not roping horses in a rodeo. I'm pitching."

He invited me to the club. I wasn't pitching until the next day. I taxied there that evening and took a seat at the ringside table Eddie had thoughtfully reserved for me. He came out of the audience singing, "May I Sing to You?" and I started to feel right at home. I had a feeling it was going to be a long night.

Next day, I was at the ballpark feeling pretty good—all things considered. My manager was the owner of a famous family name: Alomar. Before long he'd have two grandkids in the bigs. (Bet I don't have to tell you their names.) Now he told me, "Mickey, we're at ten thousand feet here. The air's pretty thin. You've gotta get your lungs adjusted to it. Better run in the outfield before you pitch."

Reluctantly, I followed his advice. But about the fourth inning, my stomach started to feel a little queasy. I wondered what was going on. I didn't think it was the altitude. And I've always been a steak-and-potatoes guy, so I didn't touch the salad the night before. (I knew the salad had to be rinsed with an iodine solution if the produce was local, and I've never been a fan of oil-vinegar-iodine dressing.) I didn't drink the water. I knew better than that, and besides, beer tastes better.

I kept pitching. In the fifth inning as I lifted my right leg and went into my windup, Montezuma's Revenge smote with the full force of the Mexican Army, conspicuously staining both my honor and my trousers. Unfortunately, the Reynosa uniform is white. Correction. Was white. The crowd was not insensible to my dilemma. As one, Mexico City fans rose to their feet and taunted derisively, "Señor Meekey Mouse poo-poo!" I staggered to the sidelines.

I doubled up in agony, and now I was throwing up, too. I was struck by the realization that in addition to beer I'd had a goodly amount of tequila at the Hilton. The tequila was fine. (Lick salt on back of hand, suck lemon, shot of tequila. It's a ritual. It's fun.) But the ice cubes it sat in? That was it! Frozen Mexican water, and it melted. As the ambulance rushed me to the nearest hospital, I muttered again, "I've gotta get out of here."

This time I did something about it. Contract be damned. I borrowed $100 from Eddie, taxied to the airport, and caught the first plane home. I knew it was the ice, but I never drank another tequila again. Except when I was too drunk to know the difference.

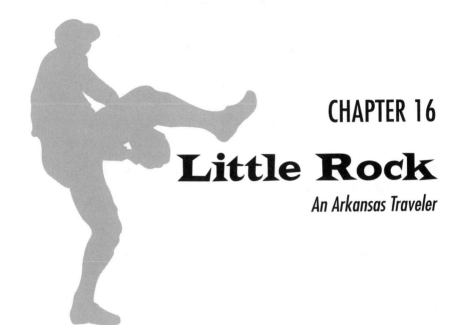

CHAPTER 16

Little Rock

An Arkansas Traveler

I could never say no to an old friend, and besides, I needed a job. I had no money. With Babs and the kids I was reduced to living with my mother-in-law, who hated me as much as I hated her, and not just because I called her "the gestapo in bloomers." So when Fred Hatfield, who'd played third base with me on the Red Sox and stabbed many an embarrassing line drive that could have gone for a triple, phoned to ask me to pitch for the Arkansas Travelers of the Southern Association, I gave him an automatic yes.

"I'm managing an indie club for an owner who doesn't have much money," Fred had confided, "but by the time we're playing and get people to the ballpark, we'll all make money. I got a chance to win with you and get back to the majors. You gotta help me, Mac."

We trained in the Everglades. (Would you believe two alligators roomed with me? No? I didn't think so. But we had more of them watching us than we had people watching.) There was no money for uniforms yet, so we practiced in street clothes and leftovers. The shortstop's shirt read "Birmingham." The left fielder's read "Memphis." Hatfield's said "San Diego Wild Animal Park." Mine said "Hooters."

We were mostly drunks who'd seen better days and run out of ballclubs, and we had to borrow balls, bats, and uniforms for our first exhibition game, but something clicked and we killed that team and just about everybody else we played. We had one guy who used to be with the Giants but looked like he might have played for Bellevue along the way. He walked through the hotel lobby in a tuxedo jacket, stiff shirt, bow tie, top hat, and shorts, leading a pet frog on a string.

Ace Reynolds, a big, tough bayou dockworker spraying center field with tobacco juice, would've hit .350 in the majors, but your dog can catch the ball better. We discovered that, like Phil Rizzuto, he was scared of crawling things. So one afternoon, just for fun, we put a rubber snake out there. Big Ace beat the record for the 100-meter dash, and maybe he was a little embarrassed, because we didn't see him 'til the next day.

We played a game in Atlanta. By now the owners had raised enough money so we were all getting paychecks and wearing the same uniform. Walt Dropo's businessman brother, Milt, came to the ballpark and was aghast.

"What are they paying you a month?" he asked.

"About a thousand."

"Dammit, Mickey, come with me. I'm starting a fireworks business. I'll give you a piece of it and make you a ton of money."

That could have solved a lot of problems. After the game I went with him to his hotel, but somehow Fred tracked us down. "Mac," he begged, "you can't do this to me. With you on the team I've got a chance to win the pennant and manage in the majors. I'll take you with me."

Money talks, but Hatfield's baseball voice talked louder. I turned to Milt. "Fred's right," I said, "I can't do this to him." Milt shrugged. When the Travelers' bus left, I was on it. Milt Dropo's company filled a huge warehouse in Chattanooga. His business took off like a skyrocket, and he made millions. But regrets? I have none. I won 13 games, lost only 1, and helped Fred's team win the playoffs and the pennant. And I know what the truth is. I'd rather wear a uniform than a Brooks Brothers suit.

Fred never did get to manage in the majors, and he certainly couldn't take me with him, but baseball works in mysterious ways. Like flowers and fever it happens every spring, and when it did in '61, John Buick, the skipper of my Miami Beach charter fishing boat before I had to sell it, took it upon himself to drive to the St. Louis Cardinals camp to talk to manager Solly Hemus.

"Mickey's in great shape and he can throw," he told Solly. "He went 13–1 with Arkansas last season, helped them win the pennant."

"I've got the best pitching in the league," Solly said, "Ray Sadecki, Bob Gibson, Curt Simmons. But I like Mickey; so what if he beaned me a few years ago? Tell you what. I'll give him a shot. I'll give him a room and some meal money and we'll see how things go. Just tell him to get to camp before I change my mind."

I had a helluva spring. I *was* in great shape—even cut back on my drinking because, at 32, I wanted to make it bad. Solly had me throw batting practice first and, putting aside the old Ted Williams advice—not applicable in my desperate straits—I pitched as though it was a ballgame. I guess I overdid it. Stan Musial put up his hand after the first fastball. "Mac," he implored, "I know you're tryin' to make the club, but I'm an old man. Slow down. You'll f'g kill me."

I got everybody out, even my old pal and nemesis Bob Nieman. At 34, Bob (reminder: the slugger who set a never-to-be-broken rookie record by hitting homers off me in his first two at-bats in the majors) was hitting a solid 8 for 17 when the Cards traded him early in the season. And then he hit .354 for Cleveland.

In the last game of spring training—after which I either stayed with the club or got dumped—I pitched five shutout innings and walked only two. Nieman, this slugger who hit me like he owned me, missed three right down the pipe. I would have fainted on the spot except for one thing. Before the game Bob said quietly on the sidelines, "Just put it over the plate, Mac. All I'm gonna hit is air."

That night over a beer, he asked, "How'd you like that, roomie?"

"I loved it," I said exuberantly. "I'm back in the bigs. Solly came through. After the game, I signed a Cardinals contract."

"That's great." He grinned. "Alright Mac. You owe me. Give me back my f'g $300."

"Are you kidding? Those fastballs I fed you put you in the record books."

CHAPTER 17

St. Louis Blues

Back to the Bigs

Now I was wearing red birds on my shirt. A Cardinal (whose name I am not courageous enough to reveal because he still swings a mean bat) had a little something going with a starlet. We were playing the Pirates, and he'd gotten her a box seat. He came up to the plate and this ditzy blonde jumped up and shouted, "Hit one out for me, honey." He stepped out of the batter's box, turned around, and smiled. His smile faded. Oops.

He had spotted his wife in the box right in front of the blonde. Where in the hell did she come from? She was supposed to be in St. Louis vacuuming the living room rug. She must have flown in to surprise him. Some surprise. He made a quick decision. He would sacrifice his batting average for the sake of his marriage. Mr. X stepped back into the batter's box, took a strike, swung ineptly at one out of the strike zone, took a third strike, and jogged back to the bench with his head down as fast as he decently could. At his next at-bat he repeated the performance—anything to get the game over.

Later I could imagine his wife asking, "What's the matter, honey?" And his reply: "Oh, it's that smoke from the steel mills. I must have had something in my eye." Two somethings, actually. Oh, we were reprobates all right. But his wife never caught on. Anything can happen at a ballpark. She thought it was just another enthusiastic fan.

Actually we had a pretty good bunch of hitters. Curt Flood hit .322 for the club. Bill White hit 20 homers. Ken Boyer hit 24 dingers and batted .329. And at age 40, with a final lifetime batting average of .331 still two years away, the amazing 22-year Cardinal, Stan the "Man" Musial, was still clouting the homers that would add up to 475.

I don't know how he did it, but Stan was the only player I ever saw who could hit a change-up as easily as a fastball. He'd just hold his bat back, time the pitch perfectly, hit a line drive, and start running. Being on the same club was a pleasure. I didn't have to pitch to him.

My pitching was the best it had been in years. What I'd learned to do with skill instead of speed in Mexico and Little Rock was working in the big leagues as well, and I felt like I had "Comeback of the Year" in my pocket. Solly was using me as a spot reliever and closer, and halfway into the season I'd pitched 27 innings in 19 games and had a 1–0 record and four saves. Not exactly Hall of Fame stats, but I was starting to feel good about myself.

The save I enjoyed most was against the Cubs, and it wasn't mine. It was the umpire's. It was a year when Chicago's coaches, as acting managers, played off-key musical chairs all season long in owner P. K. Wrigley's revolutionary "college of coaches" experiment. Vedie Himsl (no, I didn't spell it wrong) managed 31 games and was replaced by Harry Craft. Craft lasted 16 games and was replaced by El Tappe (yep, that's the right spelling, too), who clenched his teeth for 96 games and was dumped 11 games short of the end of the season for Lou Klein. Not a one had a winning record, but then, with the exception of George Altman who hit .303, no player came close to batting .300.

Somewhere in that mess, we were playing the Cubs when whoever was manager at the time got thrown out of the game and, coming out of

Yankee manager Casey Stengel said it loud and clear in 1956 during spring training in St. Pete, without his trademark double-talk: "The fourth spot in the rotation is McDermott's, but he's got to earn it." That determined jaw and steely glance tell you I wanted it badly. But there's many a slip 'twixt the beer glass and the lip.

From the personal collection of Mickey McDermott.

This is the moment every batter dreads—a fastball headed right for his head. That's Solly Hemus about to be beaned in a spring-training game. Talk about forgiveness: when I was looking for a job a half-dozen years later and he was managing the Cards, he signed me anyway. "After what you did to me," he said, "I don't know why I'm doing this." (Well, like I said, I hit him in the head.)

Photo courtesy of UPI.

The Cardinals were my sixth and last major league team. One of those little birds told me I was gonna be comeback pitcher of the year. I could've been, too, but a fight with a hotel dick at 4:00 A.M.— he shouldn't have called my fiancée a whore — earned me a pink slip instead of a trophy.

From the personal collection of Mickey McDermott.

Later a TV and film star, Paul Gleason bummed around with me in my heavy drinking days. When we got down to "D" ball, he used to wake me up with a garden hose to the kisser when it was time to go to the ballpark. Missing from the picture is beat poet Jack Kerouac, who hit the road with us when we traveled and costarred with us in a major dance hall donnybrook (see page 216).

From the personal collection of Mickey McDermott.

***Sic transit gloria!* You didn't think I knew Latin, did you? Here I am, age 40, pitching batting practice for the California Angels. I was a great choice, too — hell, nobody hit bats better than I did.**

Photo courtesy of TV Sports Mailbag.

Why is Harmon Killebrew of the Twins standing respectfully beside me at the annual spring-training Old Timers' Day in Phoenix? Hell, he only hit 564 more home runs than I did. But with the 1955 Senators, I outhit Killer by 63 points (well, he was only 19 at the time).

From the personal collection of Mickey McDermott.

Here I am with Frank. We just had a crooning contest, and guess who won? (See page 232 to find out how I almost got Swiss-cheesed by his bodyguards.)

From the personal collection of Mickey McDermott.

The Ted Williams Museum's annual golf tourney is about to begin. Left to right, that's me in the San Francisco togs (I led the league in stolen towels and warm-up jackets), Mickey Vernon (who had a great 20-year career), and Walt Dropo in his Salvation Army best. (Don't hit me, Walt! I'll never say it again.)

From the personal collection of Mickey McDermott.

I don't know why Eddie Fisher, my old fifties singing superstar buddy, is smiling. When I sang at Steuben's in Boston, I stole half his act.

From the personal collection of Mickey McDermott.

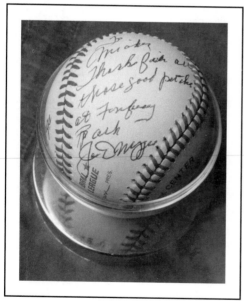

Instead of showing you the ball Joltin' Joe autographed to me at a baseball benefit, I should probably be embarrassed and hide it. But if my Arizona Lottery prize money ever runs out, it should fetch a pretty penny in an eBay auction.

Photo courtesy of Jack Kurtz.

nowhere, coach Leo Durocher took over as king for a day. Durocher was not National League umpires' choice for Mr. Congeniality. His "Leo the Lip" moniker was well earned. Now the Cubs were threatening, and I came into the game in the ninth to protect our lead with two men on and two out.

On the PA system I heard, "Now batting for the Cubs: Andre Rodgers." The name meant nothing to me, but the kid at the plate called out, "Hey, mon, thanks for the ticket to the Willie Pep fight." I stared. What was he talking about? He sounded like he comes from the Islands. He looked like he came from the Islands. Then it came to me. He did come from the Islands—from Nassau in the Bahamas.

I'd seen him only once before, and that was maybe 10 years earlier. I was in Nassau with Willie Pep, a boxer and good buddy who was there on the fateful day when I married Babs. Willie was a real scrapper, for about 10 years one of the greatest-ever world featherweight champs. At the moment he was as broke as I was and needed to pick up a purse, which is why he was booked for a pickup fight with a kid named Billy Lauderdale. He asked me to come along to make sure he got a fair shake.

"Here," he said before he entered the arena, "take this gadget and clock the people as they come in, so the promoter don't rob us." It didn't really matter because after the fight—which was stopped in an early round with both of poor Billy's eyes closed and his ears looking like prize-winning county fair cauliflowers—Willie went to the Colonial Inn, grew his $2,000 purse to $10,000, said, "I'm gonna break the bank!" and then lost it all.

Anyway, I was standing there clocking the paying customers when this handsome young kid, maybe 14 or 15, came along.

"Hey, mon," he said, "you let me go to the fight? I got no money, mon." He stopped and stared at me. "I know you, mon. You're a ballplayer. I'm a ballplayer, too, mon. You should see me play. Someday I'm gonna play in the major leagues."

I chuckled and said, "Good for you, son. Now go in and have a good time." That was the end of that. But not quite. Sonovabitch. He told me he'd make it to the big leagues and here he was—and, small world, I had to get him out to win the game. Before my windup, Durocher called time.

He knew this was my first National League team, and he was gonna do his best to rattle me. He jogged out to plate umpire Jocko Conlon and gave him the old lip: "Now you be sure and make that American League sonovabitch come to a complete stop."

Conlon dismissed him and walked out to the mound. He was red in the face, furious at Durocher for trying to show him up. "Mac," he said, "you want to win this game?"

"Sure. It'd be my first in the league."

"All right, I'll win you this one. I hate that little sonovabitch, Durocher. Now listen up. Just give me a complete stop. I know it's different in the American League, but in the National that's what the rule calls for. If you don't, Durocher will be all over me."

I came to the mandatory complete stop and hurled the first pitch. It missed outside by a good three or four inches. I was just wasting a pitch to make him hit mine, but Jocko threw up his right hand: "Strrrike!" Durocher came up the top stair of the dugout and screamed epithets at the ump. I came to a complete stop and threw my second pitch. It was inside off the plate, and Andre had to step back. "Strrrike two!"

Now Durocher was out of the dugout and toe to toe with Conlon. He jumped up and down, cursed, fired insults, kicked dirt. Finally, he went back to the dugout. Conlon was fighting to keep from laughing out loud. He could eject him, but he was having too much fun torturing him. I pitched again. "Strrrike three!"

Durocher streaked out of the dugout fighting mad, but Conlon, laughing all the way, had already turned and ran for the tunnel. Game over. Poor Andre was standing there holding his bat and looking bewildered. In the clubhouse, Cardinals ballplayers were sharing the last laugh with me.

"Geez, Mickey, what have you got on Conlon? How in the hell did you get those calls?"

"Easy. He hates Durocher."

"Join the club."

There is just one thing wrong with this Durocher-Conlon story. According to official baseball history, Durocher wasn't there. He didn't

take over the Cubs until 1966. But geez, that Phil Wrigley was always exper-
imenting. Maybe that was the day he decided to give Leo a tryout. All I
know is I can still see that scene clear as the view from the Sears Tower. Leo
had to have been there. Hell, even if I was hallucinating, it's a great story.

It was shaping up as a great season, but my elbow's shape was not
exactly great. I won a couple of games with pinch-hits, but one night Solly
inserted me to hit, and on the first swing my elbow locked. Another bone
chip playing fast and loose. He had to put in a pinch-hitter for the pinch-
hitter.

Meanwhile, Babs and I had finally divorced and I was looking for a
pinch-hitter myself. On a charter flight to the West Coast, the stewardess
(that's what they used to be called) came down the aisle to take drink
orders. Linda was very pretty, and I wanted to get her attention, so I ordered
in double-talk—a trick simply rearranging words in a sentence that I picked
up listening to Casey Stengel—and totally confused her. When she came
back with the tray, I said (I am ashamed to say), "I hate to tell you, but
you've got a booger hanging from your nose." Well, that got her attention.
She dropped the tray. By the time we got to wherever we got to, she had
forgiven me. I asked her out, she accepted, and pretty soon we were an item
and talking about when and where we were getting married.

We were an item that led inexorably to my downfall. Sure, I was
doing a helluva job out of the Cards bullpen as a reliever, but I didn't let
that interfere with my drinking and raising hell. By the All-Star break,
what Solly had called "the best pitching in the league" in spring training
wasn't doing well enough to satisfy the Busch family, so he got the sack.
Coach Johnny Keane, who was very much into discipline and the opposite of easygoing Solly, took over. We didn't call him "Mr. Keane, Tracer
of Lost Persons" for nothing. (Remember that old radio show? Oh, I forgot. You're not that old.)

I came back to the hotel one night about 3:00 A.M. after having been
in a joint with Musial, Kenny Boyer, pitching coach (and ex-darned-good
pitcher) Howie Pollet, and maybe half the club. They all went home early.
I, as was my custom, lingered 'til the last ice cube melted. I wouldn't say I

was boisterous at that point, but I wouldn't say I was quiet as a Roman Catholic church mouse at a Mass either.

Linda Biggio had just come in on a flight, and I called her room and invited her to mine for a chat. Patrolling the floors, the house detective came upon us just as I was about to usher Linda, charmingly attired in a Hawaiian muumuu, into my quarters.

"You can't bring that hooker into your room!" the house dick said belligerently. (The correct verb would have been *take*, but it seemed the wrong time to make an issue of it.)

"She's no hooker. She's the lady I'm gonna marry," I retorted. Those words didn't seem enough to repair the pain and injury his insult had caused Linda, so I popped him. Not to be outdone, he pulled out his billy club and gave me a very fat lip. Then, still not satisfied, he went to the house phone and woke up Johnny Keane to report my late arrival and negative attitude toward authority.

Keane was a little grouchy being aroused at that time of the morning—I don't blame him—which may have contributed to his irritable mood during the clubhouse meeting he called the next afternoon. He tore into me in front of the whole team. Having already decided to can me, I suppose he figured he might as well make an example of me in the hope that that would bring some of the other high fliers on the club down to earth.

I listened patiently while he delivered the sermon I guess I deserved—how generous the club had been to give me a chance when no one else in the majors wanted me, and here I was repaying them by playing wild-ass playboy. When he finished and it was time for rebuttal, I wanted to say, "Why don't you get on No. 6 and some of the other guys who were with me?" But I looked over at them, saw their red faces and hangdog looks, and decided there was no point in bringing Stan the Man and the other guys into it. Besides, they'd all gone to bed early.

I just said diplomatically, "Fuck you, Keane." Then, indicating the two cardinals on the front of my uniform, I said, "I never hurt these birds. But if that's the way you feel, I'm ready to turn in my uniform—as soon as I get my paycheck." At which point he reached into his pocket and handed me a pink slip to speed me on my way.

It was a mistake. On his part. On my part, too. I finally had everything together. If I'd stayed, I really think I'd have won that "Comeback of the Year" award. The Cards under Keane went nowhere—fifth place that year, sixth the next. OK, in '64 he finally did lead the Cards to a World Series victory over the Yankees. But when he took over the same pennant-winning Yankees in '65, the best he could do was take them to sixth that year before being axed in early 1966.

Live by the ax, die by it. But I couldn't rejoice in his down-and-out fall. I'd been down and out too many times myself.

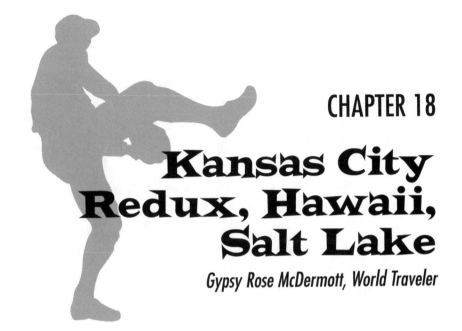

CHAPTER 18

Kansas City Redux, Hawaii, Salt Lake

Gypsy Rose McDermott, World Traveler

What, I wondered, when from my bar stool I bothered to wonder, was next? I needed a job, but who needed me? The answer came from the guy who'd hit me best in the majors. Hank Bauer, once my Yankees roommate, threw me a lifeline from Kansas City, where he was now managing the A's. (He liked me. Why not? I threw him a lot of home-run balls.) Ironically, my biggest mistake turned out to be opening the telegram inviting me to join the team.

I was throwing some clothes into a suitcase when the phone rang. This time it was Freddie Hutchinson, who'd managed me at Detroit and now, managing the Cincinnati Reds, was in the thick of a pennant race. (He wanted me? I guess some people never learn.)

"Mickey," he said, "my club's got a shot at the World Series. I hear that K.C. is picking you up, but I think you can help us. You've got Series experience. I'd like to have you in my bullpen." (Sweet music. I hadn't heard that in a long time. I loved it.)

Hutch continued, but now the music was starting to dim. "Have you signed a contract yet? Or accepted verbally?"

"All I got is a telegram from Lane in Kansas City."

"Did you open it? Did you comply with it?"

"Well, sure I opened it. And I called Hank to thank him."

"Damn. Lane will use that against you. But I'll see what I can do. Maybe they'll let you go."

They wouldn't. That is, GM Frank Lane wouldn't. Not that he wanted me that bad. He just hated Freddie that bad—from when he'd been GM of the Cardinals and Hutchinson had been his manager. That had been a marriage made in hell, and now Lane had a chance to get even. Which he did. Sorry, McDermott. A deal is a deal.

I went to K.C. resigned to the missed opportunity for another World Series ring and a shot at the big pot but not exactly ecstatic about going to a ninth-place team instead. And, between binges, that's the way I pitched. Which is why *The Sports Encyclopedia* for baseball summarizes my brief tenure with K.C. this way: Maurice McDermott, W-0, L-0, SV-0, G-4, IP-6, H-14, BB-10, SO-3, ERA-13.50. I led the league in nothing but stolen towels.

Could I have hung on 'til the end of the season? Could I have turned things around? Ah, sweet mysteries of life. I'll never know. Returning early one morning from my usual round of revelries, I pushed the elevator button in the lobby. The doors slid open and there was my worst nightmare: the GM. Lane minced me instead of words: "What the hell are you doing coming in at 4:00 in the morning, McDermott?"

It was a fair question. But, ever the wiseass, I had one for him: "What the hell are you doing going *out* at 4:00 in the morning?"

He brushed past me without reply. I hit the sack. Next day I found Hank sitting in a chair in the lobby opposite the elevators.

He got up and put his hand on my shoulder. "I heard what happened, Mac. I'm sorry. There's a note in your box. A little pink slip."

Suspended. I packed my bag and went home—this time to Cucamonga (yes, there really is a Cucamonga, and all the time I thought it was a disease), California, home of my recently acquired second wife, Linda. I would not, alas, be watching the World Series from the Cincinnati bullpen. TV would have to do. And, oh yes, I'd have to look for work.

Work? I hated the sound of the word. Pitching was never work. Anything else was. And compared to striking out the cleanup hitter or hitting a home run off Mike Garcia, or even just horsing around in the locker room with the guys, it was pretty damn boring. But I had alimony and child support to pay and a new wife to explain my latest suspension to, so it was time to get serious. For a little while anyway.

Jobs. Jobs. Jobs. After baseball I had a million of them. My first honest employment—if you can call selling cars honest, and I have to because I want car salespeople to buy my book, too—was for my buddy ("Gee," you may ask, "is everybody your buddy?") Jay Littelen who managed the joint. I sold a couple of cars to ballplayers from the L.A. Angels. In fact, I think my record at Jay's Ford agency was: sales, 2; wrecks, 4.

By a happy coincidence—although, come to think of it, this is probably how he became my buddy—Jay managed a semipro club in Ontario, which was next door to Cucamonga. (I know, it should be in Canada, but it's not. Relax. Stuff like this happens in memoirs.) He liked having a salesman (OK, OK—salesperson) who could pitch and play first base, but because the work was on commission and, oh, how I hated to get up in the morning, the income was more a trickle than a stream.

After a year of that and Linda having to take jobs as a waitress at pizza joints, a guy came in to sell advertising time for the Ontario station. I was getting tired of not selling cars, so I accepted his invitation to meet the station manager and take a shot at selling ad time. Selling Joe's Café on trying radio ads turned out to be even more boring than what I'd been doing, and the appointments were earlier in the morning. I tossed out the box of business cards with my name on them and went back to sleep.

I should have known that Madison Avenue South wasn't for me. In Sarasota one winter a few years earlier, with Babs working as a dental assistant in her uncle's office and me unemployed as usual, Lew Burdette had introduced me to a friend who wanted to put up billboards for his version of Cypress Gardens. When he showed me the box of engagement rings he kept in his office drawer and bragged that he was engaged to some of the sexiest broads in the county, he struck me as a lad whose sharp edges might be a problem for me later on. But it looked better than what my mother-in-law wanted me to do when we were living at her mansion in Miami Beach: "Out of bed, you lazy bastard. Get out in the garden and start pulling weeds." (Goodness, I could have gotten sunstroke. But I did it. It was either that or stay at the YMCA.)

"All you've got to do," the entrepreneur explained, "is find sites for advertising signs and sign the people up. I'll do the rest." That didn't sound too hard. I'd drive around, find a likely corner spot, offer the owner of the home or store $50 a year, get him to sign a contract, and move on. The first lady I signed up lived just off the Tamiami Trail. I had no idea what kind of signs I was selling, so when she asked what they were and where they'd be placed, I was pretty vague. "They're just signs," I said. "Like when somebody's running for office, I guess. They probably put them up on the telephone pole."

The hell they did. The following week, she called hysterically. "They put this huge billboard in my backyard," she said. "My view is blocked and my neighbors are furious."

All I could say was, "I'm sorry, lady. I didn't know. But there's nothing I can do. You signed a contract." I really was sorry, but I was glad she didn't belong to a gun club. Just in case she did, I avoided her neighborhood.

I didn't have to worry about billboard sites for long. My next introduction was to a couple of guys high up in the Teamsters union and, because nobody doesn't like baseball players, they got me a union card and a job taking tickets at Hialeah racetrack, county fairs, places like that. Ticket taking may sound like minimum wage, but not when there's a Teamsters union involved. Pretty good pay—$250 a week and you don't even work up a sweat.

So now in Cucamonga (I still can't say it without laughing), I phoned the nearest Teamsters local, told them who my connections were and how fine my ticket-taking skills had been honed at Hialeah, and wound up with a job doing the same at the Santa Anita clubhouse where the celebs and big bettors wined and dined. Cash flow at last. Pretty good hours, too. They don't race horses in the morning. And I was a growing alcoholic. I needed my sleep.

University of Southern California coach Rod Dedeaux—he's famous for bringing along Mark McGwire and a lot of other major leaguers—woke me up one morning to invite me to play in the annual USC vs. Ancient Warriors game at the college. They invite major leaguers who can still walk to come and play. ("Do I get paid?" "Yep.") The answer was, "I'll be there in my walker."

The USC ace, a kid named Bill Lee, later to famously wear a Red Sox uniform in the seventies and join the Expos as Bill the "Space Man" Lee, was on the mound. I leaned into a fastball and drove it over the fence. Being upset when someone does that to you is par for the course. I should know. But Lee looked more than upset.

After the game, the coach came over to our bench with a big grin on his face. "The kid is going crazy," he said. "He's saying, 'You know who hit that home run off me? Some f'g gateman—an old man taking tickets at the Santa Anita clubhouse. I recognized him. I was there a couple of weeks ago. I can't believe it. A sonovabitch of a ticket-taker hit a homer off me.'" I had a Mickey McDermott trading card in my pants pocket. I wrote him a message: "I hit home runs off better pitchers than you'll ever be." I gave it to the coach to give to him.

Some years later, I was doing a fantasy camp with a bunch of other players, and Lee was one of them. He apologized. "How the hell would I know you were a famous pitcher?" he says. "All I knew was I saw you taking tickets at the track." There was a big party at the end of the week, and here came the Space Man—who I found out was more genius than Space Man and a helluva guy—wearing a tux with a pair of sneakers. "You gotta be comfortable," he explained. I understood completely. Another McDermott. A nutcase just like me. But with my tux I wear patent leathers.

Except for hitting the occasional home run against a college kid still as green as a three-leaf clover, it looked as though my brilliant career in baseball was over. But then came another phone call. (I seemed to get a lot of them.) It was Bob Lemon (who apparently had forgiven me for hitting a home run off him when he pitched for Cleveland) calling to invite me to join a club he was managing in the Triple A Pacific Coast League— the Hawaii Islanders. I knew he couldn't invite me without L.A. Angels GM Fred Haney's approval and that Haney was probably thinking, well, we can get him cheap, he's an old pro, and if a miracle happens and he finds his fastball again, maybe he can help us.

Lemon knew I could still pitch a little. "Don't go out to any bars tonight," he told me halfway into the season. "Get a good night's sleep. The owner, Gene Autry, is in town with Haney and the Angels manager, Bill Rigney. You've been doing pretty good so far. I'm pitching you tomorrow against Salt Lake City. You've maybe got a shot at going back to the big leagues. Now don't blow it."

I've got big ears, but they weren't listening. That night I was at Duke Kanakanoko's nightclub as usual, swigging my favorite cooler, concocted out of 10 different kinds of rum, which has earned me the name of "Mickey Mai Tai." I led the league in drinking them, but I was going for the record and had put away about 10 when the hostess sat Gene Autry and friends, including my manager, at a ringside table only a couple of pineapple lengths away from me.

The timing could not have been worse. My pal Don Ho, the singer famous for the song "Tiny Bubbles," chose that moment to step to the microphone and say helpfully, "My pal Mickey McDermott, the great Boston Red Sox and Hawaii Islanders pitcher, is in the audience. He is also renowned as a singer. Mickey, how about coming up here to sing a song for these good people?"

I am sitting there elegant in Bermuda shorts, a Hawaiian shirt, and open-toed wedgies. The only thing I forgot to wear was a lei. And a bathing suit. In front of my table, an artificial waterfall with a paddle wheel misting it sparkles and spins in a pool. Don had given me my cue, and I know that for me the shortest distance to the microphone would not, in my condition, be a straight line. But, hey, if Autry likes my singing, maybe next winter he'll book me into a tour of his burger joints.

I stand up a trifle unsteadily, take a deep breath, and aim myself at the stairs leading to the stage. I miss the turn, lose my balance, and topple into the pool, screaming "Help!" at the top of my lungs. I thrash around trying to get back to my feet but succeed only in catching one of my sandals in the waterwheel. It slides off my foot and begins to circle cheerfully in and out of the waterfall. It's a helluva ad for the wedgies, but not too great for me.

I wade out, creating a picturesque waterfall of my own on the dance floor. Autry, Haney, and Rigney are laughing so hard that their table is in imminent danger of collapse from being pounded on. Lemon, who was noted for his dry sense of humor, something I could really use at that moment, leans over and says, "Gee, Mac, I didn't know you could swim."

They all get up and leave. I wonder if my next job is going to be backup to Max Patkin, the Clown Prince of Baseball. I know it isn't going to be with the L.A. Angels.

Actually, I was not going to be with the Hawaii Islanders either. The next day I learned that I wasn't pitching—which maybe was a good thing because I wouldn't be sure which of three home plates to pitch to. (Actually, I'd be smart enough to pick the middle one.) And the following day I learned that I had been released. Autry was a pretty good drinker himself. He may even have equaled me in DWIs. But he and his guys clearly didn't believe their pitchers should drown themselves in drink and waterfalls the night before a game. On my birthday, my suspension made *Sports Illustrated* on its milestones page: "Happy birthday to the thirsty Irish thrush."

As usual, there was an enabler friend-in-need to come to my rescue. This time it was Bob Kennedy, who was Ted Williams' flight instructor in World War II, a real straight-arrow who roamed the outfield for five major league teams. Now he was managing Salt Lake City, and he rashly offered, "Fly back with us and I'll sign you when we get there."

Bob had a helluva club, including Joe Nuxhall, who pitched his first major league game at 15 but who's been an announcer for the Cincinnati

Reds for the past 30 years. The players were the usual mix—young guys on their way up or not going anywhere fast, sprinkled with old guys and ruffians like me to help season them. I was told that Salt Lake City was dry. That was a problem for me, but, of course, the club traveled outside its desert. On the other hand, Salt Lake seemed like a great opportunity to sober up and stay that way. Unfortunately, the town was full of charter clubs where all you had to do was tell them at the speakeasy peephole that you were a charter member to get in. Out the window went good intentions. I joined three of them.

I finished the season with Kennedy's club, was gently informed that there would not be a next season for me in Salt Lake, and worked back home not very successfully as a time salesman for a local radio station that winter. And then came McDermott's last hurrah.

Tom Sheehan, formerly the GM of the Minneapolis Millers, who fortunately had a long memory and hadn't forgotten my striking out 18 of his players in a game some 20 years earlier, invited me to join the Eugene, Oregon, club he was now managing. It was all over and I knew it. I was 36 years old and down to A ball, below Double A Scranton where I started 21 years ago, for gosh sakes. But I loved to eat, and I still loved baseball. Besides, I couldn't turn down $800 a month. And he wanted me to "help with the kids." That part I liked.

The kids didn't need help with wisecracks. Tom didn't grow a lot of hair on his head, but he had a jungle on his upper body. As he was about to step into the shower after a game, one of his kids asked, "Gee, you gonna take a shower with your sweater on?"

Sheehan was pretty funny himself. When one of the kids asked, "How the hell did you get McDermott here?" he answered, "I found him in the newspaper. He was in a circus and they were shooting him out of a cannon." I almost believed him. If when they fired me from the cannon I had landed on my head, that would have explained a lot.

The older and crankier I got, the less I liked being called out on a bad pitch. That happened one day, and I called the umpire every name in the book and a few that, even these days, don't get published a lot. But he was kind to old horses, and he knew that next season I was set to be an assistant pitching coach and batting practice pitcher for the Cal Angels. So he just grinned, wagged his index finger, and said, "I'll tell Gene Autry on you." I grinned and wagged back: "Oh yeah? I'll tell Roy Rogers on you!" That ended the debate. We both broke up.

In owner Gene Autry, I finally met my match. He was a happy-go-lucky lovable guy, but he was even deeper into his vodka bottle than I was into Scotch. He sideswiped so many cars in Beverly Hills he could have wallpapered his bedroom with DWI summonses. (But I think when they did the stats, we were tied.) He finally had to get a driver. And he never could get my name straight.

"Howdy, Lew." I'd look puzzled. "Lew Burdette, right?"

"No, no, Mr. Autry. McDermott. Mickey McDermott."

"Oh, right. Sorry." But next time I was Burdette all over again. (Well, the cops in Sarasota mixed us up, too.)

Actor Scott Brady, who was doing *Shotgun Slade* on TV at the time, told me not to take it personally. "I did a show with him once at Madison Square Garden," Scott told me. "He pranced down the aisle on his horse and rode up a ramp to the stage to sing 'Back in the Saddle Again.' The horse was trained to rear when he hit a certain note on his guitar. But Gene was loaded as usual, and playing the song he hit a wrong note—which happened to be the note that cued the horse to do his thing. Gene had no idea what he'd done, but the horse was a better musician. Recognizing the note, it snorted and reared before Autry expected it. What could I say? 'There goes the world's most famous cowboy flying through the air like a bullet from his six-gun. Watch out below. Here he comes in for a three-point landing. In the box seats.' Lights out. Act over."

When his horse Trigger died, Roy Rogers had it stuffed. If Autry's horse could talk, would it have arranged to stuff Gene?

The job with the Angels was a gift. I'd first met Tommy Ferguson when he was a freckle-faced clubhouse boy for the Boston Braves. He'd risen steadily through the ranks to become a VP and traveling secretary for the transplanted Braves in Milwaukee, leaving the memory of the thousands of pairs of dirty socks he'd washed for ballplayers far behind. Fred Haney had brought Tommy from Milwaukee to the California Angels as traveling secretary. Maybe I'd done a good turn or two for him, because now he did one for me.

Bob Lemon, a real student of the game, was the pitching coach, and he didn't need much help, so pitching BP became half of what I did. With my experience hitting bats when I was pitching, they knew I'd be perfect for the job. The other half was charting pitches from the stands during the game—noting what got thrown to each hitter and what and where it got hit—and filing a report for Bob and manager Bill "Specs" Rigney to use next time around.

Maurice McDermott, BP pitcher. It was hard not to think about how far down I'd parachuted, but, hey, I'd been cooking this crow for years. Now I had to eat it. The occasional wise guy made it even less digestible. As Ted Williams had told me long long ago, BP isn't for the pitcher to show off; it's to loosen up the hitter's swing and get his eye on the ball. You don't fire bullets; you throw apples and oranges. One cocky kid took exception to that. "You're making it too easy, old man," he called out. "For cryin' out loud, put somethin' on the damn ball."

"Oh," I said, "is that right?" I put something on the ball—and aimed it right over his ear. He hit the ground and got up cussing. "Want to do something about it?" I asked. "I'll be in the clubhouse." Old men do get grouchy sometimes. But that shut him up.

All good things come to an end. (Actually, I learned that a lot earlier.) I spent all of '67 and '68 with the Angels. But after an eight-year run, with the club standing at only 11–28 in the '69 season, management politely terminated Bill Rigney. The new broom, Lefty Phillips, swept out all Bill's coaches, too. You would have thought he'd have spared a fellow lefty. But, no. Once more I was looking for a job. And with Cal Angels BP out of my life, I'd thrown my last pitch in the majors.

CHAPTER 19

Life After Baseball

Didn't You Used to Be Mickey McDermott?

Now I had good reason to regret not paying attention to the tips from big shots I'd had easy access to when I was a hot shot.

I was sitting on the bench with Birdie Tebbetts. We were playing an exhibition as the Birdie Tebbetts All-Stars, alongside of Mr. Speaker of the U.S. House of Representatives, Boston's own John McCormack, who was a dear friend of Birdie's wife, who was (yes, this is an awful lot of who was-es) the secretary to the governor of Massachusetts. Mr. Speaker—who had just learned how little we get paid for these exhibitions and how badly we need the dough in the winter—spoke. Sympathetically. And I can still hear his voice:

"Birdie," he said, "tell your ballplayers to pick up a stock called Arco Oil. It won't cost them much—25 cents a share. Take my word for it. It's going through the roof." None of us had sense enough to risk a quarter. That was another hamburger. Arco later hit it big. Not for me though.

Ty Cobb did appearances for a new product called Coca-Cola, a hometown Atlanta company, and wisely got paid partly in stock options. They say Cobb acquired and bought so much stock he practically owned the company. Lefty Grove was another good listener who was at the right place at the right time with the right attitude and became a multimillionaire.

I had my chance again when the Yankees won the World Series in '56. A bunch of us were invited to a big do in Georgia by Governor Folsom under the auspices of the American Life Insurance Company. Billy Hunter, Jerry Coleman, Yogi Berra, Phil Rizzuto, Bob Turley, and I made the trip and were paid in stock options. Turley, a very smart kid, opened an office in Atlanta to sell insurance in the off-season and was soon flying around the country in his own private jet. Hunter did it in Baltimore and made a ton of money. They offered me Miami, but it sounded like work. At 27, I was old enough to know better, but I thought, what do I know about business, and I was too lazy to learn. Business? That was for businessmen. I was a baseball player. All I wanted was to have fun. But now the fun was over, and reality had set in like sidewalk cement.

I knew I didn't want to work in a clothing store again. I'd tried that in Poughkeepsie one winter when I was still with the Red Sox. I wasn't bad at selling, but I was better at buying—so long as it was at cost—and my buddy Billy D. Fitzgerald, who owned the store, lost money on me. I'd say (especially if it had zoot suit shoulders and pegged pants), "Wow! This looks great on me but I can't afford it," and he'd say, "OK, OK, take it already."

I didn't want to front another baseball camp for kids. My friend Jack Miller had run the business part of two of them for me in Poughkeepsie and in New Hampshire—two places where my name still meant something. We had 70 or 80 local kids for a weekend on an empty high school field at $60 a head (bring your own lunch), with Johnny Pesky and Rick Dempsey, the Yankees catcher, working the field with me. Well, most of what I did—it was the drinking again—was fight with Jack. As far as I know, none of our kids made it to the Hall of Fame. We were babysitters for stressed-out parents, but we did teach the kids a few tricks, made some money, and had some fun. I'll never forget the cute little kid who took me by the hand, looked up with a puzzled look on his face, and said, "Mr.

McDermott, where's right field?" I gently walked him out there where he stood, doubtless hoping everyone would hit to left.

Pete Rose's fee was $35,000, and I don't know what Hall of Famer Johnny Bench got paid, but $1,500 for two weeks at a fantasy camp in Florida sounded sweet to me and Walt Dropo one winter. The promoter did a helluva job—350 people at $3,000 a pop on four or five diamonds with hockey legend Bobby Orr and major league coaches like the Braves' Pat Corrales thrown in for good measure.

To my surprise, a bunch of young women and a couple of old ladies signed up for the camp. Being totally inappropriate, lewd, and politically incorrect comes naturally to me, so of course I asked the friendliest of them, "How can you play? You ain't got any balls." She should have clouted me over the fence for a home run, but she just laughed.

I heard no laughter from the wife of a guy in his sixties who signed up for camp at the last minute, hit a grounder in his second at-bat, fell running to first, and broke his leg. "Some vacation," his wife fumed. "I'll never let him talk me into anything again. He's in a cast and we spent two weeks in the hospital." We had a lot of seniors who looked like they belonged in wheelchairs instead of uniforms. I was proud of them, but with all the pulled muscles we needed more doctors than coaches.

One 82-year-old acted as much in love with the game as he must have the first time he played as a kid on a sandlot. He didn't get hurt, but it was fun watching him running circles under a fly ball before he caught it. We were yelling, "Put a helmet on before you get killed." And sunburns. I could have made a fortune selling lotion. The dentists in town did with all those fantasy campers catching line drives and grounders with their teeth. And oil of wintergreen perfumed the air as a couple of girls, licensed masseuses, set up a little tent on the sidelines and cleaned up giving rubdowns to muscle-challenged fantasy campers at $20 per.

When it was all over, Dropo and I picked up our paychecks, shook hands with the promoter, and drove to Sarasota. Apparently he had overdone the fees for the main attractions. I don't know about theirs, but our checks bounced so high I'm surprised the Air Defense Command didn't shoot them down. We got back in the car and drove back to camp. No trace of the promoter. Of course. He had, to use a fancy but appropriate word, absconded. We chased the sucker all over Fort Myers, finally cornered him, escorted him under duress to the bank, and collected our $3,000 in cash. He was lucky we didn't run him over when we left. But with a sleazebag like that, you don't want to soil your tires. I said, "We've had to chase you all over Florida to collect our paychecks. At least give us a couple of T-shirts." He said, "Sure, but they'll cost you $25 each." With the fees he paid to the big names, he must have lost his T-shirt. I don't believe he ever ran a camp again.

Then, back in Cucamonga, opportunity knocked big time. At a bar (where else?), I met a well-dressed successful-looking guy who was actually happy to meet me. "Mickey," he said, "I know a Mexican who wants to open a music bar in Scottsdale. We could use your name over the door. The area's full of ex-ballplayers. From all those spring trainings, you're well known in the area. We could maybe make some money."

Money. It even spells beautifully. I said yes so fast (well, of course, I said I had to talk it over with Linda first) he must have thought I hadn't seen a picture of Andrew Jackson in months. (He was right. I thought he wore a T-shirt.) But it worked for a while. We opened just in time for spring training and had ballplayers in there by the yard. (You think I was the only one who drank too much?) With my bartender pouring them beer on the house, they kept coming, and the tourists and locals followed. Linda and I bought a big house and a big Cadillac and then we found out that my Mexican money man had been stealing money here, there, and everywhere, and an FBI posse was out looking for him to string the varmint up from the nearest palm tree.

That, plus the fact that my owning a nightclub is like a guy with a can of gasoline trying to put out a fire, and all of a sudden we were in the middle of the desert with no money, no job, and a mortgage too heavy to carry. What could I do? I drank the inventory.

Now it was good-bye house, rent the cheapest apartment we can find, and back to waitressing for Linda, who, despite the fact that I'm very cute for the first half-hour when drinks are being poured, was getting very tired of living with a ne'er-do-well in 10 consecutive years of penury. (That's OK. I liked all my wives, but I followed the general rule that after 10 years it was time to trade them in. It didn't take them half that long to want to trade me in.) Linda said, "So long, it's been good to know you." And she was on her way back to Cucamonga with divorce papers in her suitcase.

At another bar (actually the one that was mine for about six months), I met a guy who was in construction. "Can you hit a nail on the head?" he asked. I admitted that I was more likely to hit a thumb, but it was my thumb so he didn't care. He hired me. Now I was swinging a hammer and contributing to lowering the water table, and the overpopulating, of Scottsdale and its environs. I toted that wood, nailed that panel, got a little drunk, and landed in jail. Well, the first three parts are on target. That last part comes a little later.

In a way, until it got boring, it wasn't bad. I felt like I was doing honest labor for the first time in my life. But it was thirsty work, and as the weather got hotter and hotter, I thought, "This is inhumane; it's time to work indoors."

I moved to Phoenix and landed an entry-level job in security. (Now I was down to minimum wage.) They gave me a uniform that almost fit, a shield, and a gun belt (can you imagine me with a gun?), and pretty soon I was guarding jewelry stores, airports, and, the last place, a fancy phone company corporate headquarters.

Once I had to go to the bathroom bad. I took the elevator up to their cafeteria, made the most of the men's room facilities, and picked up a cup of coffee. A suit approached me with an ugly look on his face.

"You can't come in here."

"Really, why not?"

"Because I say so. I'm the manager. This cafeteria is for phone company employees. You're only a security guard."

I wanted to hit him, but I got good advice from the common-sense department in the back of my head. Instead I took off my gun belt and threw it at him.

"Here," I said. "Now you're the security guard." I walked out of the building. And the job.

Fortunately, my baseball pension now started to pelt me with money—only $350 a month because I took it early, at 45—but $100 a week can go a long way if you like canned tuna. Anyway, it was enough to eat on, and people like to buy drinks for ex-ballplayers who have a story or two to tell about Williams, Mantle, and DiMaggio. My good fortune, such as it was, continued when I met Betty Owens, who had a good job at Motorola, and I moved in with her. That took care of the rent.

It wasn't all sweat and insecurity. There were lots of good moments and good times. Like the time when out of right field Ted Williams got me invited to a banquet in Manchester all expenses paid. Then out of left field, they invited me to sing a song—my old Steuben's "Making Whoopee" parody—which I did. Then they gave me a plaque for tying Babe Ruth's record of 10 consecutive wins for a lefty at Fenway Park. "Thank you, but what do I need a plaque for?" I asked. "What I need is a check."

I was fast running out of options. I mean, how much lower can you go than minimum wage? Then Walt Dropo came to town for a fireworks convention, and we went to watch the Oakland A's in spring training. We dropped in at the cocktail lounge of the hotel where the team was staying, and there was Billy Martin, who'd been managing the Yankees for the past five years 'til his latest run-in with George Steinbrenner evicted him to Oakland.

"You need a job. Why don't you go talk to Billy?"

"Ah, he's got enough on his mind. I don't want to bother him."

"If you won't, I will," Walt said. He came back a couple of minutes later. "Billy wants to talk to you."

"What'd you tell him?"

"He's gotta help you out. You're a good baseball man. And you've been sober for a year. Which you have." Which I had. Betty had kept insisting it was time for rehab, but after a day in the joint I decided I could do it better myself and quit cold Wild Turkey.

"So what did he say?"

He said, "He's as good a baseball man drunk as he is sober. Send him over. I'll buy him a drink." Which he did. But I stopped at one.

Billy's the same guy who put Joe DiMaggio on the A's roster as a coach for one day, to give him an extra year so he'd be eligible for a retroactive raise in his pension from $400 to $700. Now it was my turn.

"You doing anything?"

"No. I'm broke."

"Not anymore. Come to the ballpark tomorrow. You're gonna be my scout." He nodded to Dick Wiencek, the scouting director. "Put him on the payroll for $25,000."

"I can't give him 25," Wiencek protested. "They'll shoot me." They settled on $1,500 a month. Hallelujah. I was back in baseball.

I was assigned to cover Triple A—Phoenix, Las Vegas, and Albuquerque. (Somebody help me spell this town.) A scout doesn't just look at batting averages and ERAs. You read body language: how does he pick up his glove, how does he wear his uniform, and is there spring in his walk or lethargy? Most of all you look for heart. There are a lot of kids with good arms, but they don't all have what is very appropriately called intestinal fortitude. Will you see a puddle on the mound when the bases are loaded?

The kid who impressed me most was a relief pitcher with the Albuquerque Dodgers. He was the nicest boy you'd ever want to meet—clean-cut and religious, with guts and heart. My report said this kid could start in the big leagues this afternoon. He's smart. He has great control, a greater arm, and he has a lot of balls. The only problem was that the L.A. Dodgers knew it. He was a do-not-trade. They already had Orel Hershiser nailed.

I covered colleges, too, and Arizona State University—which was a hothouse for up-and-coming young players like Reggie Jackson, Ron Santo, and Rick Monday—was one you ignored at your peril. I couldn't ignore young Barry Bonds, but my report on him was a bouquet of roses with a brick inside. "He's got all the tools in the world," I wrote, "but he's a dog. A showboat who doesn't want to play."

By my next report, he'd turned around 205 percent. I don't know if Bobby Bonds heard about my report or figured it out for himself, but he took his son in hand. Papa Bobby, the only college coach I know of who went straight to the big leagues, is very stern but a good teacher. Whatever he said, Barry responded. He started to run out ground balls, chase flies, and—not a bad thing either—hit home runs.

Maybe the greatest college kid I ever reported on I scouted sight unseen. The USC baseball coach, Rod Dedeaux, called me again. "I've got a kid who can hit the baseball a mile," he said. "He's been pitching. That way I could hide him from the other scouts." I wrote him up and passed on my report. One of the A's heavyweight scouts followed up. That's how Mark McGwire signed with Oakland. Was he an overnight success? No. It took him two nights. When he came up in '86, he hit only .189, but he had a not-bad-at-all three home runs in just 53 at-bats. The following season, he exploded: 49 homers and a solid .289. Going through some old papers, I found my original report. I had to write a book to get credit for that.

The Oakland gig ended for Billy—and so for me—at the end of '82, but this time, at the beginning of the beginning of the end, I knew what I wanted to do next. I phoned my old pal Tino Barzie in Las Vegas. (Remember Tino? You first met him 17 chapters ago at Scranton managing Tommy Dorsey's orchestra.) Tino had been coming through for me with $100 here, $500 there whenever desperation set in.

"How much?" was his first question.

"No, Tino. I've got a great idea. You're gonna make back all the money you ever lent me."

"You got an idea on how to make money? I'm hanging up."

I got right to the point. "How about you and me become baseball agents?" He listened as I told him how everybody was starting to hire agents, and there couldn't be a better team than McDermott scouting for talent and Barzie running the business side. He was in with both feet in five minutes.

"Start traveling and making connections."

"I need some traveling money."

"How much?"

"Fifteen hundred should do it."

"Go to the airport at 10:00 A.M. to meet the Riviera's jet." I was there. The pilot handed me an envelope. "Who the hell are you?" he asked. "You must be pretty important for Mr. Barzie to wake me up at 6:00 A.M. to fly you a check."

Tino owned a piece of the Las Vegas Riviera and managed singer Pia Zadora on the side. (Or vice versa because, like most performers, she required hand-holding and quality time.) Tino knew more about negotiating than the U.S. secretary of state. He'd owned a couple of minor league teams and he loved baseball. Plus, Billy Martin loved him and would quietly tip us off to players who needed representation. But we had to walk softly. The word *agent* frightened front-office types. If you used it, the clubhouse door slammed in your face. So Billy set the ground rules: "Remember, you're not an agent. You're a counselor."

Billy called me one day to say Tony Armas was being wooed by an agent he didn't like. "Get down here," he said, "and we'll have a meeting with Tony and get this other guy out of the picture." When I got there, Billy said, "Come with me. We're having a meeting with Tony and some of the other players."

"Where?"

"In the outfield."

"The outfield?"

"Yeah. There won't be any spies out there."

Billy addressed the group. "You guys are all gonna need agents. I got the best guy in the whole world right here."

It was the worst thing he could have done. He could have been fired. But he cared more about his players than about management. We signed six or seven of them.

Armas was getting $220,000 a season, which embarrassed me a little when I considered that it was $201,000 more than my highest salary. Tino told Oakland's GM, "I want five years and a million a year for Armas." The GM almost swallowed his Adam's apple. "What! You'll kill my franchise." Tino settled for three years at $3.3 million.

Tony was in Venezuela. Tino, master of the grand gesture, shipped Tony a Ford Thunderbird, flew to Miami to meet him, and then accompanied him to Oakland for the meeting that would make him one of baseball's first millionaires. At Tino's insistence, the GM cut two checks for the $400,000 due on signing. One was for $70,000. That was Tony's. Tino wanted the agency's 10 percent commission up front. Our check was for $330,000.

At the end of the '82 season, Billy was among the first to know that the Oakland A's were about to post a For Sale sign. "We can buy the club for $7 million," he told Tino. "But one thing. I want a five-year contract to manage." Tino didn't go for it. "Nah," he said, "it ain't worth it. That club ain't goin' anywhere." It sold for $10 million then, and later for $100 million. It would've been better than winning the lottery, but the A's boat left without us. Nobody guesses right all the time.

Meanwhile though, the agenting was going great. We went for the superstars. Tony Armas came with us, and so did Mario Guerrero. Then Alejandro Pena, Candy Maldonado, and Marty Barrett. We'd wine and dine them, and Tino would take them to the Riviera for three or four days. You won some and you lost some. We thought we had Rickey Henderson. He enjoyed his Riviera vacation and then said see you later and went with another agent. A lot of agents were stealing from players. Eventually the commissioner's office did background checks, which should have been done in the first place. But nobody wrote fairer contracts than Tino. With the younger players, he didn't take any money until he got them up to $100,000. And he wrote in a clause that enabled them to cut out after three months if they weren't happy with us.

I traveled with a Cuban shortstop named Mario who had played with Oakland. We'd get in the car and drive, scouting minor league clubs all over the country. Mario would make our case in Spanish with the Hispanic players who were starting to become a force in the majors. They were comfortable with him. He'd played with them. He spoke their language.

We had 20 to 25 clients in two swings of a bat, including 10 who became millionaires. But once more fate frowned. We were about to extend our reach into basketball and football when Pia put her size 4s down. Running her, the hotel, and the agency was spreading Tino too thin. She felt neglected. Tino took stock. Something had to go, and it was our agency—for a couple of reasons, one of them being me. "Mickey," he said. "You're drinking too much. I can't work with you like this. You need to go into rehab."

He was right. I had a suite at the Riviera and the power of the pen. I could sign tabs, and I signed a lot of them. One night the tab came to $1,700 for booze. Tino had to ask me about that one. It was hard to find my head inside my hangover. "Oh," I explained, "yeah, I think I know what happened. I think I said, 'Buy the bar a drink' a couple of times. I guess the bar was longer than I thought."

I never had to sell my blood. Tino always came through—which I guess, now that I think of it, made him my principal enabler. But with me he meant well. He justified the handouts by using me for do-me-a-favors. But in my condition, he wasn't doing himself a favor. Like when Pia, who does not travel light, needed a long parade of suitcases and garment bags moved from the Riviera in Vegas, which her husband Meshulam Riklas owned, to their home in Malibu. Tino spelled it out for me: "Take the ones in the sitting room. Leave the ones in the bedroom." Of course, I gave the bellhop the order ass-backward. I drove them all the way to Malibu Beach, was politely informed I had screwed up yet again ("Geez, Mickey, can't you do anything right?"), and had to drive back and do it all over again. I passed the same Greyhound bus so many times they started to wave greetings.

There was always someone who wanted to help me get in a winning groove. Singer Jerry Vale was sure his agent could get me lots of singing gigs. He offered to help me put a new act together—half songs, half patter. "You could do Vegas," he said. "A lot of people know you. But you gotta work at it. Get a voice coach, pick songs, get arrangements made." There was that word again. He could have stopped the speech after "work." That's when he lost me. I was having too much fun. It was me and pitching all over again. I was happy to take my turn in the rotation. But work with a coach on another pitch in between? Maybe next week. Voice coach. Pitching coach. It was all the same to me.

A Funny Thing Happened on the Way to Cooperstown

When I needed a few bucks, I could always open my mailbox. Some outfit publishes a book with every old ballplayer's address in it. So there were three or four letters every day with Topps and Bowman's trading cards in them and a request for an autograph, along with a $5 or $10 check. Most of them were from "fathers" asking for autographs for their kids but actually fronting for dealers. If I was particularly hard-pressed for funds, I'd sign and return and keep the money. The ones from kids—the handwriting told you the difference—I did as freebies.

My signature can make a collector rich. I'm the last number on the set of the most valuable Yankees trading cards and, because I was too lazy to sign and return cards and instead just let them pile up with unopened mail, my signature was the hardest to get. Collect a complete set of mint condition 1956 originals and, because that was the year of Larsen's perfect game and Mantle's Triple Crown (and my World Series single through the middle?), you've got something very special. Without my signature, the set is practically worthless. With it, it's suddenly worth around 35 grand. Makes a man feel important. And very much in demand at baseball card shows.

All a baseball player has to do is live long enough and he becomes a minor celebrity and gets a free dinner at Major League Baseball Players Alumni Association golf tournaments. There are still people on the side asking, "Mickey who?" But a lot of people say they remember you, and that feels good. Better than my old ex-superstar singer friend felt when he got in a cab one day and the driver asked, "Didn't you used to be Eddie Fisher?"

CHAPTER 20

A Cast of Characters

My Most "Unforgettables"

Baseball is too serious today. Once it was a game of colorful charac-ters. Now it's a game of sullen millionaires. Businessmen in base-ball uniforms. (Or am I, on my $1,400-a-month pension, just jealous?)

Gone are the days when Dizzy Trout, a big red bandana for wiping his eyeglasses trailing from his pocket, would turn around after a pitch, bend down, and, when the catcher returned it, catch the ball between his legs. Bud Selig would probably fine him for having too good a time.

Gone but still remembered are clubhouse guys like Johnny Orlando of the Red Sox who knew that the socks and jockstraps it was his job to wash—even of the great ones—stunk, and he took no crap from any-one. The first time Lou Gehrig didn't leave a tip for the clubhouse kid in the visitors' locker room, Johnny gave him the benefit of the doubt. OK, he forgot. When it kept happening, Johnny took matters—and an ice pick—into his own hands. From then on, Gehrig had to play with gaping holes in his athletic socks. Live and learn. He started tipping club-house guys.

A Funny Thing Happened on the Way to Cooperstown

Gone but not forgotten is Casey Stengel, the king of triple-talk. When I went into his office in St. Pete to sign with the Yanks, I was gonna hit him with a little double-talk, but he did it to me first. He got me so confused I signed the contract without checking the money page. When I looked at it later, I found out he'd cut my salary by $1,500 to a big $17,500.

I hold no grudge. He was even more of a character than I am. When he was called to testify before the House Antitrust Committee on how baseball owners ran their show, he rearranged words and phrases in the same reasonable-sounding but totally unintelligible double-talk he used on sportswriters. What congressman wants to admit he doesn't understand what you're talking about? None. They finally gave up and dismissed him. Mickey Mantle followed. The chairperson asked, "Mr. Mantle, what do you have to say on this subject?" Mickey calmly replied, "The same as Casey." And off he danced.

Gone is Bob Swift, the Detroit catcher whose specialty was even more effective than the hotfoot. I was sitting in the Detroit bullpen—the only one in the majors shared by both teams—a 19-year-old kid in my first time up with the Sox, my right hand resting on the bench. I felt a sudden stab of pain on the back of my hand and looked down at it bewildered. What in the hell? All Swift had done was casually extinguish his cigarette on my wrist. "Oh," I was assured. "Bob does that to everybody. Relax. He won't do it to your pitching hand." I had been initiated into the fraternity.

Gone but not forgotten are drinking buddies Billy Hoeft (a 20-game winner in '56) and Harvey Kuenn (a lifetime .303 hitter) of the Tigers. When management—probably an executive who believed in celibacy and abstinence for his players, if not himself—put a tail on them to see how and where they misspent their nights, they caught on fast. One night they pulled their cab over and stopped the one behind them containing the private detective they'd spotted following them from saloon to saloon. "What the f'k do you want to follow us for?" said Hoeft. "Make it easy for yourself. Just come with us."

Two weeks later, the P.I. went to the Tigers front office. "They keep buying me drinks," he said. "They're upset if I turn them down. I can't say no. They keep me out half the night. They're turning me into an alcoholic. My wife wants to divorce me. I'm sorry. I can't keep this up. I quit."

Gone is the horseplay, probably not as funny as we thought it was then, of pitcher Jack Urban, who mooched a supply of firecrackers ("just for July 4, Milt") from Walt Dropo's entrepreneur brother. Jack, usually limited to whoopee cushions in the hotel lobby ("you should've seen the look on that old geezer's face!"), ran riot. He opened a hotel window and fired a rocket into traffic. He accidentally blew a toilet bowl apart with cherry bombs. And he scattered explosive pellets onto a crowded dance floor, startling and scattering the serenely fox-trotting populace who probably thought it was Al Capone's Valentine's Day Massacre redux.

Gone is jolly Jackie Price, the Cleveland Indians shortstop, whose pride and joy was the satchel full of big and little black snakes he carried along on road trips. (Well, it couldn't have been easy to get a snake-sitter.) Bob Lemon told me, "I should have known better than to go to breakfast with him. We sat down in the dining car, and I didn't notice he was carrying his little black satchel with him. While I was looking at the menu, he stuck a big black snake under his shirt and unbuttoned the top couple of buttons. When the waitress came in to take his order, the snake stuck its head out and the waitress took off screaming down the aisle."

That was nothing. One night en route to Chicago when things got boring, Jackie opened his satchel around 2:00 A.M. and dumped all his adorable little serpents in the middle of the aisle. They slithered into the dining car and had cooks defending themselves with meat cleavers. They slithered into sleeping cars. One lady—probably more than one—almost had a heart attack in her berth. Somebody pulled the brake cord, and the train shuddered to a halt in the middle of nowhere.

The conductor came back to see what was happening. Everybody knew: "Oh, Jackie Price is at it again." The conductor was not amused. He ordered Jackie to collect his pets. (How Jackie tracked them down I don't know. Maybe he had a flute like the Pied Piper.) Then he threw Jackie and friends off the train out in the country miles from the nearest town.

Somehow he made it to Chicago in time for the game, but I have no information on how he accomplished that feat. I like to think he arrived in a wagon pulled by a team of black snakes.

By the time he got to Cleveland for his single season in the majors in '46, Jackie was already 33. He didn't last long. Maybe because that was a little old for a rookie. Maybe because he collected only three singles in his 13 at-bats. More likely because—unlike having a roomie who drank, which was tolerable—having a roomie nutty enough to slip a snake into your pillowcase if you used his shaving cream was a risk nobody I know, not even me, would be willing to take.

But Jackie's career had just begun. He put together a comedy baseball act and worked regularly all over the minors and majors. I don't think his war surplus bazooka stayed in the show after he almost killed an old lady in the stands with it. But he was mighty impressive catching fly balls from a jeep. And he broke a lot of bones and probably teeth hanging upside down to catch line drives.

Where is the psychological warfare creativity of Mel Parnell, who, as this book proceeded, corrected something I wrote about him in the Introduction? I, along with everyone else in the American League, believed his story that he had this great natural slider because a line drive had broken a knuckle on his left hand at Louisville. Turns out that's only half true. A knuckle was broken all right, but it was on his ring finger—which he didn't use to pitch.

"Actually the slider I developed grips the ball with the thumb and the two fingers closest to it," Mel explained. "The rumor started with a *Saturday Evening Post* writer who was trying to compare me to 'Three Finger' Mordecai Brown. I told him what I'd told a lot of pitchers and hitters, too—Johnny Sain, Allie Reynolds, Hank Bauer, and Tommy Henrich—who asked me how I threw the pitch that runs in on a right-handed batter. I wasn't about to tell pitchers who'd copy it or hitters who'd lose their fear of it, so I just invented that story about a broken finger. I finally told Allie the truth one night at a banquet after we'd both retired."

Jimmy Piersall's been doing a radio show in Chicago for 11 years, but when he played right field for me with the Red Sox, he was more fun than a truckload of today's players. He'd stand on the foul line and lead a cheer. The fans would enthusiastically join him in: "Yay, Piersall!"

In Yankee Stadium, when the Yanks were beating our bats into tooth-picks and Jimmy was feeling equal parts frustrated and playful, he hid briefly behind the Babe Ruth memorial. Mel Parnell, on the mound in relief as I remember it, looked around and wondered, "Hmm, where's my outfielder?" Knowing it was unlikely that Jimmy had been kidnapped, he went into his windup, confident that if the ball was hit to him, Jimmy "the Shadow" Piersall would reappear. A few pitches later, when Jimmy got into a heated discussion with Ruth's statue, an umpire accused him of making a farce of the game. Jimmy, who believed that authority figures could be too authoritarian, was unawed. He asked, "Did you ever see your-self umpire?"

Long before the story of his life, *Fear Strikes Out*, became a book and a movie, Jimmy and I, young Red Sox hotshots at the time, were invited by a department store in Salem to do a personal appearance. No money was to pass hands. Instead we'd be allowed 10 minutes to take anything we wanted from the store. (The only area off-limits was the jewelry depart-ment. Too bad.) This appealed to the shoplifter in me. The answer was, "Sure. Why not?"

We drew two thousand people, did our song and dance, and then got down to business—which wasn't going to be easy in a crowded store. Jimmy prepared like Eisenhower on D-Day. He scouted out the quickest routes to departments he was interested in. I borrowed a car and parked it in the lot. He borrowed a station wagon, backed it up to the entrance, and brought along an assistant to unload the three shopping carts he used in rotation. He even brought a list of sizes for his five (now there are nine) children.

I headed for the men's department and filled my arms with suits, shirts, topcoats, and hats, instantly achieving the pinnacle of my fashion career as an equal even to Handsome Jack Kramer. Jimmy captured a playpen, a high chair, and complete wardrobes for his kids. "Gee," his wife said later, "you even remembered socks."

When he singled off Satchel Paige one day, Jimmy cheerfully ran to first base backward. Even ol' Satch scratched his head about that one. Years later, playing for Casey Stengel's 10th-place Mets, Jimmy did even better. When he hit his only home run of the season, with loyal Mets fans cheering him on, he celebrated by running the bases backward all the way. I doubt the umpires said anything. It sure isn't in the rule books. And at the Polo Grounds, home of a team that lost more than twice as many games as it won, with the team's highest batting average Frank Thomas' .260, and pitchers with records like 4–14 and 5–22, baseball was more of a circus than a sport anyway.

I can't believe anyone's ever topped Jimmy's stunt at Birmingham when the home-plate umpire called him out on a bad pitch. Jimmy screamed. Jimmy hollered. Jimmy jumped up and down. Then Jimmy reached into his trousers pocket, pulled out a dull black pistol, aimed it point-blank at the umpire, and pulled the trigger. I wasn't there. I wish I had been. I'm told that the ump looked at the pistol, exclaimed "Ohmigod!" and fainted dead away—just before a spurt of water from Jimmy's pistol hit him dead center in the chest protector.

I often felt like I needed protection from the umpires myself. (Actually, after the honeymoons were over, my first three wives all became umpires. They took turns saying, "You're outta here!") I had a reputation: "He's wild on the field and off." So any close pitches went to the batter—particularly a Joe DiMaggio. I could throw the ball right down the middle on 3 and 2, and if he decided to take it all the way, I wouldn't get the call. It was the same for Ted Williams. If it was off the plate a quarter of an inch, a call that a control pitcher would have gotten would be an automatic ball for me. I'd do my automatic hollerin' and cussin' of course, but the only ump I couldn't get along with was Ed Hurley, who hated pitchers anyway.

At that time the doubleheader was still alive and well. One game started at Fenway at 11:00 A.M., and when it ended there was a two-hour break. McCarthy pitched me in the second one, his theory being that my fastball would be even tougher to hit in twilight and under the lights. When the first game ended, Birdie Tebbetts invited me to a late lunch. He had invited a big jolly gent I'd never seen before.

"I'd like you to meet my friend Bill. He's a watch salesman."

"Great. Can you sell me a couple wholesale? One for me. One for my girl?"

"Anytime."

I was on the mound. I got them out in the first and the second. In the home half of the third, I came to the plate to hit. I was poised, waving my bat, waiting for the pitcher to release the ball. He was taking too long. I stepped out. Just then I heard a voice behind me. "Wanna buy a watch, kid?"

I turned and stared. He was wearing a mask and chest protector but I recognized the build and the voice. It was Birdie's "watch salesman," and the joke was on me. "Sonovagun," I said. "You're Bill McGowan." And the Yankee pitcher had no idea why we were laughing our heads off and, led by Birdie the comedian, so was the whole Boston dugout.

Another season. Another doubleheader. And this time—maybe hoping bright sunlight would help me find the plate—McCarthy tried starting me in the first game. It was 1950. Birdie was 37 now, the oldest guy on the club and in his last season, sharing the catching with Matt Batts, who was hurt, and our third catcher, another veteran, 35-year-old Buddy Rosar.

Bill Summers, aging, overweight, and a veteran of too many campaigns with the biggest butt in the league, was umpiring behind Birdie. After four or five innings, I threw a pitch very wide of the plate. Bill called it a ball, and Birdie unexpectedly disagreed. He turned around. "Hey," he said, "that was a pretty good pitch." I couldn't hear the rest of the conversation, but I got a report from Dom DiMaggio, who got it from Birdie.

I threw another wide one. Birdie argued harder. Somehow I located the plate and whipped in a strike. Birdie didn't look particularly happy about that. I threw another ball. Birdie sprang up. This time he argued the call like they were married—unhappily. Summers said, "Birdie, I don't know what's wrong with you today." He took out his whisk broom, bent methodically with great effort, and, giving himself time to think, swept home plate. He straightened up.

"Birdie," Summers said, "I know what you're doing. It's a hot, miserable day. You think you're going to have to catch both ends of the doubleheader, and you're trying to get thrown out. Well, it's not gonna work. I have to be here, too, and my equipment is just as heavy as yours. So let's you and I get together and get along." And they did.

Poor Bill. He was a good guy, and what happened to him shouldn't happen to your worst enemy. He was getting old and tired, too tired to walk around to the front of the plate to sweep it. He just ordered the catcher and the batter out of the way, leaned down, and brushed it from behind. Unfortunately, that created a clear field of view for a newspaper photographer who snapped a shot of Bill just as his trousers and his boxer shorts split simultaneously, leaving the Summers jewels, both of them, exposed to both sunlight and camera lens.

To make matters considerably worse, the photographer sold his prize candid photo to a Massachusetts beer company, which promptly decided to adorn its next year's calendar with this very funny (to everyone but Bill) photograph. I'll say it again. Poor Bill. Every bar he went into, there was his anatomy. Raising hell got him nowhere. Neither did threatening a lawsuit. He was a public figure, and his nuts were in the public domain.

The Red Sox player I most wish I'd played with isn't Jimmie Foxx or Babe Ruth or Lefty Grove—though that would have been great—but a colorful character named Jim Bagby who pitched for Boston the year before I joined the club. Actually I feel as though I played with him. That's because ex–Boston pitcher and later scout "Broadway" Charlie Wagner told so many great stories about him in the dining and lounge cars on the long train rides between cities.

Bagby's record wasn't dazzling: 97–96. He's remembered for two things—his sense of humor and his "handicap." That was a cleft palate, known in those days as a harelip, and it didn't handicap him in the least. He talked funny. Well, not funny, just with a kind of nasal lisp like Bugs

Bunny. But nobody was more popular. Not (surprise!) even me. And the stories. Yes, the stories.

Bagby was in the bullpen during a game with the Yankees. He warmed up again and again, finally got hungry, and ordered a hot dog from a passing vendor. Just as the kid returned, Cronin signaled for Bagby. The bullpen coach said, "Jim, you can't eat that now. You're in." The kid said, "What am I gonna do with the hot dog?" Bagby said, "Wait a second." He turned to the bullpen coach. "Who am I pitching to?" he asked. Replies the coach: "DiMaggio, Henrich, and King Kong Keller." It was the famous Yankees Murderers Row. Bagby turned to the kid. "Wait here with the hot dog," he said. "I'll be right back."

Bagby was in the dugout. The Red Sox were playing Detroit. Ted Williams was the hitter. Hank Greenberg was playing first base. Two men on, nobody out in the seventh inning. A bunt was in order to move the runners up, but Theodore Samuel Williams never bunted in his life. Greenberg, who had been in the military for a couple of years and maybe forgot that, edged in a little closer, thinking bunt. By the third pitch, Hammerin' Hank was up so close he could almost shake hands with Ted. Bagby moved up to the top step of the dugout. "Hey, Henry," he shouted, "you get in any closer and you're going to be talking just like me."

Bagby was with the Cleveland Indians, rooming with the great third baseman Ken Keltner, another McDermott who was out late every night. At 24, Lou Boudreau had just become the youngest manager in baseball, and he had to prove he was in charge, so he announced that he was doing a bed check every night. Boudreau called. Bagby picked up.

"Where's Ken?"

Bagby thought fast. "He's in the bathroom shaving."

"At 2:00 A.M.? Get him on the phone." This was, of course, not possible. Keltner was out having a very good time. Bagby waited a decent interval and then picked up the phone again.

"Yeah, Lou," he lisped. "This is Kenny. Whaddya want?"

You don't get to be manager with a 75 IQ. Not usually anyway. Boudreau snapped, "You and Kenny are both fined $500."

Bagby was in an ice cream parlor. "What will you have?" asked the waitress. Bagby said, "I'll have an ice cream soda." The waitress slapped his face. Bagby was stunned. "Ouch!" he said, and then suddenly realized she thought he had cruelly mimicked her speech impediment. "Geezus, lady," he cried, "I wasn't making fun of you. I got one, too."

Bagby was on the train pulling into South Station in Boston. There was a rush to the phones. Somebody yelled, "Married men first." Bagby called his wife: "Hi, Mary," he lisped. "Can you guess who this is?"

Actually, there's a third thing Jim Bagby will be—and would like to be—remembered for. That's the day DiMaggio came to the plate against him having established a record 56-consecutive-game hitting streak. Bagby poured it on and sent him back to the dugout hitless at-bat after at-bat. Keltner was at the hot corner when DiMaggio lashed a vicious line drive down the third-base line. Kenny thrust up his gloved hand in instant reflex self-defense, accidentally spearing it. "Geezus, roomie," Bagby said, "I hope you have good insurance. That ball was hit so hard I thought it was gonna go through you and come out the other side." DiMag's streak was over, and Bagby and Keltner had ended it.

I hung out with a lot of crazy guys over the years, but the one who takes the cupcake is Paul Gleason, now a Hollywood star—in *Die Hard*, as the villain in *Trading Places*, as the angry high school principal in *The Breakfast Club*, and in *Arthur*, *Tender Mercies*, and a ton of TV shows. But he was a hungry 11-year-old kid looking for handouts when I first met him.

I was about 22 and I was walking through a mall in my Red Sox jacket when this cute street kid said, "Where'd you steal that jacket?" (Today anyone with $75 can wear one, but they didn't have major league franchise stores then.) "I didn't steal it," I said. "I play for them." The half-pint-sized con man got right to the point: "You know, my family don't like me. They threw me out of the house. Got a fiver on you?" I took him home. Later I threw him out, too, but we've been buddies ever since. In fact I helped get him his first job—batboy for the White Sox.

Fast forward. Paul was in college quarterbacking the Florida State team to a 7–3 record. He and his football buddies copped a naked mannequin from the window of a women's dress shop. They drove down the 79th Street Causeway between Miami and Miami Beach in a top-down convertible pretending to beat "her" up while horrified drivers snuck furtive looks. (This was before cell phones, or they'd have heard police sirens in two minutes flat.) At the top of the Haulover Bridge, they pulled over, bopped her some more, yelled, "Swim you bitch! Go ahead, swim!" and tossed her out of the open car into the bay.

Cars screeched to a halt. People were shouting, "Those awful men in the convertible. Did you get their license plate? They undressed that girl and raped her. Then they threw her off the bridge!" A half-dozen dismayed fishermen glimpsed a gorgeous but battered naked lady plunging into the drink, and they dove in to save her. Fishing rods were flying everywhere. Quite a scene. And can you imagine the look of chagrin on the face of the hero who saved her? Well, he'll be telling that story to his grandchildren.

Paul played some minor league ball at second and short. The Red Sox gave him a $30,000 signing bonus and later released him. He got a bonus from Cleveland and played in its farm system. They released him. He was about to get a bonus from Washington under the name Billy Gleason when farm team director Hal Keller, who got around, recognized him. "Oh, that was my twin brother," Gleason explained. (Nice try, Paul.) But Keller wasn't born the day before yesterday. He checked social security numbers, and Billy/Paul was handed his walking papers. Although a bit short of cash, he didn't walk home. He simply "borrowed" the team bus and drove it home. That was Paul in those days: my younger twin brother, a wild man and a screwup. You never knew what he was going to do or pull next. That's why we get along.

Paul's life is a better movie than some of the films he's costarred in. Maybe more like *All My Children*, the soap he appeared in for three or four years as Dr. David Thornton. He was making $400 a show, not bad at five times a week, but when the producer negotiated with the other actors for the following season's new full-hour format but didn't seem interested in him, he flew back to his L.A. home. Then a buddy at another network said, "Hey, did you know a survey has you number three in popularity of all the characters on all the soaps?" Paul realized the soap's producer was playing cat and mouse and he could name his own price.

When that sly executive phoned to say, "We can offer you $500," Paul, ever the smart quarterback, said coolly, "Have to think about it," called his agent, and said, "Tell them I want $1,250 a show, plus my own dressing room, plus a private phone, plus a limo to take me to and from the show, plus, plus, plus." He found out later that when the agent called, he had said, "I know this is a crazy demand, but I have to make it. My crazy client insists." The reply was what he expected: "What? No way!" But two days later, the soap capitulated to all demands, and when Paul returned to New York, he learned that the producer, who could have had him for $750, had been fired. (Way to go, Paul.)

Flashback. He was out of work. I was out of work. We were so broke we were eating peanut butter and tomato sandwiches and driving a bank clerk nuts by cashing in a jar full of pennies. We patronized 15-cent beer joints for the free peanuts. And (yet another true confession of how low a hungry guy can descend), we sold hubcaps, sometimes not waiting 'til they fell off the car.

Then in a factory above Biscayne Boulevard with an elegant view of Burdine's Department Store, we got a job on an assembly line. We had to put Ping-Pong balls in boxes, and the damn line was moving so fast it was like that classic *I Love Lucy* episode with the candies. After half an hour, Paul said screw this job. Too stressful. We opened a window and tilted the assembly line toward it. There was a busy avenue out there with cops directing traffic. Suddenly it was snowing Ping-Pong balls. Balls were bouncing off policemen's heads and passing cars in the middle of downtown Miami. Everybody was bewildered, looking up, trying to figure out what was going on.

There was a traffic jam and angry honking as cars stopped to harvest dozens of elusive little white balls. It was a good thing it was before 9/11, or all South Florida would have panicked. We turned up the speed on the conveyor belt. The balls shot off the belt like white musket balls. We took off. Two days later, we went back to the agency that hired us and collected our paychecks. They added up to $13. Not even a living wage. Cheap bastards. It served them right. Great advertising stunt though. They should have paid us double.

Eventually Paul paid for his sins, but it was the wrong sin. He was headed south with his buddy, Frank the Tank, driving a clunker through a rural north Florida hamlet with its post office in a general store, when he was pulled over. Not for speeding. As a suspect in the post office robbery earlier that day. Paul protested, but he and Frank were misidentified in a lineup and shoved into the local lockup. No lawyer. No phone call. Just a sentence. Next thing he knew he was wearing leg irons in a chain gang and cutting grass on the highway with no way out for the next 10 to 20, watched by hawkeyed, shotgun-totin' guards who'd as soon shoot him as smile at him.

Suddenly Paul remembered the beautiful words he'd heard uttered a few years earlier by Governor Leroy Collins at a banquet honoring the Florida State football team. "You boys ever need anything," said the governor, "just let me know." Paul finally managed to make a phone call. After some anxious moments he got through to the lieutenant governor, who relayed the news to Governor Collins, who informed the sheriff that he had made a grievous error. After a week on the chain gang, Paul and Frank were abruptly, though not apologetically, released.

I met Jack Kerouac, the beat poet, through Paul. I had no idea who he was, what he did, or how famous he had already become. He dressed like a bum, and I thought he was one. "I want to write a book about you," he said. I laughed.

"Don't laugh," Paul told me. "You'd be lucky if he put you in a poem. He's a great writer." It wasn't until I saw a 90-minute documentary about him 40 years later that I believed Paul. Who knew? The beat generation.

At the time I just said, "Come on, Paul. Let's go to the movies. I don't want him hangin' around." But Kerouac hung, and he was an interesting guy. A good listener. A good storyteller. And I got to like him.

A Funny Thing Happened on the Way to Cooperstown

We were at an all-time low point. I was the pitching coach for the Class D Orlando team, and Paul was playing third base. I was drinking heavily, sometimes even in the morning. I'd fall asleep on the screened porch of the dump we lived in. When it was time to report to the ballpark, the only way Paul could wake me was to douse me with cold water.

Kerouac and Frank the Tank would drive with us in our station wagon when the club went on road trips. Kerouac would sit with the African-American people in the segregated bleachers, always half stoned, always wearing a raincoat with a fifth in one pocket and a notebook in the other. "Whaddya doing up there?" I finally asked. For a poet his answer made sense: "Just picking up the local lingo."

The three of us were at an American Legion Hall one night in a little redneck South Florida town with Paul dancing very close to a sexy local lady. This did not please her husband, who suddenly appeared and wanted to take a swing at Gleason. Kerouac, who was a strong guy and played football for Lou Little at Columbia, grabbed the husband's wrist and yanked him to his knees. Then the jealous husband's buddies started throwing punches. We were mixing it up pretty good, windmilling fists all over the dance floor in a grand donnybrook reminiscent of a B western saloon fight—much like one Paul appeared in on *Gunsmoke*—when we suddenly heard police sirens.

Paul shouted, "Let's get out of here!" Before he finished the sentence, two guys ganged up on Frank the Tank, who was instantly out of there—on a direct route through a plate-glass window. We headed for the car, stopping only to pick up Frank and explain to the cops that we were innocent bystanders and we had to take our poor injured pal to the hospital. We got in the car and roared out of there.

I turned to Kerouac. "Where were you when we needed you?" He gave me an injured look. "Where was I? I was pinning down the guy who started the fight."

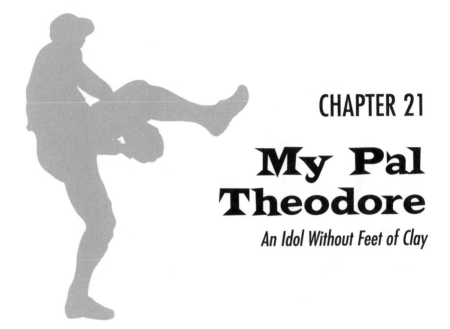

CHAPTER 21

My Pal Theodore

An Idol Without Feet of Clay

Ted Williams liked me before he even met me. Right off the bat. Not because I'm likable. Because we both came from poor families. The day I met him in Sarasota spring training he looked at my battered suitcase held together with a leather belt and the pants that were too short to hold a growing 18-year-old boy and said, "I heard about you, Maurice. You're a poor kid, huh?"

Ted's family was even poorer than mine, and with an alcoholic father and a mother marching off every day with the Salvation Army, he didn't have an easy childhood. When we ate breakfast together, he always seemed to be making up for lost meals. Two steaks. A half-dozen eggs. Protein. Part of his plan to put on the muscle that would put the ball where he wanted it—off the wall or over it. The Williams Diet got the same results as the Atkins Diet. At 6'4" sportswriters called him the "Splendid Splinter."

The writers said he was aloof, but he just seemed that way. Ted was intense, and apparent aloofness was just a by-product of intensity. He lived in a tunnel. At the end of the tunnel, said this man whose swing was described as "poetry in motion," would be the day that this Tennyson with a bat walked down the street and heads turned and, in hushed respectful tones (because respect is what a kid growing up in hand-me-downs wants most in the world), people said, "There goes the greatest hitter who ever lived." The bronze key chain I carry says he achieved that goal. It bears his likeness, along with the half-dozen words that were all he ever wanted in a eulogy: "The Greatest Hitter That Ever Lived."

The entrance to the Baseball Hall of Fame in Cooperstown says it without words. Inside you'll find a bust of every player elected to that exclusive club. But only two get the royal treatment. Two life-sized statues stand on either side of the entrance to welcome arriving visitors. "The first time I walked in and saw them," Ted told me, "tears came to my eyes. Can you imagine that? Just Babe Ruth and me?"

I told a lot of Williams stories in my Red Sox chapters, but I can't do this book without a special chapter just for Ted. He wasn't "just another guy" in the cast of characters in my life, he was an amazing man and a loyal and generous pal. Brilliant, too. And not only in explaining how and why a curve curved and a slider slid. All he had was a high school education, but Johnny Pesky, who was in the preflight V-5 program with him at Amherst College, told me that when it came to the courses in navigation and math, students with college educations wrestled with complicated problems that Ted "got" in minutes.

What he didn't get was military etiquette. Bob Kennedy told me the story of the evening a group of baseball fan generals came to the Officers' Club especially to have the honor of an introduction to the very junior Lieutenant Williams. Ted had one drink with them, said, "Good night, boys; it's past my bedtime," and made a quick getaway.

More than once, Ted lectured me on what I needed to make myself the ace on any staff. Lefty Gomez's advice to me was, "When you start to pitch, nobody's looking at your feet. Edge up a little. That little edge of inches is what made me great." Ted went beyond insider tips. My missing link was obvious to him, something built into every cell in his brain, every muscle in his body: self-discipline. He'd schooled himself never to swing at a pitch outside the strike zone. Umpires trusted his 20-10 vision more than their own. If Williams took a pitch, they knew they had to call it a ball. Ted never let up either. We were beating the hapless St. Louis Browns 29–4 one night. Ted went up to the plate in his last at-bat as though it was a 2–1 ballgame. And, if I remember correctly, he bought himself another hit.

Ted's goal was so much more ambitious than my goal—which was at age 18 just to make the ballclub—that I never forgot his. At the foot of the master, I should have learned from it. It wouldn't be bad to walk down the street and hear myself called "the greatest pitcher who ever lived." If I'd worked half as hard at the art and science of pitching as Ted did his whole life at batting, I might be able to say hello to a Mickey McDermott bust every time I visit Cooperstown. Or, better yet, take my picture with it.

Something else I never forgot is what he told me years later, shaking his head in a way that was part respect for what I did and part regret for what I didn't, "Bush, you had better stuff than anyone I ever hit against." What he said when I was with the Senators and pitched against him was just as telling. I hit him in the back with a pitch. "Bush," he said from first base as he reached around to rub it, "where did you get a knuckler?" We both knew I didn't have a knuckler. I was just wild. As usual. Well, we had one thing in common. Ask him about a game 10 years earlier, and he could tell you who was pitching, the score, the count, and who was smoking in the dugout. Total recall. I've got that, too. Don't ask me where I put the car keys though.

I achieved my first goal six times—with six different clubs—but not a lot more. Ted achieved his big time. So big that one game playing for the Senators, when I hit a home run that beat the Red Sox—to dead center and (take a bow, Mickey) the longest hit there by a pitcher since Babe Ruth—I had to look hard just to find my name in the papers I bought the next day. I saw Ted later at his hotel apartment. "Geez," I said, "I hit a mile-long home run and beat your ass and there's one line in the papers about me: 'McDermott also hit a home run.' I won it and the whole article is about you." He grinned. "Well, Bush," he said, "you gotta be a star."

He never stopped kidding me about that. When the Sox came to town to play Washington, I pulled into the Senators parking lot in my clunker, an old 1940 Oldsmobile with black smoke gushing from the tailpipe. The Red Sox bus pulled up nearby, and the players were straggling out. Ted strolled by my car.

"Hi, Theodore," I said. He stopped to greet me, looked over my elegant vehicle, rolled his eyes, and said, "Geezus, Bush. I told you pitchers were all dumb, dumb, dumb. Pitchers drive clunkers. Home-run hitters drive Cadillacs."

I got a chance to be a young pitcher driving a Cadillac of my own when Rocky Palladino, who owned the Latin Quarter in Boston, offered to pay Ted $12,000 a week to do nothing but fake playing the piano at the club. "Mickey," he implored, "we'd pack the joint. He's your pal. He'll do it for you. Tell him there'll be a guy behind the curtain who'll do the actual playing. All he's gotta do is move his fingers and smile."

It was a crazy idea, but there was a new Cadillac in it for me if he said yes. I found Ted and got down on my hands and knees and scraped the floor in a Shah of Persia–type bow. Then I relayed Rocky's offer.

"Are you alright, Bush?" he asked. "Are you running a 106 fever? That is the dumbest thing I ever heard. Why, I wouldn't last 10 seconds and they'd run me out of town." Being the best piano player in the world wasn't in Williams' future, and the Cadillac wasn't in mine. Oh well, I could keep on borrowing Pesky's wheels. And, until the unfortunate-to-say-the-least episode with his brand-new Johnny Pesky Day Lincoln (see page 67 if you fell asleep reading that story), I did.

No reasonable request, however, was turned down by Theodore. Before Babs came along (and, OK, after our marriage was terminal), I was not unwilling to oblige the occasional fair damsel who, blinded to my many flaws by my fastball, expressed interest in wrestling with me. I had a roomie. Ted, who was in a different salary bracket, rented quarters in a hotel not far from Fenway Park—at a time when rooms were $10 a night, and he probably got a celebrity rate.

"Ted," I asked one night when I actually won a game and a shapely blonde in a box seat sent me a note expressing an interest in celebrating quietly with me, "can I use your room?" He didn't have to ask what for. He only said, "Yeah, but get out by midnight."

He gave me the key. The girl and I separated outside. She went in first (no use getting into trouble with the house dick), and five minutes later I followed and met her at the room. I turned the key in the lock and she went in first. "Umm," she said, "very nice." I followed and was about to whistle appreciatively, but I smothered it. It wasn't a room. It was a suite.

The lights were low. Candles flickered romantically. A tray of hors d'oeuvres awaited along with champagne chilling in an ice bucket. And Earl Garner was playing whispering piano just for us from a gently circling LP. (Do I have to explain that? I hope so, because I'm hoping this book isn't being read just by senior citizens. Anyway, that's what we danced and made love to before CDs—the long-playing record familiarly known as the LP.)

Later I looked at my watch and realized time really does fly when you're having fun. Oops! Three hours past midnight. Baseball's greatest hitter was sleeping on a couch in the hotel lobby? This would be the last time Ted lent me a room. Or anything else. Oh, well. I rolled over. Might as well stay the night.

Next afternoon in the clubhouse I went up to my patron as red in the face as a groom caught cheating on his honeymoon. (Or a bride.)

"Ted," I asked, "where were you? All you had to do was knock on the door."

"Bush," he replied, "I know you. No way you'd be out of there by midnight. I rented another suite." Now there was a buddy for you.

Let me not make the case that Ted was a perfect gentleman. There were flaws. Like the time he invited me to have Sunday brunch with a lady friend. "She is not only a real beauty," he said, "but a real lady. So kindly mind your manners, be on your best behavior, and for chrissakes, no swear words."

I arrived wearing my best suit and tie, knocked politely, and greeted the tousle-haired blonde knockout seated at the room service table with Ted with the gentlemanly discretion of Little Lord Fauntleroy. One thing I'm not gonna ask: "Did you guys sleep well?"

Ted introduced me. I yanked gently upward on the creases of my trousers and took a seat at the table. The girl didn't even know I was in the room. She was just staring at him. Then Ted said, "Bush, for chrissakes, pass the f'g butter." She didn't even notice. She was in heaven. But he gaves me the Williams look—half betcha-didn't-expect-that and half gotcha. And I—the object of an elaborately planned Williams prank—relaxed and said, "You sly sonovabitch!" and fell off the chair laughing.

Everybody and his uncle wanted to sign Ted up for endorsements, but except for a few, like bread and a soft drink, he turned them down. He did sign up with Sears Roebuck for their line of fishing gear and rifles. But he insisted on trying them out first. That's why Fenway Park turned into a shooting gallery one Saturday morning with Ted and Tom Yawkey sitting in Yawkey's box and firing two shotguns the company had sent him for testing.

Yawkey dispatched GM Joe Cronin's 12-year-old grandson, Corky, to Fenway's roof to startle into flight the thousands of pigeons that watched ballgames without buying so much as a single bleachers ticket. The assassins kept up a steady fire for an hour or so in a replay of the Boston Massacre. By the time we got there to play the Browns, the field was wall-to-wall feathers, and Friends of Animals was ready to declare war.

The game was played in a gray fog. Players were cussin' and sneezin'. Ladies up in the stands were plucking feathers from their hair and probably not thinking about saving them for their Easter bonnets. And that was after the grounds crew, having hired extra people to handpick the feathers, had done its best to clean up the mess. That night it was a lot harder than usual to keep track of balls and strikes. The NRA swat team of Yawkey and Williams—especially, I suspect, the owner himself—had shot out half the scoreboard lights.

Most of Ted's shooting, during the Korean War, was a lot more serious than that—though if I were a pigeon I'd have taken it pretty seriously. In his home in Islamorada, the living room walls were wall-to-wall baseball photos. But the one he was proudest of was a photo with President George H. W. Bush. It sat smack in the center and was autographed, "To Ted Williams, a great ballplayer and a great American." Now that Ted's gone, I'd guess you'd be able to see it in the Ted Williams Museum.

It was the last part of that caption that he prized the most. I know that because when Red Sox management attempted to pull strings to keep him from flying in the Korean War, he blew his cap. In World War II he'd felt cheated out of combat. Ironically, graduating first in his class made him a flight instructor instead of the combat pilot he wanted to be. In '52, Ted hated the idea of spending his prime baseball years in Korea and missing the chance to break every hitting record in the books. But it was just something you did for your country. In a declaration every bit as ringing as "Damn the torpedoes, full speed ahead" and "We have just begun to fight," Ted said, "I'm a baseball player second. I'm a marine first."

Ted's military career came damn close to ending his baseball career. And his life. Flying wing for his commanding officer John Glenn (right, that John Glenn), Ted's F-9 was struck by hostile fire and caught fire as he was attacking a North Korean pillbox.

"I knew," he said, "if I ejected that with my long legs and that tight cockpit, I'd leave my kneecaps behind. That wouldn't help me running bases." Instead of ejecting in enemy territory, thinking fast, he aimed the nose of his fighter upward and took it well above 10,000 feet where the fire put itself out for lack of oxygen. Later, it must have reignited somehow. He didn't realize his plane was afire 'til he flashed in for a landing. Guided by a buddy flying beside him, with his instruments, brakes, and landing flaps shot out, Ted piloted his crippled jet back to base, came in for a belly landing at 200 mph, blew his canopy, and scrambled out. He said he was pretty sure he broke Mickey Mantle's record sprinting to first as the plane exploded and disintegrated behind him.

A Funny Thing Happened on the Way to Cooperstown

The North Koreans didn't get him, but a stroke finally did. One minute he was in bed. The next minute—actually hours later—he woke up on the floor with his peripheral vision gone. After that this handsome man's health disintegrated slowly. He looked sick. He lost weight. His face became drawn. He wasn't handsome Ted anymore. He was walking with a cane when I accompanied him to a baseball card show in Vegas. I opened a glass door for him at Bally's. He was right behind me, and when I stepped aside to let him pass, the door whacked him in the head. "Geezus," he said, "now he's trying to kill me."

His health worsened and I hated that. I phoned him one day. We chatted, and then I said (I don't know what made me say it, but I'll never be sorry I did), "You know something, Theodore, I always loved you." Now I've done it, I thought, certain he'd hang up. No such thing. "Bush," he said quietly, "I love you, too." How about that for two guys who always prided themselves on being macho? Walt Dropo, sitting there with me and listening to the conversation, wondered about that. "Geez," he said in a disgusted voice, "why don't you two get married?"

George Bush Sr. once pinned a medal on Ted for being a great American. He should have been buried in Arlington Cemetery with a 21-gun salute instead of in a freezer in Scottsdale. Emceeing a Ted Williams Museum banquet, I once introduced him as "the man John Wayne wanted to be." Ted liked that. "Damn, Bush," he said. "Great line. Let's go on the road with that."

Whatever road he took, I wish him well. If I'm lucky, someday I'll be pitching to him in heaven.

CHAPTER 22

Night Games

Riding a Train Going the Wrong Way

O K. This is the chapter I wish I didn't have to write. The "painfully honest" part. You've probably figured out by now that I prefer "uproariously funny."

I won't say everybody in baseball 50 years ago drank like I did, but I sure had a lot of company. Sammy White, for example. There I was pitching against the Yanks on what was not one of my best days. No hangover. Nothing like that. I hadn't even started drinking yet.

I was just plain out-of-this-world wild, and every base had a Yankee standing on it.

Sammy walked slowly to the mound as I stood there with my head hanging wondering if I ought to take Theodore W.'s advice and become an outfielder. I assumed Sammy was coming out to try to calm me down. That was a waste of time unless he was carrying a syringe loaded with 500 mg of Valium. Sammy stared at me for what seemed a full minute. Finally he said impatiently, "Get this guy out. It's almost cocktail hour." He turned, plodded back, and squatted wearily behind the plate.

And Ellis Kinder. For pitching, he was a great role model. None better. But drinking? Well, yes, that too. I once got a phone call from him in the middle of the night.

"Congratulate me, Mac," he said. "I just got married."

"You what? Geez, Ellis. Did you forget Hazel? You're already married."

"I am?"

Hazel was a very forgiving lady. I'm sure when he sobered up she accepted his apology.

Should I blame my drinking problem on my genes? Maybe. Who else has an Uncle Thomas who plowed his New York Central train right through Grand Central Station and into the Oyster Bar? Luckily, it was a dead run returning empty. It happened in the middle of the night, and the station was empty, too. But the maintenance crew picked oysters off the locomotive (maybe even ate a couple of dozen) for quite a while.

I can't say no harm done. The station was a mess. But you know that line about how God protects babies and drunks? Well, Uncle Thomas got out with nothing worse than a few scratches. When he asked, "Where's my bottle of rotgut?" (from which, of course, he had been cheerfully imbibing on the long boring ride to Grand Central), the answer, alas, was, "It broke." The good news was that he hadn't knocked down the Commodore Hotel. (Can you imagine, "What's that train doing in my room? What's the next stop? I'm getting off.")

You could get water in the clubhouses on hot summer days, but cold beer was the beverage of choice. Rheingold (or whatever the clubhouse guy picked up by the case) had a taste to it. We were thirsty. The water was room temperature. The beer was on ice. Drinking was no big deal in those days.

Everybody drank. Even the pilots on our charter flights. (FAA rules were a lot looser back then.) I went on one plane after being out all night with the pilot. When he got behind the controls, his eyes were so crossed he couldn't see the runway. We thought we were social drinkers, but that was the booze talking. We were alcoholics. Not, as I joked it away, victims of Alkyheimer's Disease.

When we landed in Havana on a Miami Marlins International League flight, pretty hostesses with trays of margaritas, compliments of El Presidente Batista, greeted us at the terminal with "Welcome to Cuba." A lot of us couldn't stop at one. I camped there. Well, you had to settle your stomach after a bumpy flight. So did our shortstop, and later that day he took it on the chin—close to it anyway—when he caught a routine ground ball with his eyebrows. "Get that drunk out of there!" growled manager Pepper Martin.

I wish Pepper had been managing instead of Stengel a few years earlier when our Yankees bus made a stop at Mama Leone's in Ft. Lauderdale during spring training. "You've all been on good behavior the past month," smiled Casey. "We didn't have to bail anybody out of jail. So management is springing for a good dinner."

Ah, that veal parmigiana! But management forgot the wine. We didn't. On the way out we passed a tall pyramid display of Chianti bottles in their familiar rustic straw wrappings. As he passed, Mantle grabbed one from the bottom. The rest of us played follow the leader as, displaying New York Yankees reflexes Casey had to be proud of, infielders and outfielders alike caught the toppling bottles before they hit the tile floor.

We must have had 50 bottles on the bus (for which, I'm sure, Mama billed the Yankees), but they were empties by the time we arrived at Palm Beach to spend the night before driving to Vero Beach for an exhibition against the Brooklyn Dodgers—as it turned out, our World Series opponents seven months later.

We were still thirsty at Palm that night. Hank Bauer climbed over the bar and announced that the saloon had a new bartender. "You just sit there," he told the doll he replaced, "you're gonna earn some real money tonight." He announced a new price schedule—$7 for a beer—and two or three hours later gave her all the money.

By the time we got to the ball field for our game, the whole club was playing in an alcoholic haze, and from the stands we smelled like wine country. I was pitching—the Gallo Brothers would have been proud of me—but strangely my fastball didn't have its usual bite, and my change-up, which I gave up on almost immediately, refused to do anything but change down.

The first nine batters either doubled, tripled, or drew bases on balls—with one exception. Canny Walter Alston had loaded the order with right-handed hitters with Duke Snider the only lefty. Him I struck out three times in one inning. One inning? Yep, that's no typo. The one felt like nine though. Jackie Robinson, Roy Campanella, Pee Wee Reese, Carl Furillo, and their mates scored 17 runs off me. As my ordeal continued, I cast pleading looks at Casey Stengel on the bench, which he should have read as, "Get me out of here. I could get killed!" But every time I caught his eye, he looked the other way, and I didn't have to see his face to read it: "Let the punishment fit the crime."

When I struck out Snider for the third time and the final out, I went to the bench a happy man. It was over at last. Not quite. "OK, son," said Casey. "It's back to the clubhouse for you." He paused. "But I want to see you run there." (I huffed and puffed through the first 200 yards. Then, looking over my shoulder to be sure he was watching the game, I trudged the rest of the way.) Later, Stengel said (he didn't always double-talk), "This is the drunkenest bunch I ever managed. But boy, can they play!" When they're sober.

I did a lot of laughing off the bad results of too little sense and too much drinking. I papered over the pain it caused in messed-up marriages and too-often-fatherless children with sitcom lines delivered in saloons to my drinking pals: "My first two wives were stewardesses. Every time I got on a plane, I got married. Next time I'm taking the train." I dismissed the blown saves and opportunities just as clownishly: "You know, guys, it's a good thing we play mostly day games. They're more convenient. Longer cocktail hours." Or, in later years, "Playing on six teams in 12 years ain't such a bad thing. When the World Series comes around, I've always got a home team to root for."

Oh yes, the marriage business. Mother-in-law jokes are politically incorrect and very old hat these days, but the fact is my first mother-in-law fit the caricature. Living with her—which Babs and I did from time to time when the money ran out—was no joke. I got along great with my father-in-law, a wealthy criminal defense attorney who'd represented mobster Al Capone and friends. He didn't get along that well with Mrs.

Riley either. "Mac," he'd say, "you've got to be careful. The goddamned old lady is after you."

The first time I met the family, I slicked my hair and dressed to the nines, but she wanted a Palm Beach socialite for her daughter, not some flash-in-the-pan southpaw. She'd been out to get me ("I'll put a stop to this!") from the first. After her plots failed and the wedding took place, I, always the big spender, bought a fishing cruiser (proudly named *The Bosock*) and moored it at the hotel the in-laws owned on Indian Creek, the Riley Adobar.

Returning from a successful morning cruise with three trophy sailfish aboard, I found a yacht in my parking space. Well oiled—well you can't go fishing without a few cold beers to counteract the hot sun—I stormed ashore where Mrs. Riley was conducting her regular weekly noon tea and luncheon with ladies whose bank accounts contained no deposit entries under five figures.

I told her, not politely, "Get that boat out of my spot." She said, "Do you know whose boat that is? It's Dan Topping's." I said, "F'k him, too. If that boat's not moved in the next five minutes I'm going to ram the dock. And maybe that yacht with it." (There I was busily digging my own grave again. I didn't read the *Wall Street Journal*. How would I know that Topping was Del Webb's Yankees ownership partner?)

It wasn't moved. (Topping was probably out on the golf course.) Time ran out. I missed the flagship of the Yankees fleet—fortunately—but rammed the dock. It failed to collapse, but Mrs. Riley's party did. Teacups and pince-nez flew through the air and shattered like mobile homes in a hurricane, and the ladies fled in disorder. The episode did not endear me to Mrs. Riley. In retrospect, its resemblance to my encounter in the Fenway Park parking lot a couple of years later with Mrs. Yawkey, another club owner's wife, tends to confirm what rehab people say about alcoholics. They (I should say we) have a tendency to self-destruct.

No matter how much I drank (and, ordinarily, I didn't drink before a game), I always got to the ballpark on time and gave 100 percent. Or, at least, the 70 percent I had left in me.

But I had roomies who knew when to "say when," and they didn't always appreciate me. With the Yanks, I roomed briefly with Tom Morgan. That ended abruptly when I came in loaded and fell asleep in bed with a cigar in my hand. I wasn't totally stupid. My hand hovered unsteadily above a bedside ashtray. But a piece of memo paper in the tray ignited, a spark flew onto my pillow and burned a hole in it, and Tom woke up, put out the fire—he should have poured a pitcher of water on me, too—and moved out the next morning.

Well, I wasn't anywhere near as dangerous as heavy-hitting Red Sox first baseman Rudy York. His cigarettes torched so many beds that when people passed a hotel with smoke streaming out the window, they'd automatically remark, "Oh, I see Rudy's back in town." (Come to think of it, Rudy was Native American. Could he have been sending smoke signals to Cleveland?)

It took a while for the club secretary to find anyone willing to risk life and limb as my roomie—even among drinkers like one of my Yankee buddies who parked his car at high speed in the middle of a highway telephone pole at 6:00 A.M. He survived with barely a scratch, claiming he fell asleep at the wheel. The crazy Chamber of Commerce actually asked permission to put up a plaque on the pole naming names and commemorating the event while welcoming tourists to St. Pete, but the front office, suddenly publicity shy, vetoed the plan.

I exulted in running in the fast lane. Dating Rosemary Clooney. Playing golf with Perry Como. Welcomed warmly (when I wasn't in my belligerent drunk stage) by Frank Sinatra, Jerry Vale, Tommy and Jimmy Dorsey, Charlie Spivak, Eddie Fisher, and Nat King Cole. Even Jimmy Cagney.

I went out to dinner with my friend Jackie Miller, who owned the funeral parlor in Poughkeepsie where I slept in a spooky guest bedroom near the attic while running my baseball school for kids after the season. Sounds funny, I know, but it was a multipurpose funeral parlor. It served its primary purpose, of course. But for buddies in need of a place to crash, Jackie ran it like a hotel. He was also the biggest bookie in Poughkeepsie.

With coffins downstairs, leaves rustling eerily in the trees, and stairs in the old frame house squeaking, I thought I was in *Inner Sanctum.* (Here we go again, youngsters. That was a spooky radio show from my childhood that turned a 10-year-old's blood into ice water.)

It was the middle of the night, and a phone rang off the hook. What in the hell was going on? Finally I got down the stairs in my long johns and turned on the lights. The phone was still ringing, but I couldn't find it. It stopped and another started. I couldn't find that either. Finally I looked in the mahogany caskets. There were stiffs in two of them and telephones in three others. I didn't know where Jackie was, so I took the bet for him.

This was no joke. You can't make up stuff like this. Once Walt Dropo came to town to give the baseball clinic kids the benefit of his wisdom. Afterward I said, "Come on. I want you to meet Jackie." We go in the front door. No Jackie. We call and tour the place. No Jackie. "Maybe he's in the basement," I say. "Let's take a look." The lights are on. We troop down the stairs. There's Jackie doing a postmortem, a surgeon's saw in one hand, the top of a skull held high in the other. "Holy shit!" Walter exclaims. He turns and pounds back up the stairs. I follow. Looking pale, he turns to me. "That's awful. Don't ever do that to me again." I'm sympathetic, but it's hard not to laugh. "I don't think he felt it, Walter," I say.

Now back to dinner with Jackie. We were talking about Bill McCarran, who signed me for Boston, and the name of the director of Red Sox farm clubs, George "Specs" Toporcer, a .279 lifetime hitter with the 1920s Cardinals, came up. Jackie said, "Did you know he grew up in Hell's Kitchen [primer for young folks: once the toughest section on Manhattan's West Side, home to "The Dead End Kids" of the movie of the same name] with Jimmy Cagney? And, by the way, did you know Cagney has a country house about a mile from here?"

We were at a restaurant in Millerton, a rural area sprinkled with big stars, big money, and rich people's homes. Cagney, it seemed, had bought a little horse ranch in its wide-open spaces. I—feeling good after a good dinner and a few drinks, not three sheets to the wind, just barely one and a half—instantly said, "That so? Let's pay him a visit." Jackie sensibly replied: "You can't go there. They'll shoot you. Are you crazy?" I said, "Of course I am." We went.

We drove around 'til we found it. Good news. The gate was open. There was no guard on duty. I knocked on the door. Cagney, wearing a cardigan, opened it. I towered over him. I did a Bogart: "Hello, Sweetheart." He looked at me aghast. He backed up and looked around like he was about to go for the shotgun. What, he was thinking, is this nut doing in my doorway? I didn't mind getting shot but not in my pitching arm. "No, no, Mr. Cagney. Before you throw us out of here, I'm Mickey McDermott of the Red Sox, and Specs Toporcer, your old pal from Hell's Kitchen, was the guy who signed me."

Cagney's expression changed. "Mac," he said warmly. "Come on in." And we spent an hour happily talking baseball with Mr. Yankee Doodle Dandy. When we left I thanked him for not shooting me.

My boozy impulsiveness didn't always work out that neatly. When I was coaching with the Cal Angels (who, by the way, I did not help to win a World Series), Jilly Rizzo, who'd led a charmed business life since stopping a bullet for Frank Sinatra, opened a new restaurant in Palm Springs. I was staying at the Melody Ranch in town, and one of the bellhops there was a nice kid who worshipped Sinatra. "Did you ever meet him?" I asked one morning. "No? Well, I'll introduce you to him."

That was in the morning. At night I was loaded, but a promise was a promise, so I took the kid and taxied to Jilly's. I saw Frank at a table with three or four pretty ladies. I walked up behind Mr. Wonderful, bent over, and administered a friendly bear hug. He struggled to get loose. The band stopped playing. The bellhop, standing near the door, shouted, "Mac, look out behind you." I looked. Frank always traveled with three or four guys who packed iron. Their hands were in their inside pockets poised for action. It occurred to me that I would look better without holes than with them. I released Frank. He turned around, took in the whole scene, and said, "Jesus Christ, Mac, you almost got shot!"

That didn't stop me from introducing the bellhop. Later I told him how what happened reminded me of the story Shecky Green told in his act of what happened to him one night at the stage door after he told one too many jokes knocking Sinatra. "Three hoods were beating the shit out of me," said Green. "Frank saved my life. He said, 'That's enough.'"

You can't drink and drive the way I did without spending time in the slammer. Oh, celebrity buys you a break sometimes, but not forever. A state police car pulled me over crossing a bridge in New Hampshire. The trooper gave me a stern lecture, then asked for my driver's license. When I fumbled it out of my wallet, he looked up curiously and asked, "Are you related to Judge McDermott?"

"No," I said, "but I wanna be." The trooper was a Red Sox fan who remembered seeing me pitch many years earlier. "Sorry, Mr. McDermott," he said, "but I've gotta cuff you. Once you're stopped, it goes into the computer." Next stop was the slammer, where I chilled out overnight and faced Judge McDermott next morning.

"Please," I said, "don't let this hit the papers."

"Why?" he asked, toying with me. "Who are you?" I told him. "Mr. McDermott," he said, "I want to see you in my chambers."

Inside my hangover, I felt a flash of hope. I followed him eagerly. Nope. "Mr. McDermott," he said brusquely, "when you were a star for the Red Sox, you were my cousin. But now you're a common drunk. I'm running for Congress this year, and I don't need you." I guess not. But for the sake of the family tree, he let me off for overnight time served and a $200 fine.

I met a lot of judges. Some were tougher than others. One gave me a choice: 90 days in the cooler or 90 AA meetings in 90 days. It wasn't a tough choice to make, but I went to a lot of meetings hungover. I hated AA meetings. They work for a lot of people. I know that. Not for me they didn't. Partly, I guess, because I'm too much of a rebel for organized anything. Partly because I hated listening to guys telling how they knifed their mothers and stole the rent money or locked grandma in the cellar and hocked her silver. I almost wished I'd taken the jail time.

Betty sentenced me to rehab. Rehab? That was for alcoholics. I was just a binge drinker. But every fifth day when I was sober, Betty pounded the guilt thing into me. "You're getting worse and worse," she shrilled. "You gotta go to rehab!" I knew she was right. When my favorite bar in Phoenix opened in the morning, I was there to greet the guy with the keys. I sat there on that same stool all day until last call. I'd do that three or four days until I was too sick to drive. That day I'd be married to (yes, that again) the toilet bowl. Two sober weeks when I was too sick to look at the stuff would follow. Then the cycle would continue. Finally I checked myself into Good Sam in Phoenix.

After the first week, they threw me out. Too flip, as usual. I told a counselor, "Stop trying to get in my head. You ain't gonna find anything, so give up." Well, I told Betty, I lasted longer than that one day at Saint Joe's. But one more binge and another dozen lectures from Betty and I checked back in to do the last three weeks, swearing to behave. About three weeks into treatment, Betty came in for the required family therapy. The counselor looked at her, listened to her, and finally said, "Mrs. McDermott, you're an alcoholic." (Well sure. We had to stay drunk to tolerate each other.) Betty did not take kindly to his assessment. "I am not an alcoholic," she said alcoholically, and stormed out.

Most of the nurses were caring, but one ball buster there reminded me of my first mother-in-law. The patients, looking like a scene out of *One Flew Over the Cuckoo's Nest*, lined up for a urine test one morning, and I was late. She got on me: "Every time I look at you, you're up to something. You disappear at night, and I don't know where you are. Now let's have that urine, and no nonsense!" I came back with the urine cup a few minutes later. "Here's your damn urine test," I said, extending the cup. "Ugh!" she said, drawing back. "Don't give me that filthy thing. Put it on the counter."

"Oh, come off it," I said, "it's not filthy." I threw my head back and emptied the cup. "Are you crazy? How can you do that?" she demanded. I exited laughing. One of the nurses followed me. "I know what you did," she accused. "The oldest trick in the book. You poured apple juice from the fridge." I replied, "No comment."

Next stop, the staff shrink. "Maurice," he said. He was a Frenchman and liked the sound of my name. "Maurice, you know exactly what you do."

"What do you mean?"

"You know what I mean." His report on me read, "His ego will not permit him to admit he is an alcoholic." In French or English, he was right about that. And I didn't like the next stage when I saw it up close—the man who came in seeing cockroaches, snakes, and frogs everywhere he looked, including his bed. I was afraid they'd move from his bed to mine.

"Let me out of here," I said. I went in an alcoholic, and I came out an alcoholic. I still wasn't ready to stop drinking.

I wished that I could drink like the DiMaggios. Dom and Joe fit the true definition of social drinkers—a couple of glasses of Chianti and they'd toddle off to bed. Give me two drinks and I was there for four days. The funny thing was that I might be miserable, but I never got to the point where I fell into depression. Puzzled drinking buddies would wonder, "Don't you ever get depressed when you drink?" Hell, no. The only depressing part was the headache.

Oh, once in a while I'd think about what a mess I'd made of my life and the gift from God I'd thrown away. But where Eddie Fishcakes was depressed about stardom gone and money gone with it, I was lucky—anyway, happy-go-lucky. I enjoyed people. Jail's supposed to make you think twice. I even had fun with the Mexicans in the Durango jail—about which more shortly.

This does not mean I was consistently fun to be around. Walt Dropo, who had reason to know because he was on the wagon when I was drunk, tells me I was a friendly, likable person until the fourth or fifth drink flipped a switch in my brain and I became, first, an obnoxious bore and, second, downright cantankerous. I'd start singing, and I'd be ready to fight anyone who said, "You've had enough." Or, even worse, "too much." In fact, I was probably my father all over again—a good-hearted guy who changed into a pugnacious brawler the minute those alcohol fumes filled his tank.

I kept right on wisecracking about my bad habits. When I played with Camilo Pascual in Mexico, he shook his head. "Meekey," he said, "you shoulda been in the Hall of Fame four times. But, no. You go like this: 'Boom-a-la-boom-bala-boom!'" (English translation: "You played games instead of baseball.") "But always in tempo," I retorted. "Right, Camilo?"

At a bar, a baseball buddy would say, "A lot of guys drink to get rid of their inhibitions. So Mickey, why do you drink? You're already nuts. You never had an inhibition in your life." Jimmy Piersall agrees. A few years ago when he was working as an outfield coach for the Cubs in spring training, I handed him a ball and asked him to autograph it for my collection (eBay, here I come!). He obliged with, "Dear Mickey: And they call me crazy!"

I blamed my troubles on destiny and the Big Dipper. "You are who you are," I'd pontificate from the bar stool. "Guys like Mantle and Sinatra, they're born stars. God sits up there and says, 'You, you, and you—go get tuxedos.' The rest of us? We just slog along."

I lost my identity and took on a new one. I became a character actor— the dumb left-handed drunk. I was on a train going the wrong way, and I didn't know how to get off. That was serious, but being serious hurt too much, so I did funny. Turned everything into a joke on me. The clown laughing on the outside and hating what's happening to him on the inside.

There's no such thing as a good drunk, and I don't condone drinking. Mine or anyone else's. But the drinks for a major leaguer were always on the house, and the broads were, too. In the beginning, I wanted to work hard at my trade, wanted to be the best since Babe Ruth. Slowly but surely, so slowly I didn't even notice, I settled for instant gratification.

Distant goals like the Hall of Fame grew more distant and meant less to me than sitting ringside at a Sinatra performance in Vegas or Atlantic City. Or singing on a bandstand. But succeeding in show business without really trying doesn't happen. So I wisecracked about that, too. "I gave up singing," I told my pals, "when I got sober and heard myself." But Ted Williams was wrong. I had plenty of self-discipline. I could always go that extra mile to find a bar. He never said it, but we both knew it—slowly but surely I lost my fastball in a bottle of Scotch.

In my life after baseball I could have gotten any number of good jobs on my own or through Tino. With a baseball name, everyone wants to hire you. But who wants to trust a drunk? Only Billy Martin. In the winter of '89, he passed through Phoenix, and we got together. "I'm going down to see Steinbrenner," he said, "and I'm gonna get my job back as manager. I want you in the booth. You have a great voice and you're funny. You'll be a great color guy." Ooh, McDermott commenting on baseball games. And on TV. That meant big paydays. I liked the sound of that.

I was ready to sing, "Happy Days Are Here Again," but I sang too soon. Some bad news hit me hard: Billy Martin was a passenger in a truck that slid on a patch of hidden ice and skidded into a tree in his yard. At only 61 years old, Billy died instantly. I'd been sober for a year. I went back to drinking.

Tino Barzie said he was nervous every time I showed up in Vegas, afraid that it would be the same old story. He gave me an RFB card—room, food, and beverages—the kind reserved for high rollers. It was the beverages he worried about, and what was going to happen next. What happened was worse than a fight at the bar, of which there were several. I was in the Riviera's nightclub one night, and Paul Anka was doing his thing, following some singing with nostalgia talk and a film clip. I got impatient. "Stop the home movies and sing, you Arab bastard," I shouted from where I was sitting on a beverage cart in the back. Two security guards hurriedly surrounded me. "Sir," one said politely, "we have to take you to your room."

"You can't," I retorted. "I don't have a room." I did. In fact, I had a suite. It was just my routine wise-guy retort. "You've got a room now," the guards said as they hustled me out, destination Las Vegas drunk tank. Rudy Guerrero, the captain, stopped them. "That's Mickey McDermott," he said, "leave him alone." They left me alone all right. In my suite to sleep it off. They probably posted a guard outside until they heard my snoring. (Oh, and Mr. Anka, this seems as good a time as any to apologize for that stupid interruption.)

There was no easy way out for me at the Durango County Jail. A judge had decided that wearing a World Series ring no longer automatically forgave my growing collection of DWI summonses. The sentence was 60 days. Sixty days with machete murderers, cop killers, felonious assaulters? Fortunately, they kept them in a separate pod. There was another for women. Mine was mostly for drunk drivers.

The boozers were in a work program—released every day under guard to saw logs, prune palm trees, stuff like that. Me, climb palm trees? No way. They're not making a monkey out of me. Fortune smiled. "Meekey," the guards asked, "you got baseball cards for my keeds?" I obliged, and they obliged. No palm trees. Instead I was given a yellow shirt and declared a "house mouse." That meant no work details, not even mopping floors (though that might have taught me a little humility), and, in fact, Betty could pick me up at 6:00 A.M. and redeliver me at 6:00 P.M.

In the evenings, for the first time in years, I read a lot. (It had been a while—probably since the invention of TV. But it turned out to be like getting back on a bicycle after you fall off. I still knew how to do it.) No Shakespeare. Mickey Spillane. And no Beauty Rest mattresses or Dux Beds. I had a lower bunk in the tiny cubicle I shared, and the bed must have had automobile springs. The first time I sat down, I bounced up and banged my head on the bed above mine.

It was the original cowboy jail, renovated sometime in the 20th century, and I kept picturing good old Gene Autry riding intrepidly to the rescue of his old Cal Angels coach, tying a lasso to a barred window, and yanking out the bars to set me free. Then I realized he was more likely to be inside the tank with me.

Anything less would have been un-American, so they let me out to play in the annual pre–spring training Old Timers' Game at the San Francisco Giants camp at Scottsdale. "Of course, we'll have to cuff you for the trip," my guard warned. He didn't warn me that I'd arrive at the same time as some of the other players. The fact that I was wearing handcuffs as I walked to the clubhouse was not lost on them. "Geez, McDermott," they wanted to know, "what did you do now?" Where were their manners? What kind of embarrassing question was that? I did my best to strike out the side.

Most of the prisoners in my section were Mexicans. Nobody remembered me from the Reynosa Broncos, and, happily, none of them had seen my last game at Mexico City. Anyway they had to be nice to someone who'd pitched in the Mexican League. I was frisked every night when I returned, so the head south-of-the-border honcho instructed me on how to smuggle treats back in. "Meekey," he explained, "they not allow to touch you in you private parts" (actually, he may have used a more colorful term), "so you can hide candy bars in your jockey shorts."

Cheerfully following his professional advice, I stuffed three of Mr. Hershey's best in my underwear and granulated coffee in a bag inside my socks. Beeg meestake. It was a 60- or 70-yard walk from the guard post to Hotel Durango, and the 110-degree heat was well beyond the melting point of both the chocolate and coffee. Walking became progressively stickier.

The guard frisked me, my legs spread, my hands against the wall. Suddenly he exclaimed, "What the hell!" My contraband had melted, leaked down my leg, and formed a sticky brown puddle on the asphalt below. He was a good guy. "Mickey," he said, "who told you to do this?" I was no stoolie. "It was my idea," I said. "I was sneaking snacks in, and now I've got chocolate nuts."

At my bunk, I could hardly tear my socks off. They were now ready to be featured as Starbucks' acrylic mocha special of the day. But I didn't get solitary. The guards wanted me around for morale purposes. Every time they saw me, they burst out laughing. I made inconspicuous Xs on the wall behind my bed to count my remaining time in stir. (Jimmy Cagney would've been proud of me.) And finally, with a clanking of keys and an echoing of boots in long, empty corridors (well, not really), they said, "Mickey, you're outta here!" And I was.

My drinking—which could not be cured by a mere 60 days of penal servitude—continued to make me everybody's pain in the ass. One night my buddy Paul Gleason came home to his Hollywood apartment after a long, hot day of wearing armor while filming *Camelot* to find the door to his apartment off its hinges and flat on the floor. Pretty audacious criminals, thought Paul. He peered cautiously around the corner. There I was, the Black Knight, lying on his couch, drinking his beer, watching his large-screen TV. "Well," I explained, "the door was locked."

Hotel Barzie in Beverly Hills was another port during my alcoholic storms. Tino not only gave me free room and board, he paid me to leave. Well, not exactly, but he never let me out the door with an empty billfold. And on weekends when I showed up at his house, drank his liquor, and passed out on his couch, he'd carry me—220 pounds of dead weight—up the stairs to a guest room. One night I woke up halfway up the stairs feeling as refreshed as if I'd just completed a six-month vacation. Or as though I were six months pregnant. "Tino," he swears I asked him, "got any doughnuts and pickles in the house?"

When I ran out of friends willing to put up with me on the West Coast, I headed east. I phoned Walt Dropo. I knew he'd understand because he'd been where I was, although not financially. When he left first base behind, he opened an insurance brokerage in Boston, and, being a college graduate and very intelligent guy with a famous baseball name and lots of acquaintances, he did very well. I mean, how could you say no to a guy that big?

Walter and I had spent a lot of time together and played a lot of night games having nothing to do with baseball. I don't recall either of us ever being available as a fourth for bridge, but we were always ready for a fifth. One day in Boston, he misstepped and toppled down the escalator at Filene's Department Store. Apparently it's true that the bigger you are the harder you fall, because Moose's skull confirmed that—step by bloody step, all the way down to Filene's Basement. By the time he hit bottom, the bloodshed included a large clot on his brain. The surgeon who operated was not optimistic, but this Moose was tough. He pulled through, recovered fully, and, lesson learned, hasn't chug-a-lugged anything stronger than orange juice in the 20 years since. At this point, to be sure you don't think this book has an unhappy ending with me dying of cirrhosis of the liver or something, I guess I should confess to 11 years of sobriety of my own. And the funny thing is, when my Stevie and I (did I forget to tell you I'm on my fourth and best wife?) go out for a beer, I can't finish mine.

Moose had hit bottom hard, and I would not have a soft landing either, but I still had a way to go. Now I phoned Walter: "Betty threw me out," I said. "Can I spend a weekend with you? After that, I'll go back to Poughkeepsie."

"Mac," he said, "what's a friend for? I'm living alone. I've got no obligations. Stay as long as you like."

Oops. Wrong thing to say. We'd been roomies in the bush leagues. Now he would let me share his swanky terraced apartment overlooking Boston Harbor with a choice view of Fenway Park as well. It was a far cry from the series of dingy fleabag hotels we'd shared traveling for Scranton.

I was still drinking. He was faithfully attending AA meetings and as dry as a martini. No, make that the Gobi Desert. After four months, Red Sox secretary Mary Trenk called me on a mission of mercy. "Mickey," she began, "there's no easy way to say this."

"It's OK, Mary," I said. "I understand. The Red Sox aren't picking up my option next season. That's OK. They haven't picked it up for 20 years."

"Worse than that," she said. "It's Walter. He loves you too much to say anything, but the fact is you're driving him nuts. You gotta get out of there."

"Mary," I said, "are you sure? How do you know this?"

"I heard it from a guy who goes to the same AA meetings. Moose is saying, 'I don't know what to do. My buddy, Mickey, has found bottles of booze in the apartment I didn't even know I hid. I don't know what to tell him. All I know is if this keeps up, I'm gonna start drinking again.'"

I got up, shaved, dressed, and got ready to give Moose some good news for a change: "I understand, pally. No hard feelings. I'm leaving."

Before I could speak, he said, "Come on out on the terrace."

We went out together and leaned against the parapet, 32 floors above the street and with a great view of the diamond we'd had so much fun on and where we'd made a kind of history together.

"Mickey," he said, "do you see the scoreboard down there? I can't quite make it out. What does it say?"

I looked. I laughed. I couldn't believe my eyes. To the right of the scoreboard was a billboard for some kind of cereal. To the left of the scoreboard was a billboard for a soft drink. And between them on the scoreboard just three words: "Mickey, go home."

A silly grin brightened Walter's face. "I didn't know how to tell you, roomie," he said apologetically. "Those three little words cost me $166.67 apiece."

"Moose," I said, grinning back while doing the arithmetic, "you wasted your $500. I already decided to leave tomorrow morning." We both broke up. In fact, we were in such a good mood, I almost went to an AA meeting with him. Almost.

Several months later, I read a troubling story about Don Bessent, a pretty good Dodgers pitcher who fed me the fastball that gave me my 1.000 batting average in the '56 Yanks-Dodgers World Series. Poor Don had been found slumped behind the wheel of his car outside a crumby hamburger joint. Basically, the cause of his death was acute alcoholism.

You'd have thought that would have given me pause. It did. I paused that night in my drinking to tip my glass in a farewell toast to Don Bessent.

CHAPTER 23

Hitting the Jackpot

A Very Sobering Experience

I woke up feeling like a sponge in week-old dishwater thinking, what in the hell is wrong with me? The sheets beneath me were soaked in warm gritty sweat. But the sweat on my body was as cold as though I'd stepped out of a steam room into a butcher's freezer.

Get yourself a glass of water, I thought. Head spinning, I climbed shakily out of bed, walked unsteadily to the bathroom, and filled a toothbrush glass. Clean, dirty—I didn't care. As I raised it to my lips, it slipped from fingers that seemed oddly disconnected from my arm. If the glass had been a baseball, it would have been a balk.

"Uh-oh," I said aloud, "I'm in big trouble."

Being alone was part of the trouble. I remembered Betty slamming the front door as she left for our cabin at Pine Top three days earlier. And I remembered my wiseacre line as she exited: "Don't forget to take the dogs."

Geez, why did I let her go? We'd been together for 23 years, finally made it legal 2 years ago, and all of a sudden she was as possessive as a teen with her first beau, suspicious of every woman I talked to. And I talked—mostly just loud genial bar talk—to a lot of them.

She'd hired a P.I. to follow me around. It didn't take a genius to spot her—a woman driver wearing a different wig each day in the same dirty green sedan, tailing me all week long every which way I turned. Oh, I had fun turning. I took her up winding mountain roads and for long rides on the interstate, whistling cheerfully, listening to country music, and hoping my wife was paying her by the mile. Once I took her through a car wash. When she came out I was waiting for her and told her off. Not politely.

But where was Betty now that I needed her? Sure, I'd done my share and more of cussing and shouting during the battle of Phoenix, but I'm no grudge holder. Ten minutes after she left, I'd forgotten and forgiven. As far as I was concerned, she was welcome back home anytime.

That's when her key turned in the lock. "Thank God," I said when she entered the bedroom, "am I ever glad to see you. Where the hell have you been?"

"You know where I've been. Up at the cabin. I heard on the radio there was a blizzard on the way, and I knew if it was anything like last year's, I'd be stuck up there at 10,000 feet for . . ." She stopped in midsentence. "Hey, you look awful. Whiter than the sheets. What's wrong?"

"What's wrong is I think I'm having a heart attack. In fact I know I am. I was just about to call 911. You gotta get me to Good Sam right away."

The ER at Good Samaritan was like the ER on *ER*, only busier, and no George Clooney. Glassy-eyed patients stacked up like jets waiting to land at O'Hare. "Hey," I told the triage nurse when she finally got around to me, "I have baseball insurance, and it pays for everything. I'm dying here. Either call a cardiologist or call me a funeral director."

One look at my graveyard pallor and she got an EKG started and paged Dr. Ali Askari, the chief of Good Sam's cardiac surgery team. Luckily he was on call and right there in the hospital. He checked the EKG. He checked me over. Then he delivered the no-frills news.

"Meekey, you are in trouble, my boy. You have badly diseased heart."

"Give it to me straight, Doc. How bad?"

"I tell you truth, my boy. Most likely you need triple bypass. I operate on you tomorrow morning. You have a 30-70 chance. But do not worry. I will do everything I can."

I couldn't see it from where I was lying down, but a 300-watt bulb lit up in Betty's head. The following morning, she walked into my room at 6:00 A.M.—after the nurse had shot me up with Valium but before the surgical team started to gather. I looked up. I was woozy, but I was pleased to see her. After that big fight we had, she could've stayed home watching Regis and Kathie Lee. But wait a minute. Who was this stocky babe with glasses who waltzed in behind her? The wig looked familiar. Sonovabitch. It was her private eye.

"Welcome to Chicago Hope," I growled. "Who's your friend and what's this all about?"

"Mrs. Bradley," she said, shoving a stack of papers in front of me. "She's our witness. Sign here."

"Ain't love grand!" I said. "I'm dying and you want me to sign papers in triplicate?" Then I caught sight of the three little words on top: "Power of Attorney."

I shoved the papers away. "This wouldn't by any chance have something to do with the $7 million we won in the Arizona lottery, would it? No way, lady. Get out of here before I get out of bed and throw you out!"

"Mickey, be reasonable. You could die on the table."

"I'm not gonna die, and you're not getting my signature. Get out of my room and get out of my life." I fell back on my pillow exhausted. The words "Sign! Sign! Sign!" bounced like a slow ground ball in my head. Betty's face slowly changed to my long-dead-and-buried father's face. There he was with that little bottle of ink eradicator in his hand, cheerfully altering the date on my birth certificate from 1929 to 1928 so he could pick up that $5,000 signing bonus from the Red Sox. I grinned at the memory of the beer truck pulling up to our front door and unloading case after case of beer for stacking in our cellar. Then the Valium took over, and I was out of there.

I woke up in the ICU surrounded by doctors and nurses. My heart was racing like I had to pitch to Joe DiMaggio in triplicate. "Meekey, my boy," Askari was saying, "your heart stops twice during surgery, while I have it outside your body. To start up again we have to shock with defibrillator. Now it is running wild—sometimes 5 beats, sometimes 250. So far I have not find right medicine to stabilize. But I think tomorrow I have it for you. Meanwhile we must hit you again with defibrillator—750 volts. Is only way to keep you alive."

I saw a machine as big as a piano with the med tech's finger on the juice button. I braced myself. An intern took my hand to reassure me. "It's going to be fine," he said. At that moment the tech hit the button. Prematurely. I was strapped down. The intern wasn't. I was a perfect conductor. With all that alcohol in my system, probably better than most. The jolt passed through my body into his. He flew through the air like a Chinese acrobat and hit the wall. He was knocked out. Askari fired the technician on the spot. My heart slowed down to a manageable 150. Everybody was happy except the technician and the intern.

Next day Askari had the medication he'd been hoping for. A little 500 mg tablet of Amocordorone kept my foolish heart stable until the following morning. They reopened my chest and Askari's partner, Dr. Shradar, my electrician-cardiologist, inserted a defibrillator. Askari hit a home run—30-70 adds up to 100 percent. I asked him how I beat the odds. He told me my positive attitude helped. That and having an athlete's body. I went home a week later wired like a General Electric kitchen. Going through airport X-ray machines is no longer an option, and, for reasons I don't quite get (could it be my allergic reaction to hard work?), I'm warned to give a wide berth to heavy construction machinery. As I walk by, TV sets turn off and women's vibrators turn on.

It's always been nice having a lifetime gold pass (admit two) to any major league ballpark as a baseball pension perk. (Of course, you have to find an empty seat, and it's useless for All-Star Games and the World Series, which is kind of annoying.) Now, as I look at medical bills totaling $1.3 million for the past eight years, I suddenly appreciate my unlimited baseball retiree health insurance. When I ask Askari, "What does the poor guy without health insurance do?" the answer is, "He doesn't. He dies." Come on, Mr. President, we gotta do something about that. (While you're at it, do something about old-timer pensions.)

Insurance or not, it was a close call. "Your heart stopped twice?" guys ask. "That's like a near-death experience, right? So tell me. Did you hover over the operating table like they say, or enter a bright white tunnel?"

"No, a dim black one," I tell them. "And at the end of it waving to me to come on in, there's Billy Martin and a guy in a red suit with a tail and a pitchfork. 'Hell no, Billy,' I told him. 'I'm not going in there with all those umpires!' "

Oh, yes. That winning ticket on the Arizona lottery that came up for discussion in my hospital room. "Where'd that come from?" you ask. Well, either somebody up there likes me, or the heavenly computer spit out the wrong McDermott. I'll tell you one thing. When it happened, it was as big a surprise to me as it is to you.

I was 63 years old. My baseball days were long over, and there didn't seem much point in whatever days and years I had left. For the first time in my life, happy-go-lucky McDermott was actually depressed. And, as usual, after three days on a bar stool, my insides were in ugly unanimous agreement that they wanted to get on the outside ASAP. The old porcelain love affair.

Two weeks earlier, being briefly sober and the fridge being empty, I had gone out to buy some luncheon meat for a sandwich. "If there's anything left over," Betty ordered, "buy a ticket. The lottery hit $23 million this week." I did, and we came so close it hurt. Four numbers out of six. The payoff? A big $55.

I looked at the bright side. "It's an omen," I said. "Take what we won and buy 55 tickets." She bought five tickets at a Circle K picking random numbers, and kept the change.

Another week went by. I was in bed as sick as a kennel of dogs. I'd been sitting on a bar stool at Betty's brother's place, Harvey's Wineburger (where did they dig up a name like that?), for two days. Betty burst in. If you'd like to write a play, here's the dialogue:

Scene One: The McDermott Bedroom

Betty: Wake up, you drunken Irishman. Get out of bed.

Me: Don't bother me. I'm sick. Give me a cup of coffee and a cigarette.

Betty: You better sit down. I've got something to tell you.

Me: I'm lying down. Isn't that good enough? What did I do now? Run over the dog?

Betty: You didn't do anything, but I did. I just hit the lottery. The good news is the pot is up to $28 million. The bad news is three other people won, too. So I only won $7 million.

Me: Only! Forget the other $21 million. You're the most beautiful broad I ever met. I feel better already. Let's go to the Lincoln-Mercury dealer.

Scene 2: The Showroom

Betty: This is the one I want. You want that Lincoln Continental? I'll buy it for you.

Me: What do you mean, *you'll* buy it? It's my money, too.

Betty: No way. You'd only drink it. It's all mine. I have the ticket and I bought it. The Lincoln is a gift. Out of the goodness of my heart.

Me: Betty, you're not only the most beautiful broad I ever met, you're the dumbest. Yes, it would've been a gift. But you made the biggest mistake of your life that night you said, "I'm tired of being your girlfriend for 23 years. I want to get married." That did it. Haven't you ever heard of community property? It's the law in Arizona. Everything we own is half yours, half mine. Especially lottery jackpots.

With the help of a friendly lawyer, we worked things out. Betty sold her tiny stucco house under the airport's jet traffic pattern, and we bought a five-bedroom dream house in Scottsdale with a pool and a circular drive-way. She quit her secretarial job and gave her brother $50,000. For reasons that escape me, she bought some land outside Las Vegas near a town called Parhump where all the brothels are. I gave my '78 Cadillac to the bar-tender who'd been pouring me free drinks for years, bought a $15,000 membership in the country club, and took up golf. That way people could stop calling me an old reprobate and start calling me an eccentric mil-lionaire. Which, of course, would allow me to keep on drinking.

But what took so long? Why couldn't God have given me all this money at age 35 and spared me all that aggravation? Then I realized I would have been broke at 36.

In fact, for the next three weeks I was well on my way to being just that. I went out and raised hell, drinking and handing out money like . . . well, like I'd won the lottery. One night I got drunk at the Elk's Club. When I got up and said, "Well folks, time for the old millionaire to go home," and wobbled toward the door, my pals said, "Mickey, we'll take you. Don't drive that damn car."

Who listens to good advice? Not me. I slipped behind the wheel, con-centrated fiercely, and managed to stab the key into the ignition. I drove a couple of wavy blocks to a four-way light and took a left in front of a car with—how would I know?—the right of way. Crash! He hit me in the tail, and I slumped back wearily in my seat, unhurt but suddenly wide awake, waiting for the cops to come.

The man in brown scanned my license, spotted my World Series ring, and asked, "McDermott the baseball player?" I nodded. He sniffed the air and said, "Geez, no need to Breathalyze you," and walked back to the other driver. "You alright?" he asked. The driver said yes. "You're sure? No injuries?" The driver said he was sure. The cop put that in the report and came back to me.

"You're a lucky man," he said. "Believe it or not, you hit a guy who's already wearing a neck brace, and he says he's OK. But when I called it in, your prior DWIs hit the computer. Sorry, but I'm gonna have to run you in." I wasn't mad at the cop. He was a good guy. If he hadn't put the other driver's statement in his report, I could have been sued for every dollar I won.

The judge was sorry, too. "Mickey," he said, "I've got to give you time, or they'll hang me from the nearest tree." And that's how (you oughtta remember—it was in the last chapter) I got my 60-day vacation at the Durango County Jail. Good thing, too. It gave me no way to drink and plenty of time to think.

Actually, the light went on at the station house while they were booking me: "Pay attention. Somebody upstairs is trying to tell you something." Finally, I listened up. And I stood there with the cuffs on thinking what if I'd killed that guy or he'd killed me? The AA meetings I resented having to go to hadn't worked for me, but one message, repeated loud and clear at every meeting, had stuck somewhere in that thick head of mine: appeal to your higher power, and you will have a spiritual awakening.

That's when I started getting down on my knees every night and praying: "God, get me out of this and I'll never take another drink." He did and I haven't. It's been a decade-plus since the last one, and I couldn't care less if I never have another.

Reactions to my jubilant phone calls to friends about my winning the lottery were many and varied. When I broke the news to Tino Barzie, I heard the receiver fall to the floor, followed by a long silence. Had the shock been too much for his heart? Finally Tino spoke: "Thank you, God. Thank you. I'm off the hook at last." I wanted to pay back all the money he'd given me over the years. He refused to accept a cent.

When I proudly handed Ted Williams a long-overdue check for $2,000 (he'd only lent me $200, but it was 30 years later and I figured he deserved the interest), he simply tore it up. "Geez, Theodore," I said, "you shouldn't have done that. It's valuable. It's got my autograph." Ted grinned. "Bush," he said, "you'll never change." Well, now I didn't want to.

Whitey Ford asked Mickey Mantle at the next Old Timers' Game, "Did you hear what happened to McDermott?" Said Mickey, "Hell, no.

What'd he do now?" When Whitey told him I'd won seven mil, Mickey sniffed disdainfully. "Goddamn," he said, "I owe more than that."

Every silver lining has a cloud. Eleven months later, Betty was diagnosed with breast cancer. She was tough. She hung in there for five years, but it finally got her. I hadn't been drinking. It seemed like a good idea to give her less trouble than I had in the past, and besides, I'd been warned that booze and defibrillators don't mix. I learned that lesson one night out drinking with Dropo (well, I was drinking, he was driving) when my alarm went off four times. By the time I got to the ER, the doctor couldn't understand how I was still alive.

I have to learn every lesson at least twice, and the second time was driving along in Vegas with my daughter and my grandson. When my heart accelerates, usually responding to a recent bender, the defibrillator gives the heart a 750-volt whack to normalize it. So I'm driving merrily along, and suddenly my built-in electric chair fires a lightning bolt.

I should have paid more attention to that public service announcement. I was not wearing my seat belt. I arched upward and—splat—my head hit the car roof, nearly turning it into a convertible. I sagged back down in my seat. I managed to steer to the side of the road. Michelle was hysterical. From the backseat I heard Daniel's voice: "Good trick, Grandpa! Do it again!" Later I resolved to wear a helmet when driving.

I was so groggy I forgot I had a phone in the car. "Michelle," I groaned, "drive me to a gas station and call 911." Within minutes the medics arrived and an injection calmed my heart down from its runaway 220 beats per minute, which was very close to "*Sayonara*, folks." They raced me to the nearest hospital where a cardiologist heard me out, checked me out, and then said, "They saved your life in Phoenix, but in view of what just happened it makes sense to insert a pacemaker, too." He proceeded to do that.

Everything was swell until a year or so ago in Cancun, Mexico, when a vacation was over and I was ready to go home. I bent over packing my suitcase. A pacemaker wire snapped. That sent a false alarm to my defibrillator, which proved how well it works by jolting me with another friendly 750 Vs. This was totally unexpected. Also rude. I almost did a 2½ gainer into the swimming pool 30 feet below. (Ooh, what a lawsuit my dead body would have had!) When I pulled myself together, I wondered if I'd die in the airplane or make it home.

I didn't, and I did. They replaced the pacemaker, and six months later they gave me the latest and coolest: the Burger King defibrillator-pacemaker combo, hold the fries. It's been miniaturized and, oh, happy miracle of modern medicine, it's the size of a silver dollar now instead of a paperback. The doctor struggled threading the wire through a vein to my heart. I had the pleasure of seeing and feeling it all because this procedure can't be performed under anesthesia. I was uncomfortable. "What's taking so long?" I asked. "It's all that pitching you did," he told me, sounding surprised. "Your musculature is still quite solid." I explained that my specialty, wild pitches, requires great strength. He said, "Pretty good for an old man." I chose to take that as a compliment.

As I lay there wondering if he would be finished by dinnertime, I figured out why a scoundrel like me was awarded as many lives as a cat. They don't want me down *there*. They sure don't want me up *there*. They want me right here making everybody miserable. And, hey, I need to stay here. Every January 27, I get another fat check from the state of Arizona. And they've still got another seven or eight payments to go.

CHAPTER 24

No Regrets (Almost)

Baseball's Designated Leprechaun Sums Up

Well, after 23 chapters, we both know for sure I'll never be a baseball icon ("something universally admired," says the Random House dictionary), but maybe a bunch of talented kids coming up can learn and benefit from the McDermott Follies of 1928 to 2000-and-something. And that, at least, is something to be proud of.

Here's the thing. Everything came easy. Too easy.

People told me I had a million-dollar arm. (With a good agent, that would be 10 million today. Even if I'd had a losing record—which I didn't.) A million-dollar arm, and not two cents worth of common sense. The problem, I guess, is that my arm was connected to the wrong guy. Guys who made baseball their craft and pitching a science and an art—guys like Sandy Koufax, Whitey Ford, Mel Parnell, Warren Spahn, Nolan Ryan, Tom Seaver—knew what to do with their million-dollar arms. I bent mine sitting on bar stools, leaning on bars. What the good Lord graciously gave me, I carelessly threw away.

So what went wrong? By now, you know as much about it as I do. I could blame my old man. I could say my lack of self-discipline came from too much rigid discipline when I was a kid. But that would be a cop-out. And, sober—which he was most of the time—he was one of the finest men who ever drew a breath.

I could blame it on early injury. I could say Steve O'Neill shouldn't have let me stay in for 17 innings against the White Sox and 16 innings a week later against the Indians. Chances are those were the games that led to that fatal "pop" in my shoulder that made me take myself out of a game against Philadelphia. But I wanted to stay in there. I was loving it. Every pitch. Every moment of proving I was Superjock. And I actually enjoyed Birdie Tebbetts, managing the other team, standing on the dugout steps calling out, "210 pitches, Morris . . . 211 pitches, Morris." Unfortunately, it was all downhill without brakes from there.

But any pitcher in baseball is just three pitches away from greatness. He needs the pitch he can count on at 2–0, at 3–0, and at 3–2. The smart ones, when they lose something off their fastball, compensate. They fill their bag with surprises—a split-finger, a knuckler, a change-up. But do you fill up that bag of tricks overnight? Hell, no. You've got to work at it. With me, it was always tomorrow. And when tomorrow came, it was the day after that. Usually because of the night before, and because I never learned the simple secret of sobriety: don't take that first drink.

I have no regrets. Well, almost none. I regret the drinking. I sure don't recommend it. I never really needed a drink to have fun. Life was fun. I have no doubt I could have had just as good a time on a glass of root beer with a cup of coffee chaser.

The thing is—and serious, hard-working people will see this as a bad thing—I never grew up. I didn't stay small and adorable like Peter Pan; I got tall and old. So call it a case of arrested development if you must, but there's still a rambunctious 12-year-old inside of me, and he's probably down on his knees right this minute chuckling to beat hell while he attempts to give the whole darned world a hotfoot.

I know. By dress-for-success, open-a-401K, cut-up-your-credit-cards, and take-out-plenty-of-life-insurance standards, my life's been a fiasco. But it sure hasn't been boring. A lot of my life's been foolish, but it's been mighty interesting. A couple of years ago, Stevie and I had dinner in Sarasota with one of my oldest friends, Dick Dombro, and his wife, Mary Ann. We sat there for three hours and, except for closing it on an occasional forkful of pasta, I didn't shut my big storytelling, reminiscing mouth once. Finally, Mary Ann, who'd been laughing her buns off all that time while looking a bit dubious, said challengingly, "Mickey, there is no way all those things could have happened to you!" I said, "But there's no way I could make this stuff up either." Case dismissed.

Dick reminded me of the time our Rat Pack—there were 13 of us, and he and I are the only ones left—drove from Sarasota to Miami to catch Johnny Ray at the old Clover Club. "All the way," Dick said, "you kept warning us not to tell anybody who you were. You said they'd pester you, want your autograph, even ask you to sing. We walked in and you announced loud enough for the whole room to hear you: 'I'm Mickey McDermott and I pitch for the Red Sox.'" Well, it got us a ringside table.

There you go. I wanted to be in show business as much as I wanted to play baseball. For one thing, that's where all the women were. For another, as a pitcher I was onstage only one day out of four or five, and now and then I got booed. At Steuben's Vienna Room I got applauded every night.

The grass is always greener on the other side of the street because you can't see the weeds. So while I wanted to be them, a lot of the showbiz people I met wanted to be me. Nat King Cole told me, "You want to be a singer. I want to be a ballplayer. Let's trade." And Jimmy Piersall was playing golf with actor Kirk Douglas one afternoon when Sandy Koufax, golfing behind their twosome, hit a drive that landed at Kirk's feet. When Koufax came up to apologize, Douglas said, "Sandy, it's great to meet you. I've got one of your autographed balls in my study." Replied Koufax, "Wonderful to finally meet you, too, Kirk. I've got one of your movie swords in my basement rec room."

Almost 20 years after I pitched my last pitch in a for-real game, I bumped into Ted Williams at a Ted Williams Museum celebrity golf tournament. (Yeah, I was still a celebrity. The older you get, the more they forget the days you got knocked out and remember the games you won. A lot of people even say, "Oh, yeah, Mickey McDermott. Aren't you in the Hall of Fame?" I wish.) "Bush," Ted said, after we'd reminisced a bit about our Red Sox years and which of our pals had died lately, "how old are you?"

"Fifty, Ted."

He slapped me on the back enthusiastically. "Fifty? Ferchrissakes. I never thought you'd make it to forty."

Well, there were nights and mornings after the nights before when I didn't think so either. And yet, here I am—74. And Ted, who—compared to me anyway—lived the life of Saint Peter, is dead. Gone but not forgotten. And he'll be remembered long after Maurice McDermott is dead, gone, and just another set of journeyman statistics in David Neft's *Baseball Encyclopedia*.

So why didn't I do right? You tell me. A psychologist friend of mine has a theory. She says sometimes the son doesn't want to outshine the father, so his subconscious does pratfalls until bright, shiny success morphs into tattletale-gray failure. Instead of the brass ring, the son winds up on the sidewalk with a tin cup. Possible. Anything's possible. But that's a cop-out, too.

I've experienced success. I've had failure. With a little luck and a lot less liquor, I could have made the Hall of Fame. Instead, I spent a lot of boozy years in my personal Hall of Shame. And if they ever build a Hall of Baseball Characters (and I'm ready to make a donation right now), I'll be there for sure as baseball's designated leprechaun and social director. Someone no one would want to write a book about? OK, so I wrote it myself—with a little help from my wordsmith pal Howie.

Back in the early seventies, when Berra was managing the league-leading Mets, I walked into the clubhouse just to say hello to Yogi. You're gonna find this hard to believe—I did. But as I strolled past players rubbing up their fielding gloves and putting on their spikes—the likes of Tom

"Terrific" Seaver, Tug McGraw, Rusty Staub, Cleon Jones, Jerry Grote, and Jerry Koosman—there was, to my surprise and no little pleasure, a friendly round of applause. Yogi grinned. "Here comes the f'g living legend," he said. OK, so it's not the Hall of Fame. But, hey, I did it without hardly trying.

So I guess the funny thing that happened to me on the way to Cooperstown was that I was having too much fun on the scenic route to want to take the straight and narrow thruway. I could have been a straight arrow. (Do not pass Go. Do not collect 200 DWIs. Go directly to the Hall of Fame.) Consciously, subconsciously, but most likely unconsciously I became a wild card instead. Sure, in hindsight I see a bunch of things I maybe should have done differently, but 85,000 words into revisiting my life, you know what? I don't think I'd swap lives with anyone. Not Nolan, not Warren, not Tom. Well, maybe Ted.

The fact is, it's been a wonderful life. A wonderful life-and-a-half. And (thank you, Frank) I've done it my way.

The best way? Probably not.

The most sensible way? Absolutely not.

The McDermott way? For sure.

Index